The American Party Battle

ELECTION CAMPAIGN PAMPHLETS

1828–1876

Volume 2, 1854–1876

EDITED AND WITH AN INTRODUCTION BY

JOEL H. SILBEY

HARVARD UNIVERSITY PRESS

Cambridge, Massachusetts
London, England
1999

Library of Congress Cataloging-in-Publication Data
The American party battle : election campaign pamphlets, 1828–1876 /
edited and with an introduction by Joel H. Silbey.
2 v. cm. — (The John Harvard library)
Contents: v. 1. 1828–1854 — v. 2. 1854–1876.
ISBN 0-674-02642-X (vol. 1 : alk. paper).
ISBN 0-674-02645-4 (vol. 1 : pbk. : alk. paper).
ISBN 0-674-02643-8 (vol. 2 : alk.paper).
ISBN 0-674-02646-2 (vol. 2 : pbk. : alk. paper).
1. Political parties—United States—History—19th century.
2. Campaign literature—United States—History—19th century.
3. United States—Politics and government—19th century.
I. Silbey, Joel H.   II. Series.
JK2260.A54   1999
324.7′0973′09034—dc21
98-50174

To my colleagues in the
Cornell University History Department

There is no other way to carry out in practice the theory of
our Republican Government but openly and clearly to declare
principles and measures and for men and parties to divide
upon them as they are for them or against them.

PRESTON KING, *1855*

Contents

Preface   xi
"Please Read and Circulate"
"To Indulge in General Abusive Declamation"
A Note on the Texts

Acknowledgments   xxiii

Introduction: Defining the Soul of the Nation   I
The Great Themes: Continuity and Change
"To Save and Exalt the Union"
"Consider Well . . . the Platforms . . . of the Parties Now Asking Your Suffrage"

Volume I

PART ONE   The Evolution of Party Warfare, 1828–1838

I   *Proceedings and Address of the New Hampshire Republican State*
Convention . . . Friendly to the Election of Andrew Jackson . . .
(Concord, 1828)   55

2   *The Virginia Address (Richmond, 1828)*   84

3   *Proceedings of the Antimasonic Republican Convention of the State*
of Maine (Hallowell, Me., 1834)   99

4   *To the Electors of Massachusetts (Worcester? 1837)*   135

PART TWO   The Jacksonian-Whig Synthesis, 1838–1854

5   *To the Democratic Republican Party of Alabama (n.p., 1840)*   169

6   *Address of the Liberty Party of Pennsylvania to the People of the State*
(Philadelphia, 1844)   178

7   *The Twenty-Ninth Congress, Its Men and Measures; Its Professions
    and Its Principles . . . (Washington, 1846)*   208

8   *What's the Difference? Cass and Taylor on the Slavery Question
    (Boston, 1848)*   238

9   *Speech of Hon. Stephen A. Douglas, of Illinois, Delivered in
    Richmond, Virginia, July 9, 1852 (Richmond, 1852)*   268

Volume 2

PART THREE   New Issues and Parties: Americans, Republicans,
             and Divided Democrats, 1854—1860

10 *A Few Considerations for Reflecting Voters (New York, 1855?)*   55

11 *The Parties of the Day. Speech of William H. Seward at
    Auburn, October 21, 1856 (Washington, 1857)*   70

12 *The Conspiracy to Break Up the Union. The Plot and Its
    Development . . . (Washington, 1860)*   82

13 *Salient Points of the Campaign . . . (Springfield, 1860)*   114

PART FOUR   The Culmination of the Battle for the
             Soul of America, 1861–1876

14 *An Address . . . to the People of the States Which Adhere to the
    Federal Government (Washington, 1864)*   153

15 *"Union" on Dis-Union Principles! The Chicago Platform,
    McClellan's Letter of Acceptance . . . A Speech Delivered by Abram
    Wakeman, of New York, . . . Nov. 3, 1864 (New York, 1864)*   186

16 *Modern Philanthropy Illustrated. How They Tried to Make a White
    Man of a Negro . . . (n.p., 1868)*   221

17 *The Three Secession Movements in the United States. Samuel J.
    Tilden, . . . the Adviser, Aider, and Abettor of the Great Secession
    Movement of 1860 . . . (Boston, 1876)*   228

Preface

The time is *at hand* when your responsible votes are to be cast.
Let no elector presume that *his* vote is too insignificant to be
needed. Let no one fail to do *his* duty.

"Address to the Voters of the Ninth Congressional
District of Massachusetts," 1860

Between the 1820s and the 1850s two major political parties took firm control of the American political landscape. Divisive political conflict at the national level raged in the 1820s, particularly in the aftermath of the controversial presidential election of 1824, and moved into high gear over the next two decades. The sense of outrage felt by those defeated in the "corrupt bargain" of 1824 and what followed when John Quincy Adams became president clarified what was at stake in American national politics to a degree not realized in the preceding decade. The issues raised in the mid-1820s were thereafter codified, regularized, and routinized by nationwide political parties. First Jacksonians and National Republicans, then Democrats and Whigs came together to confront one another in unceasing "mortal combat."[1]

The Jacksonians and their opponents developed far-reaching institutional structures to organize this highly adversarial political nation and to mobilize its voters by defining, with great vigor, what was at issue in the many elections that took place annually, year in and year out—sometimes several in a twelve-month period. As other parties subsequently appeared, as the Republicans

---

1. On the election of 1824, see James F. Hopkins, "Election of 1824," in Arthur M. Schlesinger and Fred L. Israel, eds., *History of American Presidential Elections* (New York, 1971), vol. 1, pp. 349–412; on the emergence of political parties, see Richard P. McCormick, *The Second American Party System: Party Formation in the Jacksonian Era* (Chapel Hill, 1966). Party names varied during the first decade or so of party formation. At first calling themselves Republicans, the supporters (or "friends") of Andrew Jackson evolved into the Democratic-Republican and ultimately the Democratic Party. The National Republicans were joined by other enemies of Jackson to become the Whig (sometimes the Democratic-Whig) Party by the late 1830s.

replaced the Whigs in the 1850s, and as partisan warfare took on new elements and direction, these structures of partisan conflict remained, functioned as they were designed to do, and grew even more powerful.[2]

At the center of their electioneering activities, each party put forward a set of claims about themselves and about their opponents, which they pressed with great intensity in robust polemical discourse.[3] Party leaders and candidates for office presented these claims to the electorate through speeches on the stump and in legislative halls, in newspaper editorials, in each party's central periodical (the *Democratic Review* and the *Whig Almanac*), and, in particular, in a wide range of printed pamphlets, issued in the thousands by local, state and national party organizations in each campaign season. These pamphlets were a major part of a panoply of campaign documents, from single-page broadsheets and handbills to elaborately compiled textbooks and campaign biographies, that the parties put out each year, and were at the center of the parties' mobilizing efforts.

Although nineteenth-century partisan election pamphlets varied in source, length, and type, they were alike in purpose and structure. This vast rhetorical output was designed to be a call to arms that would stoke the fires of political conflict, agitate the voters, and awaken party supporters to their duty by reminding them why they were Democrats, National Republicans, Whigs, Antimasons, Know Nothings, Republicans, and the rest. American party leaders had to canvass a very large geographic expanse of local communities and often localism in thought and outlook as well. The people had to be mobilized and brought together for successful nationwide political activity. Pamphlets accomplished that as efficiently as nineteenth-century technology allowed.[4]

The art of political advocacy, communication, and mobilization through pamphleteering was an old and well-established tradition in American public life.[5] It had never disappeared after its heyday during the Revolution, reviving

2. Joel H. Silbey, *The American Political Nation, 1838–1861* (Stanford, 1991).

3. See Andrew Robertson, *The Language of Democracy: Political Rhetoric in the United States and Britain, 1790–1900* (Ithaca, N.Y., 1995); Kenneth Cmiel, *Democratic Eloquence: The Fight over Popular Speech in Nineteenth-Century America* (New York, 1990); Daniel T. Rodgers, *Contested Truths: Keywords in American Politics since Independence* (New York, 1987); Daniel Walker Howe, *The Political Culture of the American Whigs* (Chicago, 1979).

4. Elections took place in most months of the year, except the summertime, and in most years; and voter turnout was on the rise as the party system settled in and matured. Good overviews of the emerging political environment include William Gienapp, "'Politics Seems to Enter Into Everything': Political Culture in the North, 1840–1860," in Stephen Maizlish and John J. Kushma, eds., *Essays on American Antebellum Politics, 1840–1860* (College Station, Tex., 1982), pp. 15–69; and Silbey, *American Political Nation*.

5. See, for example, Bernard Bailyn, ed., *Pamphlets of the American Revolution, 1750–1776* (Cambridge, 1965).

somewhat in the Federalist-Republican era and continuing thereafter, even as political confrontation cooled. In the 1820s, reliance on political pamphleteering was reinvigorated as newly emergent partisan leaders sought ways to meet the needs of a growing electorate and the increasingly contentious political system. After that decade, no party let an election go by without issuing a wide range of these publications.

Occasionally, one or another pamphlet would be nonpartisan, focusing on single issues or on larger themes but without arguing on behalf of a specific party. But these were unusual in the political climate from the 1820s onward. The great bulk of the pamphlets were partisan in origin and fully engaged in partisan conflict. They varied in length from four pages or so at the minimum, to the twelve, sixteen, and thirty-plus pages of most of them, to the scores of pages in the individual Democratic and Whig *Almanacs* that each of the major parties began to publish in the 1840s. Some were reprints of stump or legislative speeches already given, or letters from major candidates accepting the nomination of a party convention. Others were full-range summary statements of a party's stance in general, or about one or another specific issue.

The pamphlets were among the major tools of America's political activists in these years. To many, they were *the* major element of party warfare. As the beleagured Northern Democrats put it during the Civil War, "When a party in power violates the Constitution and disregards state-rights, plain men read pamphlets."[6] In them, party leaders found material they could use in their electioneering efforts at the popular level. Pamphlets provided compilations of useful information about where a party and its opponents stood, including extensive quotations from party members and from their opponents that could be used to demonstrate, with great force, a particular, or a general, point; they reprinted the ubiquitous formal addresses issued by state party conventions to the voters, as well as speeches by party leaders in Congress, in state legislatures, and at meetings and rallies of the faithful.

Many of the pamphlets were the work of a single writer; others were prepared by party-appointed drafting committees.[7] We know who wrote some of them, but most of the authors were anonymous newspaper editors and party leaders. The key point about them was that they were designed not to express the position of a particular writer, but to represent forcefully a collective out-

---

6. This statement appeared on the title pages of the pamphlets issued in the series "Papers from the Society for the Diffusion of Useful Political Knowledge."

7. One meeting in 1827 appointed "a general committee of correspondence" charged with the task "to prepare a suitable argumentative address on the subject of the presidential election." "To the Citizens of Washington County" (Washington, Pa., 1827), p. 1.

look. Pamphlets differed from party platforms in that they were much more than a list of desires and proposals; they were a worked-out argument that spelled out the problems the people faced, positions that were being taken, and the outcomes to be desired (and to be avoided), all presented at length, with great force.

"Please Read and Circulate"

Party sponsors aggressively promoted the pamphlets. "Please read and circulate" was a frequent request on their title page. In 1827, John Quincy Adams's supporters in Louisiana resolved that 2,000 copies of their convention proceedings be published in pamphlet form in English, another 2,000 in French. Adams's Virginia supporters that same year ordered 30,000 copies of their convention proceedings and address to be "circulated" along with other material that would "sustain the facts and principles set forth in the address of this convention." Their opponents were no less busy. "Democratic editors," the title page of one pamphlet suggested, "are requested to copy, and advertise in behalf of the Cause, the Terms [the cost] given below; and Clubs and Committees are invited to order for Distribution."[8]

When James K. Polk ran for president in 1844, he expressed his interest in this material and his awareness of its role in a particularly direct way. *"Majr. Heiss* writes me," he noted in a letter to a political associate,

> that the Pamphlet Edition of the "Vindication of E. Polk &c." will be out this week, a part of them on wednesday evening. I wish you to send 100 of the first that are struck to *Edwin Polk Esqr* [at] Bolivar, through the mail. Send them in such a way that he will only have newspaper postage to pay.
>
> Send one copy, of the first that are out to each Democratic member of Congress. When all are out send 25. copies to each Democratic member of Congress.
>
> Send 10 copies to each Democratic Elector in the Union, as far as their names can be ascertained from the newspapers.
>
> Send one copy, to each Democratic newspaper in the Union.
>
> Request *Mr. Southall* to send one copy of each one of the list of persons in this State which he has.

8. "Proceedings of the Delegates of the Friends of the Administration of John Quincy Adams Assembled in Convention in Baton Rouge" (New Orleans, 1827), p. 28; "The Virginia Address" (Richmond, 1828), p. 8; "Plain Facts and Considerations Addressed to the People of the United States . . ." (Boston, 1856).

> Send one copy to each Democratic Speaker in this State.
> Send to any others in any part of the Union whom you may think of . . .[9]

Party leaders throughout the country responded to such calls to action. Raising money to pay for printing and distribution, and securing the pamphlets from state and national party committees, party activists then circulated them as widely as they could to editors and other local enthusiasts.[10] By the 1840s, national committees of each party, such as the Whig Congressional Executive Committee, had taken charge of the national campaigns and were organizing this material and sending it out in systematic and sustained ways. As they arrived in a locality, the pamphlets were read at party rallies, reprinted in local newspapers, and passed around among candidates and the politically committed in a widening arc from state capitals to county seats to far-flung hamlets. Their contents became the basis of even more stump speeches, partisan editorials, and single-page fliers and posters dramatizing what was at stake in these fervent contests.[11]

A particular style and framework of argument were always present in the pamphlets. They were extremely repetitious, reflecting their origins in a set of core beliefs held within each party, beliefs that did not change much despite the passage of time and the rise of new issues and impulses. There was little difference between pamphlets and other sources of party ideology, newspaper editorials and stump speeches, except in tone and occasional emphasis. The pamphlets' tone was, more often than not, apocalyptic. They always conveyed a sense of impending threat, even doom. Great interests were always at stake, or "the present crisis" was always "without precedent" in the nation's history. Each such political crisis—that is, upcoming election—was one that "menaces our dearest interests."[12]

At the same time, most of the pamphlets never had the literary or intellectual qualities of earlier such publications of the pre-partisan era. They were not written by Jeffersonian political intellectuals and did not reflect the subtleties of the earlier group of writers, well-educated elites conversing with one another about the nature of power and proper governance. They did not deal

9. James K. Polk to Robert Armstrong, September 16, 1844, in Wayne Cutler, ed., *The Correspondence of James K. Polk* (Knoxville, 1993), vol. 8, pp 69–70.

10. Horace Greeley's important 1843 essay, "The Grounds of Difference between the Contending Parties," originally published in the *Whig Almanac*, was offered at $10 per thousand copies, $1.25 per hundred, and 20 cents per dozen, with "no copyright. Any are at liberty to reprint unaltered."

11. See Silbey, *American Political Nation*, chap. 3 and passim.

12. "Proceedings of the Friends of John Quincy Adams," p. 7; "Address and Proceedings of the State Independent Free Territory Convention of the People of Ohio, Held at Columbus, June 20 and 21, 1848" (Cincinnati, 1848), p. 7.

extensively, directly, or in a sophisticated way with large and abstract themes of the nature of political sovereignty and systems of government. Nor did the writers often describe a complex political world.

Rather, the pamphlets were most often cast in tones of ordinary political discourse as it had evolved in the fifty years since the Revolution. An age increasingly characterized by a raucous egalitarianism had its own kind of rhetoric and argument during its election campaigns, a polemical style reflecting the rough and tumble of the new politics.[13] They were written with specific purposes in mind by active politicians and partisan newspapermen, who were skilled in their ability to appeal to an increasingly broad-based electorate no longer outnumbered by the nation's upper classes. The writers' clear aim was to awaken and bring the voters forth to the polls in ways useful to the engaged contestants.

To do this, while the pamphleteers shouted at each other, at the same time they used all of their shrewdness, knowledge, and experience to make their shouting meaningful to their intended audience. They defined the nature of the American party battle and powerfully characterized it by offering firm explanations of the virtues of one party's approaches and the disasters inherent in those of the other side. Their discourse was usually framed in military style: armies of sworn enemies confronted each other in full battle array. Belief, commitment, and discipline were all.

What further distinguishes these pamphlets is not so much that they contain a range of previously undiscovered insights about where the parties stood on the issues of the day (there are few surprises in them for the scholar well versed in nineteenth-century party warfare); rather, the pamphlets generally confirm much of what is understood about the party conflict of the time. Historians have marked well the grounds of difference between the parties, although emphases, contested points, and often sharp differences among scholars do exist. The pamphlets contain most of the themes that scholars have identified as the core of the era's political discourse. But they served a number of practical functions as well, as Polk's letter indicates.

The pamphlets constructed a picture of the world that their authors believed was politically effective in rousing partisans to the cause. Political leaders had to find ways to touch voters, interact with them, involve them, and call them to their duty. The way they structured the pamphlets answered that need. They brought together the range of arguments each party offered and revealed much about the worldview of the contestants as they wanted the electorate to understand them.

13. See the volumes by Robertson, Cmiel, Rodgers, and Howe cited in note 3.

"To Indulge in General Abusive Declamation"

The pamphlets were forceful, reflecting their purpose to mobilize a wide array of potential voters—farmers, tradesmen, and skilled and unskilled workers who lived in the rural communities that dominated the American landscape as well as in its few urban centers. The partisan activitists who wrote them pulled no punches. They believed in the impact of sharply focused and strongly worded propaganda to affect voters. Whatever else was on their minds, the authors of these pamphlets linked their message to a general audience, the increasing number of those eligible to vote. They tried to touch the texture of personal experience.

The pamphlets contained extravagant overstatement, heated defamation, polarizing excess, and threatening and divisive imagery. Their tone was unremittingly negative, harsh, and hostile, filled with fearful images. Their authors conjured monsters: the avaricious bank, the uncontrolled despot, and later the aggressive slavocracy and the rampaging abolitionist. They personalized their attacks with aggressive incantations against the wickedness of their opponents, dire warnings about the looming degradation and collapse of the Republic if the other party won, and not a little mud-slinging, particularly against individual leaders. "It has been the fate of every man running for office in this country," a Democratic writer lamented late in the era, "to be abused and misrepresented by those opposed to him in politics." Their opponents agreed. "Slander," a National Republican pamphleteer ruefully noted in 1832, "is undoubtedly one of the crying sins of this nation. Next to intemperance in the use of liquor, it may be looked upon as our chief national vice."[14]

Occasionally there were disclaimers, disingenuous or not. "There is no intention," a Whig writer declared in 1840, "to indulge in general abusive declamation, or in indiscriminate declamatory praise. Those are but empty sounds, noisy and boisterous; but communicating no knowledge, and signifying nothing." Sometimes they did not so indulge—but rarely. The writer of the above quotation managed to remind his audience that so far as President Martin Van Buren was concerned, "the interest and the welfare of the country are the last things in his thoughts."[15]

Most often, each writer cast matters in terms of the other side's antirepublican degeneracy in contrast to their own party's commitment to the Republic's bright future. Each party made it clear that "we contend for our Consti-

---

14. "The Record of Horatio Seymour" (n.p., 1868), p. 1; "The Conduct of the Administration" (Boston, 1832), p. 13.

15. [Richard Hildreth], "The Contrast: or William Henry Harrison versus Martin Van Buren" (Boston, 1840), pp. 6, 55.

tution and our country," while the other side did not.[16] And they were usually anguished about the state of affairs they confronted given the other side's baseness. To be sure, the pamphlet writers never quite reached the same degree of pithy negativism contained in such handbills as the single-page coffin flier used against Andrew Jackson in 1828, which asserted that Old Hickory was a murderer.[17] Usually the pamphlets were more restrained. Still, they delivered their share of color, bite, and bile. As the author of the *Democratic Textbook* of 1848 wrote, the Whig opponents were animated by "a degree of desperation and recklessness unprecedented in our political history" due to their policies and behavior, which have "rendered their cause and their party appelation odious and repulsive." Modern readers may become glassy-eyed from the constant vituperation, whatever echoes of more recent times they also hear.[18]

Whatever the level of their invective and the excessive and inflated nature of the portraits they painted, the pamphlets also contained another, more substantive dimension. They reveal the consensual elements always present in a nation's political discourse. Both parties structured their appeals within the same general framework of shared values. As they squared off, each claimed repeatedly (and unsurprisingly) that it was working "to promote political objects" that each considered "vital to the prosperity of the country and the proper administration of the government."[19] On such platitudes it was easy to agree. But the parties then proceeded to sharpen the differences between them as they sought to achieve these good ends. Beyond that limited consensus, the rest of what they offered in their election discourse was unabashedly divisive.

Within broad consensual notions of republican freedom, personal liberty, and individual achievement, the pamphlet writers thought in contrasts and worked very hard to offer serious, polarizing differences in expression, outlook, and specific policy options to the electorate. The pamphlets underscored how divided the parties were in their public advocacy. Their normal

16. "Speech of Mr. Bartlett at a Meeting of Citizens Opposed to the Re-election of Andrew Jackson, Holden at Portsmouth, N.H., October 15, 1832" (Portsmouth, 1832), p. 14.

17. There is a reproduction of the coffin handbill in Stefan Lorant, *The Presidency: A Pictorial History of Presidential Elections* (New York, 1951), p. 105.

18. "The Democratic Textbook, Being a Compendium of the Principles of the Democratic Party" (New York, 1848), p. 3; Cato, "A Defense of the National Administration in an Address to the People of New Hampshire," (Concord, 1828), p. 18; "Address to the Voters of the Ninth Congressional District," *op. cit.*, p. 1.

19. "Speech of the Hon. John A. Dix, of New York, at the Mass Meeting . . . Newburgh . . . 26th of July, 1852" (n.p., n.d.), p. 1.

mode of thought and expression was confrontational. Each party's own vision, however, as expressed in the pamphlets, was remarkably coherent and consistent. Although each constantly struggled with its own factional differences, some of which were quite serious, such struggles rarely appeared in the campaign pamphlets, unless the other side saw some advantage in highlighting them to demonstrate some evil, deceptive, partisan trait and/or illegitimate activity on the part of their opponents.[20]

Some later observers have been struck by the ideological limits of what was offered in partisan discourse, that is, an alleged consensual nature of the arguments, a lack of real differences between the parties, and a sense that the discourse disguised the fact that party leaders were more electorally than ideologically driven. In their view, party leaders would say anything to win, were willing to (and did) deceive a gullible electorate, and avoided tough issues that would not pay off for them.[21] I do not share these skeptical, even cynical, beliefs.

There was less of such deceptive or consensual practices than some scholars have claimed and more policy divisiveness then is often accepted. What lay behind the parties' polarized expressions was more than electorally driven hyperbole and automatic commitment to a Manichaean perspective. The presenters of these arguments realized that they could not just say anything; they had to touch voters' concerns, fears, and hopes directly and clearly in their electioneering. The fact that their opponents were always vigorously watching their every claim prevented deviation: party spokesmen had to be consistent in their arguments or be denounced as fraudulent and deceptive by their opponents.

More to the point, despite their origins in, and their persistent tone of, narrowly partisan discourse, the pamphlets contained at their core an ideological presentation of some power, part of which was specific to a particular issue or set of policies, and part to more reflective and long-range considerations. Their advocacy proved to be a laboratory for the exploration of a range of critical issues and notions important to the nation, from the proprieties of democratic politics and the role of government in a free republican society to the nature—the accomplishments and deficiencies—of that society. Some of

20. This internal unity can also be seen in the way party representatives cohered when they voted on policy matters in the state legislatures and in Congress in these years. See Thomas B. Alexander, *Sectional Stress and Party Strength: A Study of Roll-Call Voting in the United States House of Representatives, 1836–1860* (Nashville, 1967); Joel H. Silbey, *The Shrine of Party: Congressional Voting Behavior, 1841–1852* (Pittsburgh, 1967); Herbert Ershkowitz and William Shade, "Consensus or Conflict? Political Behavior in the State Legislatures during the Jacksonian Era," *Journal of American History* 58 (December 1971): 591–621.

21. See, for example, Edward Pessen, "We Are All Jeffersonians, We Are All Jacksonians: Or a Pox on Stultifying Periodizations," *Journal of the Early Republic* 1 (Spring 1981): 1–26.

the arguments looked forward; others longingly recalled a lost arcadia in the past. Some raised questions about the role and legitimacy of parties; others vigorously defended the critical need for parties in a sprawling democratic republic.

To suggest that ideas of substance formed the mainstream of organized political discourse in the electoral and policy-making arenas is not to deny the existence of other, less laudable impulses. But the writers of these pamphlets began with the notion that there were real and very important differences within the nation and that it was the duty of the parties to clarify and present these differences without evasion, obfuscation, or humbug. They did so. As Daniel Walker Howe suggests, the party battles organized by these and similar materials "accustomed people to ferocious, *issue oriented,* political polarization."[22]

I have been reading the vast amount of nineteenth-century pamphlet literature for a very long time, trying to understand and interpret it and to consider the pamphlets' place in that century's political world. I am convinced that they are as important, and as worth publishing, despite their "narrowly" partisan origins, as pamphlets from other great periods of American history. First and foremost, though not everything in the nation's politics was electoral, a great deal was. Elections were the dominant element of the American party battle in the nineteenth century. They were the culmination of a process of defining, understanding, and resolving what was at stake in American political life.

The pamphlets were central to that process. They helped organize the world of campaigns and elections, bringing together party leaders and potential voters. The interests of the latter could be perceived, and their commitment reinforced, only so long as they could be effectively described and articulated. And they were. The pamphlet writers' rhetoric was purposive. They defined and characterized what was at issue and elaborated, supplemented, deepened, and expanded the reach of other campaign material, texturing and echoing, sharpening and codifying, with particular force, the partisan truths that were expressed in platforms, newspaper editorials, and stump speeches, all in the hope and expectation that they would thus connect to the voters in substantial and critical ways.

At the same time, the pamphlets revealed much beyond the immediacy of electoral campaigning. The clouds of rhetoric were not empty of content.

---

22. Daniel Walker Howe, "British Historians and the Second American Party System," *Reviews in American History* 13 (September 1985): 372–373. Italics added.

They always expressed many larger truths about the nation's notions about itself, its present, and its future. Their authors articulated, within an electoral context, the shape and nature of America's major ideological concerns—about liberty, about the proper role of government, and about the connections between the two—concerns that underlay and structured the partisan warfare taking place. In short, what emerges from these documents are the contours of a particular set of arguments and a particular pattern of American political discourse characteristic of a period that was itself unique. In the campaign pamphlets, the language and ideologies of an age come alive as voters prepared to make their way to the polls on the many election days in nineteenth-century America. They provide the opportunity for a fresh look at material that contains both ideological substance and electoral focus.

A Note on the Texts

Not all of the pamphlets issued in the half century after the 1820s have survived. Many that have are, unfortunately, in advanced stages of decay. That condition only underscores the usefulness of bringing them out of their comparative obscurity.

These pamphlets were not overadorned. Most were plainly presented, sometimes with a cover, often not. The texts are presented here as they were originally printed, with the wording, spelling, and punctuation—as well as typographical errors—intact.

Taken together, the pamphlets included here form an impressive record of the discourse of American political battles in a critical era, from the development of the two-party system in the 1820s and 1830s and its maturation through the early 1840s, to the rise of new issues, challenges, and parties in the late 1840s and 1850s, to their settling down in the fires of Civil War and Reconstruction. They reveal the dominant clusters of ideas, beliefs, and attitudes; they show how political leaders organized and represented these ideas to the voters and how each of the parties cohered. They reflect the variety of sources from which they came as well as the underlying pattern of beliefs held by the combatants. They give the flavor of the electoral confrontation of their time.

Acknowledgments

For sharing the conviction that this material deserves publication, I am grateful to Aida Donald and her colleagues at the Harvard University Press, who welcomed these volumes into the John Harvard Library. Aida's commitment and encouragement were exemplary. Donna Bouvier's guidance of the manuscript through the publication process was done with understanding, grace, and expertise.

Several historians of nineteenth-century American politics have helped me understand the American party battle in the period covered in these pages. Without implicating any of them in the particulars of my interpretation, I want to express my gratitude to Lee Benson, Allan G. Bogue, Ronald Formisano, William Gienapp, Michael Holt, Daniel Walker Howe, and William Shade, all of whose fine scholarship has been cogent, informative, and singularly important to me as I deciphered the play of nineteenth-century partisan confrontation.

The staffs of the Library of Congress, the New York Public Library, and the Cornell University Library were most forthcoming as I perused their collections, helping me find and reproduce material that was often difficult to locate. They too deserve my appreciation and gratitude. In particular, both Julie Copenhagen and the interlibrary loan staff she heads at Cornell's Olin Library and the staff of the Rare Books and Manuscripts Department in the Kroch Library at Cornell were relentless in their commitment to locating many hard-to-find pamphlets.

As always, my family, Rosemary, Victoria, and David, and a number of good friends, led by Glenn Altschuler and Alain Seznec, have energized and cosseted me in many important ways. I very much appreciate the warmth and constancy of their support. I dedicate this book to my colleagues in Cornell's History Department, who for more than thirty years have, by their example and in their actions, created a flourishing intellectual atmosphere that I have greatly benefited from and deeply cherish.

THE AMERICAN PARTY BATTLE

Introduction: Defining the Soul of the Nation

The bases of nineteenth-century America's partisan confrontation—the ideological and policy differences between the contending parties—always reflected specific concerns of the time. In each of the thirteen presidential elections between 1828 and 1876, and in the many off-year elections for Congress, state governorships, and other offices in that era, different issues appeared, were taken up, and were argued about, with one or another or a combination of them dominating the political arena at a particular moment. There was no shortage of such issues in any given election, and the advocates of the two major parties touched on a great many, from banking, the tariff, internal improvements, land policy, and other aspects of the nation's political economy, to foreign affairs, immigration, religion, social reform, and sectional differences, to the momentous and transforming issues raised by the Civil War and Reconstruction. The debates over these matters were constant and pointed. In their electoral discourse, the parties clearly identified themselves with contrasting positions about all of these issues without stint, as they also did in their behavior when holding office.[1] Their policy divisions formed the basic construct of American politics.[2]

THE GREAT THEMES: CONTINUITY AND CHANGE

At the same time, American political discourse had another characteristic as well. Whatever the particular policy matter discussed, there were overall con-

1. "The Contrast" is the title of at least two Whig pamphlets: [Richard Hildreth], "The Contrast: or William Henry Harrison versus Martin Van Buren" (Boston, 1840); and "The Contrast: The Whig and Democratic Platforms—the Whig and Democratic Candidates for the Presidency" (n.p., 1852).

2. There are a number of excellent studies of the various party ideologies throughout these years. For the

tinuities in the nature of the arguments offered in this great partisan debate that moved beyond the individual issue or immediate context to stretch over the whole period. The arguments offered to the electorate were always framed within a set of boundaries that encompassed similar concerns affecting the American people across an entire half century, from the 1820s through the 1870s. Pamphlet writers were always adept at crystallizing current policy issues and immediate concerns while remaining cognizant of more constant, longer-run themes in the nation's political culture. They effectively integrated, and surrounded, immediate concerns with larger arguments about the nation's future, the ever-present threats and dangers to it and to the people's liberties, Americans' expectations, hopes, fears, and prejudices, and the future course of American freedom.

These general concerns remained always at hand and were powerfully displayed in every election campaign as the clear framework of American political discourse. This was not surprising given the continuities of American political life. Battles that had begun earlier over the extent of the government's power were reborn in the 1820s, if in a quite different context. The appearance of potent issues stimulated by the Adams and Jackson presidencies and the emergence of national political parties, as well as a series of later wrenching changes on the political landscape, not the least of which was the Civil War, did not materially transform the nature of the general subjects that American political discourse focused on, nor the different perspectives that each party brought to them, whatever the important contextual differences in the specific policies being contested.

Visions of a more secure and better society achieved through political action were always the core of the pamphlet writers' arguments. They expressed first an abiding and intense concern about the weaknesses, and susceptibility to overthrow, of the American nation—about the security and well-being of a republic that was always endangered, particularly in the face of the illegitimate antecedents, goals, leadership, and behavior of most of those on the other side from the writer. In the 1820s and later, stark negative characterizations of both the opposition and the general situation abounded, including expressions of the fear of an ill-intentioned and malevolent leadership and the subsequent decline and degeneracy of the society. These remained potent organizing themes for political discourse.[3]

---

early years, see Daniel Walker Howe, *The Political Culture of the American Whigs* (Chicago, 1979); John Ashworth, *"Agrarians" and "Aristocrats": Party Political Ideology in the United States, 1837–1846* (London, 1983); Lawrence F. Kohl, *The Politics of Individualism: Parties and the American Character in the Jacksonian Era* (New York, 1989).

3. For background on the abiding concerns about the future of the republic that resonated throughout

The second organizing theme grew out of the panoply of specific issues rooted in the political economy and the social matrix of the nation. These issues, articulated usually by the Democrats (to which their opponents had to respond), raised basic questions and provoked sharp disagreements about the limits of the authority, power, and reach of the national government in America's free society. Did the national government have a responsibility to promote "development"? Did its power reach as far as the most demanding wished that it did? If not, where were its limits? These questions echoed from the first days under the new constitutional authority and had continued to be debated since.[4]

The third theme concerned the meaning, and continuing improvement, of the American experience—what was the nature of liberty in the nation, what were its possibilities and limits, and who among the partisan contestants was most willing, and best prepared, to preserve and/or extend it in the face of threatening or restrictive tendencies present on the political landscape. Who was included in the American republic? Who could participate in its decision making? What did liberty mean on this continent? Did the nation's commitment to liberty extend to its expansion to groups not usually considered full-fledged members of civil society? Should political authority be used to monitor who was an American and who was not? If so, and under what circumstances? Should such authority determine who could enter the nation and who could not? Could it be used to confront social evils and weaknesses in the society, all in the name of improvement, stability, and general welfare?

In both the electoral battles fought and the descriptions offered in the pamphlets, these basic themes were never rigidly separated from one another. Rather, the pamphlet writers tended to mix them together. Most arguments put forward by party publicists raised a number of different subjects and brought together a great deal of information that quickly and inevitably became intertwined, so that problems of political economy, for example, were rarely discussed outside of expressions of concern for the liberty of the people.

The central thrust of the discourse also varied over time among the three general themes. Emphasis on the dangers to the Republic, for example, dominated the early years of party warfare and reappeared later, during the Civil

---

this period, one should begin with Robert Shalhope, *The Roots of Democracy: American Thought and Culture, 1760–1800* (Boston, 1990); and Steven Watts, *The Republic Reborn: War and the Making of Liberal America* (Baltimore, 1987).

4. On the early background of these battles, see (among the most recent of many such studies) Stanley Elkins and Eric McKitrick, *The Age of Federalism* (New York, 1993); and J. Roger Sharp, *American Politics in the Early Republic: The New Nation in Crisis* (New Haven, 1993). On the renewed outbreak of ideological conflict, Harry L. Watson, *Liberty and Power, The Politics of Jacksonian America* (New York, 1990), is a good introduction.

War years, while disagreements over the power of government grew central in the 1830s and remained so thereafter, at the heart of the battle to define what was at stake in the evolution of the American nation. Questions about the extent of liberty in America were always present and became politically salient at a number of moments, particularly in the 1850s and thereafter. But even in these cases the themes were always intertwined and could never be rigorously separated from one another. Each theme, as it was presented, contained elements of the others. Separately and together they structured American political discourse into sharply honed and clearly articulated partisan channels. By incorporating these themes in their partisan debates, each party's pamphlet writers made it clear that the United States was, as yet, far from being a settled country, secure in its destiny and on its way irrepressibly to ever-growing freedom, prosperity and power. Rather, the pamphleteers agreed, a great deal remained to be done. There was much to be protected and preserved, and there were many things to be resisted as well if the nation was to maintain itself and realize its full potential.

"THE RUINS OF REPUBLICS"

American politicians' sense of the present's roots in the past was constantly manifested in their discourse. At the outset of the party battle in the years when Andrew Jackson came onto the scene, and frequently thereafter, values and battles from another era remained alive to the participants and shaped the substance and style of their argument. Each party structured its appeals around the traditional concerns of America's political culture and what could be learned, or should not be forgotten, from the nation's history. There were always lessons, party publicists argued, in the careful reading of the historical record. "May the people of Louisiana," that state's pro-Adams convention warned in 1827, "never permit its past to be effaced from their memory."[5] As a result, partisan discussions from the 1820s onward began as the politics of memory and never completely lost that dimension, with linkages to past events and to critical ideological marking points constantly being made and used for the illumination of current issues.

In particular, certain elements of eighteenth-century republican ideology helped shape particular aspects of the two-party battle in the subsequent political era. The system of partisan discourse in the late 1820s centered on the fragility and survivability of republican liberty in a world that was hostile and

<hr>

5. "Address of the Delegates of the Friends of the Administration of John Quincy Adams . . . to the People of Louisiana" (New Orleans, 1827), p. 23.

dangerous because of the constant presence of destabilizing political intentions and practices on the American landscape, including potent antirepublican subversion and the purported inadequacies or malevolence of some of the
nation's leadership. Republics were always in danger of backsliding due to
their own internal controversies and divisions, or of being overwhelmed by
their many external enemies. The danger was very real to those who sought to
define where they stood a decade after the War of 1812. Once the American
Republic had glowed with promise in its "earliest and purest times." But
something had gone wrong. The present looked dark. The future contained a
strong possibility of apocalypse; the very survival of the Republic was at
stake.[6]

Partisans on both sides of the emerging political divide picked up this traditional theme as a major component of their campaign discourse. Fear of
monarchy, aristocracy, fraudulent and malevolent leadership, and political
improprieties, all traditional banes of republics, formed an important part of
their calculus. As Harry Watson has written, "though Whigs, Democrats, and
Anti-Masons all pointed to different sources of menace, all were clearly troubled for the future of free government and all drew on traditional republican
rhetoric to express themselves." This is consonant with Bernard Bailyn's and
others' picture of both the later eighteenth-century worldview of American
political activists and their followers, and the potency of this theme well after
the Revolution. Some of the dark themes present in the notion of republicanism still had the power to be America's universal ideological solvent in the
1820s.[7]

While both major parties used the gloomy history of republics as the basis of
their outlook, each drew on the nation's historical record selectively and differently from each other as they assessed their current condition. The Democrats' historical analysis focused on the Federalist-Republican conflict during
the first generation of American national politics. While the Jacksonians were
particularly outraged by what had been going on since the presidential election of 1824, they were not surprised at the destructive tendencies present on
the political landscape given who their opponents were. There may have been
many differences between the political wars of the 1790s and those that
emerged in the 1820s, but the Democrats did not see them. They were still in

6. "The Virginia Address" (Richmond, 1828), p. 3.

7. Watson, *Liberty and Power*, p. 153; Bernard Bailyn, *Pamphlets of the American Revolution, 1750–1776*
(Cambridge, 1965); Milton M. Klein et al., eds., *The Republican Synthesis Revisited: Essays in Honor of
George Nathan Billias* (Worcester, 1992); Joel H. Silbey, *The American Political Nation, 1838–1893* (Stanford,
1991).

a battle with antirepublican "monarchists" who would twist the nation away from its heritage of republicanism and freedom.

The battle for America, Democrats argued, had erupted at the time of the ratification of the Constitution. Two "distinct parties" developed then and had continued into the present. Both of these parties "advocate and endeavor to carry into effect, measures diametrically opposite." Their differences were "nearly as old as the government itself," according to New York Jacksonian John Adams Dix. The people of the United States now "stand in the same attitude" toward each other "as the democrats of 1798 and 1800 did to the federalists of that day." Tennessee Democrats agreed. "The great fundamental principles of government which directed the People of the UNITED STATES into two distinct parties in 1799–1800, essentially divide and separate the two great parties at this day." The "principles at issue were the same" now as then. The differences between them were "not obliterated" by the passage of time.[8]

The Democrats saw themselves as "the disciples of Jefferson and Jackson," whose task it was "to preserve in their purity, those great republican principles, which from the earliest period of our government, it has been the great object of the democratic party to sustain." In contrast, their opponents had a dark history that they should never be allowed to hide or disavow. Democrats saw John Quincy Adams and his National Republican (soon to be Whig) supporters as the inheritors of the Federalist lust for an antirepublican centralized power sure to crush American liberties. The Whig "is the same party which, under the name of 'Federalist,' was encountered by Jefferson in the early days of the Republic . . . Scarcely a principle or a practice can be named in which ancient Federalism and modern Whiggery are not entirely parallel."[9]

All the essential elements of the case against the Federalists—their monarchial tendencies, their love of central power, and their disdain for popular liberty—appeared in Democratic discourse from the outset of this renewed party battle and gave it much of its particular bite. Their opponents' "*names* [may] have changed, but the[ir] principle is the same—an unhallowed thirst for power arrayed against popular rights." In the 1820s, for example, there was much focus on the pedigree of John Quincy Adams (as well as on his many personal inadequacies). Adams was a closet federalist as well as being a sup-

---

8. "The History of the Federalist and Democratic Parties in the United States, by a Citizen of Wayne County, Indiana" (Richmond, Ind., 1837), p. iii; "An Address Delivered by John Adams Dix before the Democracy of Herkimer County [New York] on the 4th of July, 1840" (n.p., 1840), p. 8; "Speech of Hon. John Adams Dix, of New York . . . 26th July, 1852" (n.p., n.d.), p. 1; "Voice of the Southwest: Proceedings of the Democratic State Convention of Tennessee . . . 1840" (Nashville, 1840), p. 9.

9. "Proceedings of the Democratic-Republican Convention of the State of Indiana" (Indianapolis, 1836), p. 2; "Address to the Democratic Republican Electors of the State of New York . . . 1840" (Albany, 1840), p. 13.

porter of "Aristocracy" and of "consolidationism" (concentrating power in the national government) against democracy. He and his National Republican, later Whig, supporters were "dangerous to the institutions of the country." Adams had always "inflexibly maintained . . . his monarchial principles," while "the party we oppose has again and again changed its name, but its designs are the same . . . What else is Whigism [sic] than the degenerate offspring of Federalism?" Will Americans support this member of a "degraded nobility" for president, "or will you make a republican, a farmer, and a hero, a self-made man . . . your president?" The answer was clear. In Adams's hands, the fragile republic could only, and would, fail.[10]

The Democrats added to this indictment frequent mention of the most compelling test of the Federalists' behavior and evidence of their intentions: their activities during the War of 1812, which culminated in the convening of the anti-American and antirepublican Hartford Convention. Adams and his supporters remained now in a "treaty of alliance" with the survivors of that infamous assemblage. Whiggery today, Jacksonians emphasized, was "identical with War Federalism . . . reeking with their pollution." When contrasted with Andrew Jackson's behavior then and his position now, only one question was relevant. "Will you support monarchists?" his supporters asked rhetorically. "Will you ratify the treaty of alliance which has been formed with the Hartford Convention?" Or "will you stand by those who stood by their country in its utmost peril?"[11]

But there was more to be said. The National Republicans, and then the Whigs, had added a new element to their behavior since Federalist days. Honesty in political affairs, Jacksonians insisted, was absolutely necessary for the survival of the Republic. Earlier republics had died as a result of the corrupt and dishonest behavior of their political class. Ignoring that lesson, the Whigs constantly engaged in such destructive practices. They tried to hide what they were and used "the stratagems of party" to distort and confuse what they and their opponents stood for. Their cabals were everywhere, deceiving the people in order to attain their goals. "In political warfare," Democrats claimed, "our opponents have taught us to expect misrepresentation."

10. "Proceedings of the Democratic-Republican Convention of . . . Indiana" p 6; Samuel D. Ingham, "An Exposition of the Political Character and Principles of John Quincy Adams" (Washington, 1827), pp. 3, 9; "Address of the Democratic Republican Young Men's General Committee of the City of New York . . ." (New York, 1840), pp. 4, 13; "Address of the Committee Appointed by the Democratic State Convention Which Met at Nashville . . . 1843" (Nashville, 1843), p. 8; "Address of the Jackson Central Committee to the People of Kentucky" (Frankfort, 1828), p. 11.

11. *Albany Rough Hewer* (a Democratic campaign newspaper), August 13, 1840, p. 204; "Address of the Democratic Republican Association of the Seventh Ward to Their Democratic Brethren" (New York, 1838), p. 7; "Address of the Jackson Central Committee to . . . Kentucky," p. 11.

They never retain the same name, so that "they are enabled for a time, to obscure and conceal their principles, and, thereby, to deceive many honest minded Republicans."[12]

The Whigs behaved this way because they were really not a true political party as were the Democrats, who were united in outlook and policy commitments and therefore able to compete honestly for the people's vote in a forthright, open manner. The Whigs, in contrast, were "the fragments of an ill-digested combination, united only in an unscrupulous opposition to the party in power, and faithless to each other; with no common bond of fellowship, but like a mercenary soldiery, ready to contend for him who will pay best." Their policy was particularly damaging because it was "fraught with portentious evil." Such a combination made the Whigs extremely dangerous to the American people. They were "anti-republican; . . . [their] object being to defeat the wishes of the majority . . . probably to open the door to bribery and corruption."[13]

The National Republicans of the late 1820s and their Whig successors in the next decade disdained the Democratic version of world history and the lessons the Jacksonians drew from it. "We have neither taste nor skill," one of them wrote, "for groping among the mouldering relics of dead controversies. To us, it matters very little whether a man were on the right or wrong side of a question which was put at rest twenty years ago." In fact, "the mere names of parties which have sprung up and passed away before our day, are to us nothing." There had been "no Federal party nor Federal candidate [in 1824] . . . The assertion was therefore grossly false: in the mouths of those who made it [the charge] was not merely false but BASE and MEAN."[14]

Whig explanations of what they saw as the potential for republican decline had little to do with the past battles and unhappy moments that the Democrats emphasized. Rather, the Whigs focused on the problem of civil order in the present, especially the necessity for effective civil leadership in a republic. Every anti-Democratic pamphlet seemed to include what one writer referred to as the "contrast between [candidates of] preeminent ability and illustrious public service on the one hand, and bare mediocrity and comparative obscu-

---

12. "Proceedings of the Democratic Legislative Convention Held in Boston, March 1840" (Boston, 1840), pp. 3, 5; "Address of James K. Polk to the People of Tennessee" (Nashville, 1841), p. 12; "To the People of Pennsylvania" (n.p., 1848), p. 1.

13. "Republican Legislative Address and Resolutions" (Albany, 1836), pp. 2, 6.

14. *New York Log Cabin,* (a Whig campaign newspaper), October 17, 1840; "The Northern Man with Southern Principles, and the Southern Man with American Principles . . ." (Washington, 1840), p. 32; "Proceedings of a State Convention of Whig Young Men of Connecticut" (Hartford, 1840), p. 4; "The Conduct of the Administration" (Boston, 1832), p. 12.

rity [that is, the Democratic leader] on the other." The focus was on the personal. The Whigs engaged in individual vilification of a type familiar to later generations. Both parties saw Andrew Jackson as a transformative figure, the Democrats happily, the Whigs with horror. Adams's supporters in 1828 and thereafter worried incessantly about Jackson's past, his profession, and his resulting capabilities.[15]

While the disparagement of the other party's candidates was a constant motif of the early days of the renewed partisan warfare (and would continue unremittingly thereafter), it was never confined to simple character assassination. Rather, it focused on who the candidates were and what they stood for, what they represented, what their quality was in terms of the Republic's needs and dangers. For example, a powerful early theme of those in the anti-Jackson camp was the danger of an unbridled militarism intruding into civic affairs, a phenomenon that they believed had led to the fall of all earlier republics. "Ours is a contest between civil authority and military power," a writer calling himself Cato warned New Hampshire's National Republicans in 1828, "a contest between the constitution and the sword." Furthermore, "the besetting danger of Republics, is the proneness in our natures to pay a blind and indiscriminate homage to martial renown." History was strewn "with the ruins of republics destroyed by the ambition of military chiefs exercising civil authority . . . Rome had her Caesar, England her Cromwell, France her Napoleon, Mexico her Iturbide. Let us be wiser than these nations, or at least profit by their lessons, and suffer not ourselves to be dazzled by the lustre of military glory." Therefore, Louisiana's National Republicans concluded, "if you prize the free institutions of your country, we entreat you not to founder them upon the rock w[h]ere every republic heretofore, has split." A military despotism "will overawe the exercise of our privileges, and make them subservient to the will of a tyrant."[16]

Jackson himself made this danger even worse than the historical record suggested. To his enemies, he was "altogether unfit for the Presidency, . . . his election would be eminently dangerous." His "public conduct has been at war with all our republican feelings and principles." His "whole life has evinced an arbitrary temper, not congenial to our institutions, and justifying fears of disastrous consequences, should the sword be entrusted to his hands." Jackson's "temper is impetuous, insubordinate and cruel." His is a "violent spirit" whose "disposition is ungovernable and vindicative." In short, "talents

15. "The Contrast" (1852), p. 3.

16. Cato, "A Defense of the National Administration in an Address to the People of New Hampshire" (Concord, 1828), p. 17; "To the Citizens of Washington County" (Washington, Pa., 1827), p. 31; "Address of the Delegates . . . to the People of Louisiana," p. 21.

merely military, even of the highest order, do not qualify a man for the office of President." Are we, they asked in conclusion, "already so degenerated, as to look, without horror, upon the possibility, of giving ourselves a master, and submitting our necks to the yoke?"[17]

This characterization was confirmed after 1828 by Jackson's record in office, which revealed all of his arbitrariness and lust for power, the usual characteristics of the undisciplined and dangerous military chieftain. To the National Republicans and the leaders of the emerging Whig party, Old Hickory's election had been a national disaster, it had "proved . . . to be, a *curse to the country*," distinguished by the president's "rude, arbitrary, and often absolutely unconstitutional" behavior. "If repeated for another term, [it] will in all probability be . . . [the] country's ruin." They focused a great deal of attention on Jackson's use of the veto to thwart what in their eyes was the people's will. As a result of his actions, the executive power in the United States had become "stronger than that of George the Third." The country has moved in seventy years "from despotism to despotism." In consequence, the American people had "now reached that fearful crisis in our history, when a few months will decide whether the constitution and with it the Union of the states is to stand or fall." What was at stake, in Henry Clay's words, was nothing less than "the free institutions inherited from our ancestors."[18]

Nor did Jackson's chosen successor as president, Martin Van Buren, calm the fears of his political opponents. No military man, the longtime political organizer and behind-the-scenes operator had always greatly offended the National Republican and Whig sense of what constituted appropriate leadership for the nation. His first term in the presidency demonstrated the larger danger that he and the other Jacksonians embodied. Under Van Buren, "the first American Nero," who ignored the national disasters he had fomented and concentrated instead on expanding his personal power through the growing Democratic party organizational network and his call to enlarge the American army, the country was now "but one remove from a practical monarchy!" If the people reelected him to the presidency in 1840, the Whigs argued that the country's "liberties are at an end."[19]

The Democrats slashed back, reminding their opponents as well as their own supporters that "it is often more important to examine the principles of

<hr>

17. "Virginia Address," p. 4; "Address of the Great State Convention of Friends of the Administration Assembled at the Capitol in Concord, June 12, 1828," (Concord, N.H., 1828), p. 12; Cato, "Defense," pp. 14, 15; "Address of the Delegates . . . to the People of Louisiana," pp. 7–8.

18. "Conduct of the Administration," pp. 27, 50, 86; William Henry Seward to Robert C. Winthrop *et al.,* July 29, 1840, William Henry Seward Papers, New York Historical Society, New York, N.Y.; Clay quoted in Maurice Baxter, *Henry Clay and the American System* (Lexington, Ky., 1995), p. 97.

19. "To the Whigs and Conservatives of the United States," (Washington, D.C., 1840), pp. 1–2.

that party" that has nominated someone than the alleged personal deficiencies "of the individual they propose for office." And here clearly it was the
Democrats' opponents who were found wanting, and who were the real
threatening and destructive element in the nation, no matter who their candidate was. "When time has dispelled the illusions of faction, their conduct
will appear in its true light and the only epitaph recorded on their tombs will
be, Here lie the men who were born under the only free government upon
earth, but who lived and died opposing it." The Democratic principles, in
contrast, were clearly different, recognizing the triumph of freedom in America and aimed toward the preservation of the republic and its liberties.[20]

At the same time, Democrats also attacked the Whigs on the question of
the appropriateness of particular candidates. In 1840, in 1848, and especially
in 1852, when the Whigs themselves nominated generals as their presidential
candidate, their opponents had a field day. "Why has the whig party forgotten," the young Stephen A. Douglas asked a Virginia Democratic rally during
the campaign against General Winfield Scott, "with an oblivion so complete
all that it once said about military politicians?" Remember, he went on, "we
have yet to see a professional soldier succeed as a statesman" (Jackson, in
Democratic eyes, was not a professional, but a volunteer, soldier). The answer
was clear. The Whigs simply thought that they could win by doing so. Unfortunately, whether they would win or not, the American republic could only
be the loser in consequence of the Whigs' hypocritical actions.[21]

The Democrats, National Republicans, and Whigs laid down this discourse
of danger and decline forcefully and repetitiously from the 1820s onward. At
the same time, the voice of the first of the third parties to appear on the
national scene added its perspective to the debate. The members of the Antimasonic party had a story to tell as well, a story in which they rejected the
two-party hegemony of the Democrats and National Republicans–Whigs in
American politics. But their story was similar to that of the two major parties.
They rejected neither the rhetorical style nor the substantive structure of their
enemies as they focused on the looming threats to the republic and the country's extreme danger in the face of its many enemies.[22]

Antimasons shared with their political enemies deep fears for the American

20. William R. King *et. al.,* "Address to the Democratic Republican Party of Alabama" (n. p. [1840]),
pp. 3–4.

21. "Speech of Hon. Stephen A. Douglas, of Illinois, Delivered in Richmond, Virginia, July 9, 1852"
(Richmond, 1852), pp. 6–7.

22. On the Antimasons see William Vaughn, *The Antimasonic Party in the United States, 1826–1843*
(Lexington, Ky., 1983); Paul Goodman, *Toward a Christian Republic: Antimasonry and the Great Transition
in New England 1826–1836* (New York, 1988).

republic from internal threats, although they had their own twist on what those threats were. Organized Masonry provoked an uproar among some Americans in the 1820s, an uproar powerful enough that its opponents became highly politicized and electorally potent in a number of places. Masons belonged to a secret society, and, it was charged, they ignored the conventional social commitments of the communities in which they lived. Worst of all, adherents of the masonic movement were said to have committed a heinous crime—the kidnapping and murder of William Morgan, a Mason who had publicly discussed their secret rituals—and allowed to escape punishment for it. Masonry, therefore, with its denial of law and order and its refusal to submit itself to the open marketplace of ideas and public opinion, was surely a threat to the Republic. "Freemasonry is now extensively believed by Americans to be an institution," an Antimasonic party pamphlet writer summed up, "fraught with danger to their liberties." Its practices are "subversive of individual rights and public justice." Masonry *tends to subvert Republicanism by introducing a privileged class among us, thereby giving birth to aristocracy.* Finally, Masonry was antireligious; its rites and ceremonies were "of the most revolting character, bordering on blasphemy." The American republic was indeed in danger from its power and reach.[23]

It may be argued that there was much that was obvious and conventional in such dire assertions about the political consequences of the other side's winning office. To be sure, there is some truth to that charge. But the extent and specific focus of the arguments, and the relating of them to specific people and events, suggest that there was a particular kind of reality in the discourse as well. The amount of time and energy that went into elaborating the argument about national dangers, for example, suggests something of the seriousness with which the pamphlet writers believed their audience viewed the problems of the Republic. The themes of the country's fragility and danger, so frequently reiterated in standard political discourse, framed a set of concerns that those shaping political confrontation believed were important to the American people. They were also a way of winning votes, if the electorate could be made to understand not what was at stake in politics—they already knew that—but where each party stood and what each would do, or was capable of doing, when in office. In cultural terms, such emphasis suggests a great deal about the nature of American perspectives in this period; in political terms, it reflects a continuity of concern that offered opportunities to

23. "Proceedings of the Antimasonic Republican Convention of the State of Maine . . . 1834" (Hallowell, Me., 1834), pp. 11, 13, 21.

frame politics in a singular way. The pamphlet writers followed through on those opportunities with talent and gusto.

"THE HAND OF GOVERNMENT"

Persistent fears about the daunting threats that the nation faced helped organize much of the American party battle at its outset in the late 1820s and for some time thereafter, coloring the conflict and directing it into well-marked channels. But the traditional theme of the fragility of the Republic was always supplemented by other, related matters of comparable importance. As their competition and arguments matured, Democrats and Whigs moved away from their early focus on the Republic's fragile condition to what seems to be, at first glance, the commonplace discourse of conflict between different economic interests in society and debate about the best means to deal with the widespread changes and development that were taking place in the United States.

In the midst of vast transformations of American society after 1815, fueled by the so-called market revolution and the opening of new resource areas in the west, American politicians had to deal with major questions arising from the nation's vast and rapid economic growth, including the boundaries of such growth, its needs, and its management.[24] Issues concerning banking and land policy, the nature of the tariff, and the extent of government-financed internal improvements—road and railroad construction, river clearing, harbor deepening—filled the pages of the electoral pamphlets from the early 1830s onward. Some of these matters were discussed extensively; others drew less attention. But from the beginning they all raised the same significant issue: Did the United States need a purposeful national government in this area? If so, what was its appropriate (and necessary) size and the reach of its power, and what would be its effect on other values and commitments of the society? The political parties, unsurprisingly, stood in very different corners on these questions; and, as they did on all matters, they made their points vigorously and vociferously.

The National Republicans and their Whig successors were expansive and optimistic about the national government, and they were not bashful to admit their commitment to a vigorous national authority in their election pamphlets. Their conception of the union, its needs, and its prospects was closely

---

24. On the market revolution, see Charles Grier Sellers, Jr., *The Market Revolution, Jacksonian America, 1815–1846* (New York, 1991).

tied to the positive role that they believed the government should play in national affairs. They argued that vigorous government authority was the necessary agent for the promotion, even the guarantee, of the nation's economic development. After all, suggested President John Quincy Adams's Ohio supporters in 1827, "the hand of government never touches us, but to promote the general good." A decade later, Whigs argued "that the first object of the Government should be to take care of the people." They believed that government activism opened up opportunities for every American; its opposite did not. The Whigs, as a party, "advocate no such anti-republican principle as that which declares that 'the people must take care of themselves and the government [must] take care of itself.'"[25]

Expansive credit, protection for American goods, and the financing of an infrastructure adequate for American economic growth were the mainstays of the Whig political economy—and, in their view, were necessary to meet the needs of the nation. They could not understand their opponents' failure to grasp what the Whigs contended were basic economics. The Bank of the United States was "in a manner, indispensable." To destroy it would be to cause the American people unnecessary suffering and the nation as a whole significant economic retrogression. "Banks are the life and soul of credit and of commerce, and through these means it may be confidently asserted, [they] have done more to improve the social condition of man than all other human agencies. They have everywhere been the friend of the artisan, the mechanic and the laborer. They have everywhere been identified with the spirit of liberty and regarded with jealousy by arbitrary power."[26]

To the Whigs, therefore, President Andrew Jackson was "arresting the progress of DOMESTIC INDUSTRY and INTERNAL IMPROVEMENT" through his and his supporters' opposition to the national bank, government-funded construction of transportation projects, and a protective tariff. In particular, the tariff was "the question which directs itself most strongly to the attention of the people." It was "emphatically their measure, for it is the bread and sustenance of life to the toiling millions." Government ought "to protect and cherish the Industry of the Country to the fullest extent as a matter of legitimate and necessary concern . . ." In the Whig view, "Enlightened Protection" was "emphatically the hope and stay of the toiling millions over the whole face of the earth."[27]

---

25. "Proceedings and Address of the Convention of Delegates . . . to Nominate . . . John Quincy Adams . . ." (Columbus, Ohio, 1827), p. 7; "Address of the Hon. Willis Green, of Kentucky, before the Alexandria (D.C.) Clay Club," (n.p., 1844), p. 6.

26. "Conduct of the Administration," p. 54; "Proceedings of the Whigs of Chester County [Pa.] Favorable to a Distinct Organization of the Whig Party" (West Chester, 1838), p. 54.

27. "Conduct of the Administration," p. 53; "Address of . . . Green," p. 7; Horace Greeley, "The

Jackson's opponents similarly found favor—and necessity—in the government-financed construction of canals, roads, and other transportation schemes, funds for which were raised through public land sales. Whigs regarded such projects "as calculated and intended to give employment to Labor, secure a market to produce, and contribute generally and vastly to the physical improvement of the country, and its advancement in Arts, Civilization and Morality." In contrast, the Whigs delighted in pointing out, the Democrats remained "hostile to any action of the Government designed to promote affirmatively the welfare of the People." Failing to see the absolute necessity of these things, the Democrats appealed instead—and destructively—"to the worst passions of the uninformed part of the people."[28]

To the Whig pamphlet writers' regret, conditions remained the same after Jackson, the economic primitive, left office. In the late 1830s and into the 1840s, Democrats, with their "agrarian, infidel Principles," continued to demonstrate their failure to grasp the necessaries of the new economic order that promised so much to the American people. They were "Locofocos; no other name suit[ed] them." There was "nothing good or conservative about them"; they were "the worst of destructives." The new president, Van Buren, the Whigs warned the American people, "made it the great business of his administration to obstruct your prosperity, strip you of your wealth, and overthrow your most useful institutions." Under his administration, no new appropriations were made, even for existing and necessary construction projects. "The workmen have been dismissed, and the unfinished works have been left to go to ruin." Later, in the midst of the depression that his policies had brought on, Van Buren "mocked at the sufferings he had created, and tauntingly told them [the American people] 'that they looked to Government for too much.'" The Democratic president's object clearly was "to prepare you for deeper humiliations and a worse vassalage; to wrest from you your liberties, and subject you to an iron and relentless tyranny."[29]

In the 1840s, under President James K. Polk, "Young Hickory," matters became worse. The Democrats continued to demonstrate that they remained the "BRITISH FREE TRADE PARTY—the uncompromising enemies of American labor—the friends of the British manufacturers—the foes of the AMERICAN mechanic and farmer." If Polk and his Democratic cohorts re-

<hr>

Grounds of Difference between the Contending Parties," and Greeley, "The Protection of Industry," both in *Whig Almanac and United States Register for 1843* (New York, 1843), pp. 11, 16; "To the People of Michigan" ([Detroit], 1844), pp. 1, 8.

28. "Grounds of Difference," p. 17; "Conduct of the Administration," p. 75.

29. "Proceedings of the Democratic Whig National Convention . . . Harrisburg, 1839," (Harrisburg, 1839), p. 35; "Address of . . . Green," p. 4; Concivis, *Letters to the People of the United States* (New York, 1840), letter 13, p. 96; [Hildreth], "The Contrast," p. 36; "To the Whigs and Conservatives," p. 1.

pealed the Whig protective tariff of 1842 in favor of lower rates and free trade (as they did in 1846), "we shall again be reduced to a state of dependency on Europe, and her mechanics and laborers will take the bread from the very mouths of our mechanics and laborers." Whigs contended, in contrast, "that it is the duty of the Government to foster and cherish American labor and American enterprise, in preference to the labor and enterprise of Europe." It had always been "plain that the protective tariff was a great benefit to all the laboring men, both the farmers and the mechanics." If one votes Democratic, therefore, "you will sign the death warrant of domestic industry, and condemn yourselves, your children, and your country to the direst evils."[30]

The Democrats, in their forceful disagreement to all of this, raised a familiar cry about the condition and problems of their society. The party battle, their pamphleteers argued into the 1830s and beyond, remained rooted in a basic, overwhelming situation, the ongoing threats to the liberty of Americans from too much government power. "From the beginning of time, a perpetual war has been waged by *privilege* on *popular rights.*" The Democrats were for limited government because "history clearly shows the tendency of all power to exceed its proper limits." They firmly believed that there was only one way to preserve—and ultimately extend—individual freedom. A large, or "splendid" government was always "built on the ruins of popular rights." It is better, therefore, "to concede rather too little [power] to it than to[o] much."[31]

Such advocacy underscored the Democrats' unstated belief, in contrast to the Whigs' outlook, that they lived in what a later generation would call a zero-sum universe: that the rights of the people decayed as the power of government increased. Liberty and power were opposites. Government expansion fostered undemocratic privilege: a national bank or a protective tariff created unacceptable hierarchies of power on the backs of popular rights because while these institutions enhanced the power and prosperity of some, they always did so at a major cost to the rest of society. "The only use of government," Democrats believed, "is *to keep, off evil.* We do not want its assistance in seeking after good."[32]

Unfortunately, the Whigs were incapable of understanding, or were indifferent to, the threat to the people's liberties from too much government

30. "To the People of Michigan," pp. 1, 8; "Address of . . . Green," p. 11; [Hildreth], "The Contrast," p. 37.

31. King, "Address to the Democratic Republican Party of Alabama," p. 3; "History of Federalist and Democratic Parties" p. 19; "Proceedings and Address of the Massachusetts Democratic State Convention, Held at Worcester, September 1838" (n. p. [1838]), p. 7.

32. Howe, *Political Culture of American Whigs,* p. 139; "Address of the Central Hickory Club to the Republican Citizens of the United States" (Washington, D.C., 1832), p. 7.

power. They were centralizers to their bones despite the dangers from a powerful national government. They readily accepted—and indeed wanted—an "aristocracy" in America. They "would clothe the general government with large and dangerous powers, hostile to the independence of the states and the liberties of the people." Whigs would always favor the "centralized consolidation" of power. The reason for that was clear enough given their Federalist antecedents. Like the Federalists before them, they will never understand that "a simple and frugal government will achieve more for a people, than gorgeous splendor and consolidated wealth."[33]

This theme emerged in particular, in the Democrats' view, in the long battle over the power of the Bank of the United States, a battle that dominated partisan discourse in the early 1830s and whose echoes reverberated for more than a decade thereafter. Democrats demonized the bank and its president, Nicholas Biddle, in the harshest terms possible and linked the Whigs to that demonology. They argued that their opponents were "heated to madness by their zeal for the bank." Extensive credit availability was the mainstay of Whig political economy, even if such prompted—as it did in Democratic eyes—the "extravagant speculations, the visionary projects, and the enormous over-trading of the times." Whigs always "ardently desire" to regulate money and credit as a means of promoting the interests of the privileged in the society. "This is simply the principle of monarchy, carried directly into the banking system, and indirectly into the national government."[34]

The bank question was "between the Aristocracy on the one hand, and the Friends of Equal Rights and Free Institutions on the other." Whigs were engaged in "the great work of subverting the Government of the people, and of substituting in its stead the Government of [the] Bank," of raising "a great moneyed power, hostile in its very nature to free principles, and far beyond the reach of the popular will." The presence of banks "defiles the Temple of Liberty." Its nefarious presence had become "a question for the industrious producing classes—mechanics and sturdy agriculturalists of the country—how far they will degrade the pursuits of labor, giving to the manufacturer of paper money an ascendency, which shall make labor still more tributary to the exactions of the paper system."[35]

---

33. "Papers for the People" (New York, 1852), p. 47; "Address to the Democratic Republican Convention of the State of Georgia" (Milledgeville, Ga., 1840), p. 12.

34. "Proceedings . . . of the Massachusetts Democratic State Convention, 1838" p. 6; Samuel Young, "Oration Delivered at the Democratic Republican Celebration . . . July Fourth, 1840" (New York, 1840), p. 21.

35. "Address of the Republican Members of Congress from the State of New York to Their Constituents" (Albany, 1834), pp. 3, 5, 16; Robert Rantoul, "An Oration Delivered before the Democratic Citizens of the County of Worcester . . . 1837" (Worcester, Mass., 1837), p. 71.

Because of the Whigs' advocacy of the bank, Americans were forced to engage in a "war of PUBLIC VIRTUE against BANK CORRUPTION." Only the Democrats could lead the forces of right because they clearly saw the bank as extravagant, overly powerful, corrupt and corrupting in its activities, dangerous to the nation, and unnecessary for its prosperity. "If we sum up in one grand total all the woes to which paper money, banking, and the over-extended system of credit growing out of it, have given birth, we shall pronounce it to be the most tremendous of the plagues which the Almighty in his wrath has suffered to afflict degenerate men." Something had to be done. It was the Democrats' role to restore "the government of the country to its primitive simplicity."[36]

Instead of a national bank, Democrats ultimately came together to promote an independent treasury to hold the federal government's receipts—an institution created during the Van Buren administration in the late 1830s and subsequently anchored by the Polk administration in 1846. This "dissolve[d]" the government's "unnatural and impolitic connections with the private pursuits of its citizens." And, the Democrats argued, since the country's leaders no longer deposited government money in private banks, they had at last "separate[d] the business from the politics of the country," an action vitally necessary and constitutionally proper.[37]

A high protective tariff, which the Whigs always sought, was, Democratic publicists insisted, also very dangerous to the American people's liberties. Tariffs that limited the free exchange of goods always benefited the few at the expense of the many. To the Democrats, such legislation was "one of the heir-looms of monarchy." They regretted that "in the United States; where all other liberal principles have gained such vigorous growth, protective oppression has been clung to with greater tenacity than even in Great Britain." In contrast, under the Democrats, "a just and equal revenue tariff has been established, yielding more revenue than could be raised under the prohibitory system of the Whig party."[38]

Finally, the Democrats sharply disagreed with the Whigs about federal financing and construction of internal improvement projects. Despite the many demands for federal aid in building transportation projects throughout the country (including many in Democratic constituencies), the Democrats

36. "Address of the Central Hickory Club," p. 22; Rantoul, "Oration, p. 68; *Democratic Review* 40 (December 1857): 517.

37. "Proceedings and Address of the Democratic State Convention at Worcester, Mass., June 17, 1840" (Boston, 1840), p. 6.

38. "The Democratic Textbook, Being a Compendium of the Principles of the Democratic Party" (New York, 1848), pp. 49, 51; [Edmund Burke], "Taylor Whigery Exposed," (n. p., 1848), p. 4.

maintained their position on the national government's having a negligible role in the political economy. They connected internal improvement policies with other aspects of the Whigs' reach for power, while expressing their own disdain for many of the proposals. "We are not yet so infatuated with the blessings of the credit system," one Democratic pamphleteer wrote, "as to build canals in untrodden forests, or throw railroads over unfrequented mountains at the expense of an irretrievable debt to ourselves and our posterity."[39]

The Democrats always claimed to be "in favor of a steady and judicious progress" despite their strong opposition to government intervention in the economic realm. And despite what one historian has called their "rusty ideas," the Democrats seemed to accept, however grudgingly, the presence and continued development of the emerging market-driven economy even as they challenged any government monitoring or full-scale promotion of its activities, as demanded by the Whigs. The latter, however, remained skeptical; they—and some historians since—perceived in the Democrats' electoral rhetoric much evidence that the Jacksonians did not readily accept the economic revolution then well under way in the United States or the policy and attitudinal imperatives that followed from such a dynamic society.[40]

In the Democrats' repeated underlining of their commitment to a set of diffuse populist principles and prejudices—a fear of bankers and banking, a powerful, if romantic, commitment to the producing classes, and a belief in equality of the people—Whigs found economic naïfs incapable of understanding their society and its needs and unfit to rule it as a consequence. Whig pamphlet writers sneered at such notions as the Democrats' independent treasury scheme as one particular example of their enemy's silliness. "From commerce and credit," Daniel Webster argued, "it returns [the nation] to hoarding and hiding."[41]

All of which was true enough. Traces of an anti-industrial, anti-urban cast of mind were present in the Democratic pamphlets, as were other elements of a precapitalist faith. But such "republican" commitments had been greatly stretched since their heyday a half century before, and the Democrats' arguments about economic development now took on a much more ambiguous tone in their pamphlet presentations, often because those presentations fo-

---

39. "Address of the Democratic Republican Young Men's . . . Committee of . . . New York," p. 8.

40. Ibid.; Rowland Berthoff, "Independence and Attachment, Virtue and Interest: From Republican Citizen to Free Enterpriser, 1787–1837," in Richard L. Bushman et. al., eds., *Uprooted Americans: Essays to Honor Oscar Handlin* (Boston, 1979), p. 109; Sellers, *Market Revolution,* passim.

41. Quoted in Melvyn Dubofsky, "Daniel Webster and the Whig Theory of Economic Growth, 1828–1848," *New England Quarterly* 42 (December 1969): 568.

cused on the larger theme of liberty as well as on economic development. Charges that the Democrats were precapitalist or anti-capitalist were, and are, exaggerated. Whatever the Whigs believed, there were some Democrats who were market capitalists and who expressed themselves as such, whatever their differences with their opponents.

In the 1840s, as the grounds of difference between the contending parties firmly settled in, the lines concerning the nation's political economy were clearly drawn in the speeches of two prominent party leaders. Senator William R. King of Alabama told his state's Democrats in 1840, "In short, we believe that the election of General Harrison would be the triumph of northern Federalism, bankism, and abolitionism; . . . that it would be followed by a strong Federal Government, a high tariff, a mammoth Federal bank, a system of internal improvements by the Federal Government, and by all the concommitants of Federal usurpation, which are subversive to the rights of the states and the liberties of the people."[42] King spoke only to one state's party members, but the substance and style of his oratory strongly echoed similar presentations made throughout the Union by his party colleagues. His was the voice of Jacksonian Democracy as it always presented itself to its supporters.

The Whig William Henry Seward saw things differently. "The party which is now administering the federal government," he complained to a Whig audience in upstate New York in 1848 during the Polk administration, "is a party of inaction in regard to education, industry, internal improvement, melioration and emancipation. It is their creed that the powers of government for beneficent action are very limited." To Whigs such as Seward, this was unacceptable, dangerously restrictive, and ultimately destructive of American prosperity and progress. Vigorous, positive government, from "the beneficent operation of the tariff" to "the improvement of our interior communications by land and by water," was clearly required for the nation's present salvation and future prosperity and happiness.[43]

"THE WELFARE OF THE WHOLE PEOPLE"

The ubiquitous concern that Americans had for the preservation of their republican freedom was expressed in debates over issues besides that of the

42. King, "To the Democratic Republican Party of Alabama," p. 6.

43. "To the Orleans County [New York] Whig Meeting" [August 21, 1848] and "To the Whigs of Michigan" [June 12, 1844], both in George E. Baker, ed., *The Works of William H. Seward* (Boston, 1884), vol. 3, pp. 399, 410.

power of the national government. The Democrats' constant fears for the people's liberties ultimately raised questions about the nature and extent of those liberties, and what guarantees and protection they needed. Those questions, in turn, came up repeatedly as a focus of party confrontation. The United States, most recognized, was a nation of striking social, economic, and geographic diversity, with many problems and tensions arising from that fact. Social disharmony based on class tensions, different religious perspectives, and prejudice against certain ethnic groups was a major part of the American social scene from the 1830s onward and spilled over into political discourse.

Each party disagreed about what was needed to be done and, once again, what the role of the national government should be in determining the boundaries of inclusion in America, the nature and extent of the nation's liberties, and the necessity for—and method of—reforming and improving society. For example, should the boundaries of American political freedom be expanded to include those who were on the margins of society, most of whom were denied the vote and the rights of citizens, such as wage earners who were unable to meet suffrage requirements, African-Americans, and women? Did the concern for liberty and its protection inevitably lead to the necessity for specific actions by the national government? The intrusion of nativism, conflict over slavery, and other issues of reforming the republic became part and parcel of this general concern over national meaning and popular liberty.[44]

Democrats, Whigs, and the minor parties of the 1830s and 1840s continually battered each other over these questions. Much of their discourse began with the use of class rhetoric to establish their positions. There were repeated attempts in the pamphlets to array the poor against the privileged and to construct a sense of outrage, resentment, and frustration about how things stood in American society. This was followed by exchanges over the role of others—slaves, women, and immigrants—and their relationship to the society and its politics. These arguments were persistent, bitter, and extremely divisive; in the 1850s they would grow powerful enough to permanently destabilize the existing political system.

Writers of the early pamphlets made much of their society's differences, churning up agitation about corrupting hierarchies and the inequalities that still existed in the United States. Both parties knew how to use the rhetoric of class tensions for their own purposes. The Democrats quickly claimed the

---

44. A useful introduction to these issues is Ronald G. Wolters, *American Reformers, 1815–1860* (New York, 1978).

egalitarian mantle, injecting a great deal of class resentment into their arguments. They repeatedly and heatedly asserted that too much special privilege
still existed in the nation, and that their political enemies were to blame for
such inequities. In contrast to themselves, their opponents were monarchists,
aristocrats, and/or representatives of cabals of illegitimate interests determined to do in the American people in order to promote their own elitist
aims. "From the beginning of time," New York's John Adams Dix told an
audience of Democrats in 1840, "a perpetual war has been waged by privilege
on Popular rights." Furthermore, "our political opponents have publicly
avowed their adhesion to the maxims of aristocracy." They "set up the city
against the country, the rich against the poor, the interests of stockjobbers
and speculators and bankrupt debtors against the welfare of the whole people." If anyone is for Harrison [in 1840] he will "PLACE IN POWER THE
MONARCHISTS WHO SUPPORT HIM." In contrast, Democrats were committed to protect "the rights of the many against the encroachments of the
privileged few."[45]

The Whigs also became adept in their use of the rhetoric of egalitarian
populism and ultimately developed their own appeal to the same democratic
spirit that their opponents did. At first they had worried about "the excess or
abuse of liberty" and about the Democrats' arousal of "the worst passions of
the least informed portion of the people," both of which would only lead to
anarchy or despotism. Jackson's endeavors "to stir up the poor against the
rich" were dangerous, they thought, to the nation's social harmony, a harmony that benefited all. "The capitalist," the Whigs argued, "is useful to the
mechanic, and the mechanic makes himself useful to the capitalist, each re-
ciprocally aiding the other upon the true principles of the social system."[46]

Beyond that, Whigs often condemned the Democrats' egalitarian postur-
ing in contrast to what they argued was their own true egalitarian commitment, especially about matters specifically related to the political economy.
Their policies were not class biased, as the Democrats claimed. Rather, it was
Whig policies that best aided the working classes in American society. The
Whigs claimed, for example, that mechanics were hurt by low tariffs. "Read
this table, mechanics and working men!" one of their pamphlets suggested;
"artisans and laborers, reflect on it."[47] It seemed to prove the Whigs' contention that their policies were best for the workingman.

Such repeated expressions of class-based division by both national parties

45. "An Address Delivered by Dix," p. 8; King, "Address to the Democratic Republican Party of Alabama," pp. 1, 3; "Proceedings of the Democratic Legislative Convention Held in Boston, 1840," pp. 3, 8;
"Whigery Is Federalism" (n.p., 1840), p. 23.
46. "Conduct of the Administration," pp. 60, 75.
47. "The Sub-Treasury: A Tract for the Times" (Washington, D.C., 1844), p. 13.

may have grown out of real inequities in the American economy. At the same time, there was a consensual quality in all of this rhetoric. Both sides wore the mantle of *all* of the people in their presentations. One does not find sharp class-reinforcing notions in them. Much of what was said was generalized and fuzzy; only rarely can be found coherent analyses of, or claims about, hard-edged class divisions. The tendency was to stick with one's party principles and claim that they were beneficial to all classes in society, that one's party was not particularist but had the good of everyone in American society at heart—while the other party was the prisoner of some group or misled in its policies by some basic misconception detrimental to the good of every American.[48]

Where the parties differed in social matters lay beyond class polarization and more on the question of the boundaries of inclusion. Who constituted the nation and how was "nation" defined? Who should participate in the American republic? How flexible should inclusiveness be? These questions involved matters of definition and personal behavior, including specific religious and ethnic qualities. To no one's surprise, Democrats and Whigs found much to disagree about in this area and did so with the same intensity and confrontationalism as they displayed in their debates on the other issues that defined the American party battle.[49]

The Democrats were always quick to condemn the nativism and religious bigotry that was frequently heard in the early 1840s as "contrary to the spirit of the Constitution, and repugnant to the principles of the democratic party." But they were not surprised that such attitudes dominated their opponents' outlook and belief system. "The hatred of the whigs toward our foreign-born population, comes by natural generation. They are the legitimate offspring of the party that enacted the alien and sedition laws. During the last ten years they have occasionally dabbled in the dirty waters of Nativism, and supported tickets nominated by the church-burning faction." In contrast, Democrats believed that "America has been selected out from all the world, by the God of Liberty, to be the asylum of the oppressed of every nation, and his chosen land of freedom."[50]

The Whig argument on these matters was never too far from what the

---

48. Martin J. Burke, *The Conundrum of Class: Public Discourse on the Social Order in America* (Chicago, 1995), usefully discusses these matters. "It is interesting to note," he suggests, "that in a political culture where a great deal of energy was expended in campaigning against social groupings—be they Freemasons, immigrants, Catholics, or slaveholders,—no party ran against the 'working classes,' or identified themselves with the interests of the 'nonproducers'" (p. 127).

49. See Robert Kelley, *The Cultural Pattern in American Politics: The First Century* (New York, 1979); and Michael Holt, *The Political Crisis of the 1850s* (New York, 1978).

50. "Proceedings and Address of the Democratic State Convention of the State of Ohio . . . 1844" (Columbus, 1844), pp. 8, 23; "Papers for the People," p. 158.

Democrats accused them of advocating. Some of their spokesmen made it clear that they feared that "our beloved country" was in danger of "becoming the seat of Papal thraldom." Some Whigs believed that the "despotism" of the Catholic Church was on the march, sending hundreds of thousands of its believers to the United States where they would help destroy the country. Of course, the Democrats were to blame because they accepted that outrage to the republic. To support that party was "to aid Romanism in disguise." Were any "Romanists," they asked, "not a modern Democrat?" In fact, "every catholic on the continent . . . [is] a modern Democrat."[51]

Such arguments were not unusual; they reflected what appears to be a genuine partisan divergence of view about the matter of societal inclusion. As Daniel Walker Howe has written, "the Whigs proposed a society that would be economically diverse but culturally uniform; the Democrats preferred the economic uniformity of a society of small farmers and artisans but were more tolerant of cultural and moral diversity."[52] Both parties were quick to establish the differences between them and reiterated them incessantly in their electoral discourse.

There was a major ambiguity in all of this. As has been noted, the Democrats' ideas of freedom were articulated broadly. The party was hostile to privilege and government-imposed restraint. But their egalitarian claims were also exclusive. While their defense of liberty was broad, it was always centered only on white, male liberty. They made no room for equality for African-Americans, Indians, and women. Quite the contrary: they argued *against* the inclusion of nonwhite racial groups as part of the American nation, and vehemently refused to limit slavery where it existed. All of this made the Democrats often stridently racist in their rhetoric.[53]

The Whigs, though hardly racial egalitarians, were much less ready to limit social inclusion in the nation only to whites, or to condone the existence of slavery. In the first half of the nineteenth century, the continued presence of African slavery in the nation troubled some Americans. Many of those who were so troubled were northern Whigs. Some of them took an antislavery stance early on, and, while most of them did not press their position very hard, they did hold to a different standard from that of their partisan opponents. "Slavery," Whig leader William Henry Seward told an upstate New

51. William G. Brownlow, *A Political Register . . .* (Jonesborough, Tenn., 1844), pp. 77, 78, 110, 111, 113.

52. Howe, *Political Culture of American Whigs*, p. 20.

53. See, for example, Michael Rogin, *Fathers and Children: Andrew Jackson and the Subjugation of the American Indian* (New York, 1975); and David Roediger, *The Wages of Whiteness: Race and the Making of the Working Class* (London, 1991).

York audience in 1844, "is the bane of our social condition . . . True democracy," he continued, "is equality and liberty. The democracy of the Texas party is aristocracy for the white race, and bondage for the black." But what did that mean in policy terms? As Howe suggests, some Whigs were willing to challenge slavery (or at least its extension), as Seward clearly was, and were even willing to help blacks directly as they encountered them. But the Whigs wished to do this "without having to acknowledge their equality."[54]

Some Whigs went further in their commitment, and here they were joined by some of the alternative parties' voices. The Liberty party, which contested two presidential elections in the early 1840s, appealed to the moral qualities of the American people, calling for the extension of the nation's liberty to people not then usually accepted as part of the society. This party expressed great concern about the virtue of the Republic and about its falling off into degradation. This was reminiscent of the rhetoric of the major parties—albeit with a very different cause. The Declaration of Independence was being ignored, the Constitution shunted aside, by the old parties. "The alarming influence of the Slave-power" in its "corrupt and corrupting" actions had led to a degraded state within the nation. The Liberty party therefore sought to "rescue . . . the grandest country on the globe, from the dominion of a slaveholding aristocracy." Only they, the Liberty activists, were capable of doing so: "We believe, both of the large parties have bowed down ignominiously, to slaveholders, and have thereby made the North into conquered, tax-paying provinces of slavery."[55]

As the Liberty party's presence indicated, political tensions were rising out of sectional sensitivities over slavery. These tensions were part of American political life in the 1820s and 1830s as the new party system developed, though they were not yet dominant. In addition to the Liberty party assault, southern spokesmen weighed in on the other side. The defenders of slavery were always quick to oppose any pressure articulated or exerted against their way of life. Beyond these sectional activists, many of the pamphlets issued by the main parties articulated various positions on the issue of slavery and helped to intensify the nation's sectional divide. Even before the appearance of the Liberty party, political parties used sectional sensitivity in an attempt to gain partisan advantage. As early as the 1820s, in National Republican campaign

54. William Henry Seward, "Speech at a Whig Mass Meeting, Yates County, October 29, 1844," in Baker, *Works of Seward*, vol. 3, pp. 269, 272; Howe, *Political Culture of American Whigs*, p. 20.

55. "Address of the Liberty Party of Pennsylvania" (Philadelphia, 1844), p. 9; "The Creed of the Liberty Party Abolitionists; or, Their Position Defined in the Summer of 1844, as Understood by Alvan Stewart" (Utica, N. Y., [1844]), pp. 7, 8.

pamphlets, the Jacksonians and Van Buren in particular were sometimes presented as being under the control of Southerners and acting on their behalf in such matters as their opposition to a higher tariff.

These attacks did not stop with the retirement of the southern slaveholder, Jackson, from the presidency. In the presidential races of 1836 and 1840, Van Buren and his supporters had to deal with such Whig pamphlets as "The Northern Man with Southern Principles," which made the argument that was to follow the candidate throughout his career. As a "northern man with southern principles," Van Buren, in order to be elected president, "threw himself on the platform of profound subserviency to the South, bowing and cringing to the slave power for a long course of years."[56]

Conversely, another of Van Buren's many opponents argued in 1836 that because Van Buren was from New York, he would not be as attentive to southern interests as Jackson had been, or as a Whig candidate from the South (Hugh Lawson White of Tennessee) would be. That same year the Democrats, in response to such southern Whig representations about the danger of electing a northern president, issued a pamphlet for southern consumption. "Opinions of Martin Van Buren . . . upon the Powers and Duties of Congress in Reference to the Abolition of Slavery" established the New Yorker's conservative bona fides on questions that bothered some Southerners: it asserted that Van Buren was against any federal interference with slavery as it existed and allowed him to challenge the partisan obfuscations being engineered by such Whig allegations.[57]

Democrats did not remain on the defensive. They responded to the sectional assaults of their opponents in kind. Senator William R. King's 1840 "Address to the Alabama Democrats" was particularly revealing. King claimed that a Whig victory "would bring into power a political party whose ascendency would be fatal to the rights and institutions of the South," since it would be followed by the expansion of the power of the federal government, high tariffs, a bank and all of the other "concomitants of Federal usurpation, which are subversive to the rights of the States and the liberties of the people."[58]

What is compelling here is that whatever the sectional anger manifested in these, its first appearances in the Whig-Democratic dialogue, it was well con-

---

56. "The Northern Man with Southern Principles, and the Southern Man with American Principles . . ." (Washington, D.C., 1840); "The Charles F. Adams Platform; or, a Looking Glass for the Worthies of the Buffalo Convention" (Washington, D.C., 1848), p. 1.

57. The pamphlet was published in Washington, D.C., by the great Democratic editorial team Blair and Rives. On the election of 1836, see Joel H. Silbey, "Election of 1836," in Arthur M. Schlesinger, Jr., and Fred L. Israel, eds., *History of American Presidential Elections* (New York, 1971), vol. 1, pp. 577–641.

58. King, "Address to the Democratic Republican Party of Alabama," p. 6.

tained by the existing partisan system. There was something ritualistic about the way the matter came up in party discourse, usually as a litany of complaints, a litany that became very familiar through frequent repetition, that assailed the other party for its misbehavior on the issue or its lack of understanding of what was going on. In its early stages, sectional expression was often vague, usually abstract, and always general, lacking the intense focus of a salient policy issue or a specific danger. It was usually wrapped up in, and overshadowed by, other national issues that divided the parties. As a result, whenever sectional anger appeared in the 1830s and early 1840s, it did not have the political force that its proponents wished it to have, as both the Liberty party's leaders and southern rights proponent John C. Calhoun frequently lamented.[59]

The ground began to shift in the mid-1840s. American involvement in foreign adventures helped transform what had been vague into something much more concrete and politically salient than it had been. This change did not happen suddenly or without a great deal of resistance. In fact, sectional political influences, while invigorated by the foreign policy conflicts of the 1840s, at first continued to be contained by the existing system of cross-sectional political division and discourse, which extended to foreign policy matters as well as domestic policy concerns. The Democrats, from the 1820s on, articulated a robust, often uncompromising foreign policy stance. America was always under imminent external threat, was their repetitive claim. Fortunately, the Democratic party stood on guard against aggression from both the nation's traditional and its newer enemies: Great Britain, Spain, and Mexico.

But the party's foreign policy was more than defensive and reactive. Under the leadership of Democratic president James K. Polk, there emerged in the 1840s a commitment to expand the nation's physical borders aggressively, regardless of consequences. Party spokesmen argued that under the Democrats' leadership America's "commerce whitens every sea" and "its flag is feared and respected by the most distant barbarians." The Democratic party had "presented to the Union Texas, and with it the command of the cotton supply, which . . . [was] so much more efficient than cannon balls in keeping manufacturing Europe on her good behavior." Under President Polk, "the national character has been elevated in the estimation of foreign nations to a degree never before known in the history of this republic."[60]

---

59. William Freehling, *The Road to Disunion: Secessionists at Bay, 1776–1854* (New York, 1990), and Joel H. Silbey, *The Partisan Imperative: The Dynamics of American Politics before the Civil War* (New York, 1985) explore the theme of sectional force and its limits in this era.

60. "Proceedings of the Democratic-Republican Convention of . . . Indiana" (1836) p. 5; "Papers for the People," p. 139; [Burke], "Taylor Whigery Exposed," p. 4.

But, predictably, such good intentions rapidly became the subject of intense partisan warfare. The Mexican War, which was opposed by many Whigs, had broken out, the Democrats argued, due to an "insolent foe who had dared to invade" American territory. Polk and the Democrats had repelled their audacity despite "the traitorous Whigs," who in their hesitation and outright opposition to the president's policies "reek with pestilent treason against their country" and are "aiding the cause of the enemy." Under Polk's leadership, and despite bitter opposition, the nation had acquired "the golden valleys of California and the silver mountains of New Mexico, and in them supplied . . . [the] country with a steadily improving tide of coin to meet and balance . . . [its] commercial fluctuations." Under a Whig president, in contrast, America had "truckled . . . to British power" in central America and "put our forehead in the dust before offended royalty" (the Spanish).[61]

Early on, in the 1820s, the National Republicans had been critical of the ability of the Democratic leaders to handle the nation's foreign policy, believing them to be a group of unproven politicians who lacked sufficient leadership skills and military leaders who were prone to violence.[62] In the 1840s, the Whigs were much less enthralled and exuberant than were their opponents about the flexing of America's muscles outside its borders. They had, as the Democrats claimed, spoken, campaigned, and voted against aspects of the war against Mexico. Whig congressman Abraham Lincoln's sharp questioning of the Polk administration's account of how the war between the United States and Mexico broke out was one part of a major Whig effort to draw the line against the president's foreign policy adventurism and to establish in the electorate's minds the extent of Democratic folly and "the lust for dominion" that was "now cherished by the democratic party." In contrast, Whiggery dared to "entrench itself across the path of national rapacity."[63]

The Whig presidential candidate in 1848, General Zachary Taylor, was "a friend of peace," while his Democratic opponent, Lewis Cass, was "an advocate of war." Whig leaders argued that Taylor "would stand upon our own soil to improve it." In contrast, they warned that Cass "would grasp at all the country around us." Cass, Daniel Webster claimed, believed "in the doctrine of American destinies; and that their destiny is to go through wars, and inva-

61. "Speech of Douglas, 1852," pp. 2, 7; [Burke], "Taylor Whigery Exposed," p. 2; "Papers for the People," p. 139.

62. "Conduct of the Administration," chap. 5.

63. "Address Adopted by the Whig State Convention at Worcester . . . September 13, 1848" (Worcester, 1848), p. 6; Horace Greeley, "Why I am a Whig: Reply to an Inquiring Friend" (New York, 1852), p. 6.

sions, and armies of aggrandisement." He was "a gentleman of rash politics, pushed by an ardent and rash party."[64]

In the early years of the next decade, the Whigs continued to oppose the exuberant expansionism of the Democrats in Central America as well as the latter's willingness to involve the United States in European affairs as a consequence of the revolutionary turmoil there. Expanding the arena of freedom outside America—as in the Democratic-fomented excitement over the appearance of Hungarian republican patriot Louis Kossuth in the United States in the early 1850s—was not, in the Whigs' view, America's concern. They were quick to criticize Kossuth's arrival under the auspices of the Democrats as an "unseemly interference with the peace and welfare of this country." They condemned the Democrats' attempts to whip up popular excitement in favor of the central European republican leader and blasted their rash willingness to confront Kossuth's European enemies directly and provocatively.[65]

These differences over foreign affairs were part and parcel of the normal realm of partisan confrontation. There was nothing new in such efforts in this partisan-dominated nation. But some of the dialogue that developed over the Mexican War had a much larger impact as well—in particular, as it involved the question of the expansion of slavery. Did slavery have the right to follow the American flag into the new southwestern territories acquired as a result of the war? A number of third parties took the lead in saying no and in resisting the expansion of slavery outside of its current boundaries. The Liberty party had challenged the existing partisan consensus in the early 1840s and attracted a number of votes at the margins of American political life with its rhetoric assailing the continuation of slavery on the American continent. In the election of 1848, the much larger Free Soil party added its voice to the partisan debates, demanding a major reordering of political priorities in the nation given significant disagreements over the future of the recent territorial acquisitions.

To Free Soil advocates, as with their Liberty predecessors, "minor topics" such as the tariff and the bank had now "sunk out of sight"; they were no longer relevant to the demands of the day. In their view, the old parties had become obsolete as the issues raised by the Mexican war and its aftermath had come to the political forefront. "Retaining their party names, which in years past have indicated a clear line of difference, the whigs and democrats now

---

64. "Address, Whig State Convention . . . [Massachusetts,] 1852" (Boston, 1852), p. 7; "Speech of the Hon. Daniel Webster on the Presidential Question Delivered at Marshfield, Massachusetts, September 1, 1848" (n. p., 1848), p. 9.

65. "The Contrast" (1852), pp. 22–23.

stand before the country without claiming as peculiar to themselves a single great measure of the slightest practical consequence. They propose to keep up the fight when nothing remains of their principles worth fighting for or against."[66]

The third parties' narratives indicated why this was so. They pointed to a moral failure in American life and the corruption of the older parties in the face of the moral conundrum they faced. To the minor party advocates, "neither Whigs nor Democrats *dare* look the great danger of the land in the face." New parties were needed, therefore, who would use the ballot to cleanse the republic of its failings and eradicate the dangers it now faced. Many of them were willing to use the force of government to change the way things were. They demanded that slavery "be excluded from national territories" newly acquired as a result of the Mexican War by action of the federal government. By the late 1840s, their particular weapon was the Wilmot Proviso, a congressional measure designed to prevent the further expansion of slavery into any part of the Mexican lands ceded to the United States by the peace treaty.[67]

These attempts to raise the sectional standard in place of the existing partisan confrontation did not, at first, have as great an effect as the Free Soilers and others wanted. To be sure, the Free Soilers did manage to make a dent in the normal course of American politics in 1848, with the great architect of the partisan political nation, Martin Van Buren, heading their ticket. But their efforts were largely frustrated by the strenuous efforts of the old parties to block the sectional debate and return to discussing the more traditional policy matters that divided them. These restorative efforts were at first successful. The partisan excitement over the Mexican War, and over Kossuth a few years later, reaffirmed and continued a confrontation between the parties that had become the political norm since the 1820s in the United States. The party battle that Americans had grown so accustomed to (and comfortable with) would continue on as it had done over twenty-five years, with no end possible so long as Americans in every part of the country remained as divided as they were over public policies and as willing as they were to confront those divisions at the polls on each election day.

66. "General Taylor and the Wilmot Proviso" (Boston, 1848), p. 3; "Cass and Taylor on the Slavery Question" (Boston, 1848), p. 4.

67. "To the People of Virginia (n. p., 1847), p. 8; "Address and Proceedings of the State Independent Free Territory Convention of the People of Ohio, Held at Columbus, June 20 and 21, 1848" (Cincinnati, 1848), p. 10. A useful survey of the evolution of political abolitionism and antislavery is Richard Sewell, *Ballots for Freedom: Antislavery Politics in the United States, 1837–1860* (New York, 1976).

"To Save and Exalt the Union"

A new phase of the nineteenth-century party battle burst onto the political landscape in the early 1850s, when new issues and a new major party came to dominate the American scene. The new party was totally unexpected by the leaders of the two major parties and, of course, they strongly resisted it. They continued to believe that the ideological conflict between the Whigs and the Democrats that characterized American politics in the generation after 1828 had an eternal quality to it, encompassing as it did the universal and everlasting conundrums of power, government, liberty, and responsibility. Party activists and their supporters assumed that because they were contesting such potent and unchanging issues, once the party system had been firmly implanted, its elements of discourse would remain the prime driving impulse of American politics.

"it is the destiny of associations to have a beginning and an end"

They were wrong. In the 1850s, the Jacksonian party system began to exhibit signs of aging and a need to change direction—signs that rapidly grew into a reality. New issues emerged that the existing major parties found difficult to integrate into their usual pattern of argument and operations. At the same time, the sectional impulse became so energized as to grow into a potent, and then the dominant, force on the national political scene. This time, the familiar partisan restorative efforts that had previously worked so well when cross-pressures erupted in American politics ultimately failed. The invigoration of issues that were largely outside of existing party discourse led to a potent voter realignment beginning in 1854 and the altering of the existing framework of party competition in a number of its critical components. From then on, the American party battle assumed qualities that led to a fundamental shift in its nature and direction: the emergence of two new national parties led to the disappearance of the Whigs and finally the triumph of the Republicans around a new central core of policy differences, largely sectional in nature.[68]

In this new era, much about the content and direction of American politics changed significantly. But much about the style, structure, and underlying

---

68. Michael F. Holt, *The Political Crisis of the 1850s* (New York, 1978); and William E. Gienapp, *The Origins of the Republican Party, 1852–1856 (New York, 1987)* are the best introductions to the political transformation of the 1850s.

substance of the election campaign rhetoric did not. The issues were new, and politically organized in new ways, and the rhetorical differences between the parties could not have been more pronounced along these new lines of conflict. But, even as the new party alignment took shape throughout the fifties, the earlier dipoles of conflict remained. Much of the partisan discourse continued to echo the basic ideological elements that were already embedded in American politics and that had been at play over the previous twenty-five years. The American party battle changed dramatically, but it also had a certain consistency. It continued to echo historical perspectives even as it was transformed by new and potent issues.

The political revolution of the 1850s did not originate solely with the sectional conflict, no matter how powerful that impulse later became in affecting parties, elections, and public policy. Rather, the first significant issue to roil the political waters was an old one: immigration and its consequences for the nation's future. Dormant on the national level for some time, this issue reemerged in the early 1850s with a new potency and became nationalized as it had not been since the Federalist-Republican conflict over aliens and sedition at the beginning of the century. Immigration, coupled with powerful religious and ethnic prejudice, became central matters of party warfare. The existing parties had differed over these issues earlier and continued to do so. But their expressed differences were not significant enough for some critics, who saw no alternative but to disrupt existing political habits and perspectives.

An emerging group of anti-immigrant and anti-Catholic nativists found their voice by condemning both the Democrats and the Whigs, who had, in their view, "been found wanting" in the strength of their commitment on this issue. In the nativists' view, the traditional parties "had become old [and] effete," indifferent to new dangers and increasingly alike in policy and in the way they behaved. With the members of both parties living only for patronage and to be reelected, there was no longer anything to choose between them. As one critic noted, "However wide apart might have been the points of the compass from which both parties had originally started, they had of late approximated so closely, that they had almost merged into the same homogeneous substance." Most dangerous was that, in their quest for votes and power, both parties had allowed foreign elements to become much too powerful politically. Both of them "were *the allies* of the alien faction, and too much under their thumb."[69]

69. "Principles and Objects of the American Party" (New York, 1855), p. 24; "A Few Considerations for Reflecting Voters" (New York, 1856), pp. 13, 16; Charles Gayarre, "Address to the People of Louisiana on the State of Parties" (New Orleans, 1855), pp. 2, 3, 8.

The threats to society were both real and critical, and could no longer be evaded by the political system. The decline of past republics had begun when the native population was "adulterated" by "too great an admixture" of foreigners. The evil effects of this trend were already evident. "The explosion of immigrants" entering the United States had led to vast increases in crime, pauperism, intemperance, and immorality, and, as a consequence, renewed dangers to the republic. "To what class of population are these [social pathologies] chiefly confined?" fearful critics asked. "Unquestionably," they answered, "to foreigners." Something had to be done to preserve American society, beginning with the recapture of the political system from its present leaders with one purpose in mind: "Americans should rule America."[70]

The Democrats received the most criticism from the nativists, especially because they generally supported the entry of Catholic immigrants, who were perceived by nativists to be the most dangerous element in the new tide. Nativists believed that, in the Democrats' support of Catholic immigration, the party had "degenerated into a *semi-papal* organization" that would do nothing to protect the nation from the resulting dangers. Unfortunately, the Whigs were no better. Though in the past they had often suggested their commitment to nativist beliefs and the preservation of a Protestant republic, the Whigs had slipped badly in the early 1850s, as the nativists saw it, and proved themselves miscreants to their previous commitment to cultural homogeneity. They had, nativists charged, "abandoned the old ground on which [they] had stood" to become a "counterfeit" of their opponents. Both parties, therefore, were now alike on this issue; a new party was needed.[71]

The Democrats had always been sensitive to the nativism issue and had always directly challenged the Whigs about it when it was raised. In 1848, for example, echoing familiar historical themes, they asked "our naturalized fellow-citizens" if they desired "to see the party elevated to power that proscribes you—the party that passed the infamous *alien* law . . . the party that openly leagues with the proscriptive native Americans to overthrow the democracy, who stand by your rights and privileges?" The "Puritan Federal party" (the Whigs) was, as before, trying to forbid entry to the foreign born with no legitimate reasons for doing so. Nor did this Democratic assault stop with the Whigs. When John C. Frémont ran as the first Republican presidential candidate in 1856, Democrats described him as "the representative man of caste, aristocracy, proscription, sumptuary laws, a meddling priesthood, and all that

---

70. Gayarre, "Address to the People of Louisiana," pp. 17, 30.

71. William G. Brownlow, "Americanism Contrasted with Foreignism, Romanism, and Bogus Democracy" (Nashville, 1856), p. 7; Gayarre, "Address to the People of Louisiana," pp. 2–3.

has so often proved itself at war with the principles of individualism, and the true progress of mankind."[72]

The Democrats, in contrast, Stephen A. Douglas stated clearly in 1852, made "no distinction among our fellow citizens." The party has "ever been just and liberal to all foreigners that come here," whatever their birthplace or faith. It "made this country a home for the exile, an asylum for the oppressed of all the world." The party's "creed is equal rights to all, both at the polls and in kneeling before the altars of God." Further, Democrats, again in contrast to their opponents, believed in letting people live their lives as they wished. The party was not organized "to act as a spy upon the private opinions or pursuits of men, or sit in judgment upon their consciences, or control even their outward conduct, except through the rightful actions of government."[73]

The nativist American party, or Know Nothings, as they organized and presented themselves in the national arena in the early 1850s, reiterated the narrative of political decline in order to establish their own beachhead against the dominant partisan system. To them, the country had lost its way amid the turmoil of the alien menace, was descending toward fragmentation and chaos, and was in extreme danger from the corrupting activities and failures of the major parties in the face of this overwhelming threat to American nationhood. Nothing could be expected from either of them. "Both parties have degenerated, have become unsound, and have lost the confidence of the people." Fortunately, an alternative existed that could reverse the decline. "The paramount and ultimate object of . . . [the] AMERICAN ORGANIZATION . . . [was] to save and exalt the Union."[74]

Amid this cauldron of social turmoil and loud claims about the parties' failure to deal with the dangerous problem of immigration, the sectional issue once more burst onto the scene, breaking through the bounds of conventional partisan confrontation to take over the political stage. When the issue reemerged in 1854, despite expressions that "this accursed agitation should cease" because it was "futile for good . . . and potent only for evil," its force

72. "Address of the National Democratic Republican Committee," (n. p., 1848), p. 3; Benjamin Barstow, "A Letter to the Honorable James Buchanan . . ." (Concord, N. H., 1857), p. 13; *Democratic Review* 38 (October 1856): 183.

73. "Speech of Douglas, 1852," p. 5; Richard Rush, "To the Democratic Citizens of Pennsylvania," (n. p., 1844), p. 8; "Proceedings and Address of the Democratic State Convention Held at Syracuse . . . 1856," (Albany, 1856), p. 9.

74. Gayarre, "Address to the People of Louisiana," pp. 2–3, 8; Brownlow, "Americanism Contrasted," p. 10.

was now too much to hold back.[75] Politics became complicated, then transformed, becoming more sectionalized than it had ever been.

The centerpiece of this sectional uprising was the emergence of the Republican party in the mid-1850s, as its members challenged increased southern aggression in the nation's western territories. The emergence of the party added powerful new currents to the nation's political debate—currents that moved the country further toward a confrontation about the expansion of freedom's universe. The leaders of the new party infused their rhetoric with the moralism of freedom, as had the Democrats and others before them; but they added to that a persistent and intense anti-Southernism. According to the Republicans, something had recently gone very wrong in America. The federal government no longer served everyone. It had become "the tool of the slaveholding power" and since the 1840s had continually promoted the aggrandizement of Southern interests at the expense of those of other Americans.[76]

The reason for that was very clear and very political. In William Henry Seward's words, "whatever has been at any time or anywhere done for the extension of Slavery within the United States, has been done by the 'Democratic' party." The Jacksonians were now and forever fully controlled by the slave power. If and when they controlled the federal government, their actions and policies always and unfairly benefited the South and its peculiar institution. This was unacceptable; the situation had to be confronted and actively dealt with. It was "time that the honesty of Government were renewed and its purity re-established." Republicans intended to do so and direct government toward the realization of "certain fundamental principles of right and justice," most particularly "absolute refusal ever to surrender another foot of free territory to slavery."[77]

In order to accomplish this, first, old party labels, habits, and commitments had to be overthrown. "It is the destiny of associations to have a beginning and an end," Republicans argued. They agreed with the Know Nothings that the "obsolete political issues of former years" had disappeared or lost

75. "Letter from Hon. Harry Hibbard to Stephen Pingry and Other Citizens of New Hampshire," (Washington, D.C., 1852), p. 7.

76. C. S. Henry, "Plain Reasons for the Great Republican Movement" (New York, 1856), p. 46.

77. William Henry Seward, "Speech of William Henry Seward at Oswego, New York, November 3, 1856" (n. p., 1856), p. 6; "The Man Who Doesn't Vote" (New York, 1860), p. 3; "Address of the Republican State Committee to the Electors of Rhode Island" (Providence, 1857), pp. 11, 18. The leading interpretation of the Republican ideology of freedom is Eric Foner, *Free Soil, Free Labor, Free Men: The Ideology of the Republican Party before the Civil War* (New York, 1970), but its conclusions should be compared to Gienapp, *Origins of the Republican Party,* especially chap. 11.

their centrality. Tariffs, banks, and the rest of the earlier political agenda, they claimed, were no longer at the center of affairs (although the Republicans had positions on all of them—largely reflecting those held by the Whigs). As a result of the shift in political issues, established parties could only "break asunder and dissolve when new exigencies bring up new and different policies and principles." That time had come. The existing political scene, in their eyes, reeks of a "demoralized atmosphere" that only the new Republican organization could overcome through their determination to use national power to restrict the further expansion of slavery.[78]

The Democrats vigorously countered, strongly denying their obsolescence and malfeasance, relying on their traditional themes of the necessity for limited government authority and the protection of individual liberties. They had never departed from their position, asserted to the American people as long ago as 1832, that "the only use of government, is *to keep off evil. We do not want its assistance in seeking after good.*" That position, in their eyes, was relevant then and was even more so now, twenty years later. Since slavery in the United States was constitutionally recognized, Democrats argued that no one had the right to interfere with it, as the abolitionists in the Republican party were clearly endeavoring to do.[79]

But there was more than the question of constitutional rights and the power of government at stake in the 1850s. The Democrats were convinced that the Republicans posed a particular threat to the nation's safety. The new party was prepared to go beyond normal political confrontation, even to risk breaking up the Union, since the southern states would refuse to live under such threats as the Republicans posed. "The Black Republican party is most essentially the disunion party of this country," Democrats believed, with its intention to force its own conception of right on a resistant South. As such, they had no legitimacy, posed a massive danger to the Union, and had to be put down. In contrast, the Democratic party "has ever been the constitutional, and therefore the only national party. Its fundamental tenet of strict construction, affords the only security for the protection of the States and people." Therefore, in opposing any restrictions on slavery in the territories, it "is sustaining the glorious charter of our liberties."[80]

Despite all this tumult, as new and powerful issues emerged to reshape the

---

78. "The Parties of the Day. Speech of William H. Seward at Auburn, October 21, 1856" (Washington, D.C., 1857) pp. 4, 7; "Address . . . to the Electors of Rhode Island," p. 1; "Man Who Doesn't Vote," p. 3.

79. "Address of the Central Hickory Club," p. 7.

80. "The Great Issue to be Decided in November Next! Shall the Constitution and the Union Stand or Fall, Shall Sectionalism Triumph?" (Washington, D.C., 1860), p. 19; "Speech of Col. Jas. C. Zabriskie, on the Subject of Slavery . . . 1856" (Sacramento, 1856), p. 13.

institutions of political warfare and cause a massive confrontation between regions, many aspects of that political warfare remained as they always had been. Bernard Bailyn noticed a significant ideological transformation across time in the pamphlets of the American revolution.[81] In the ensuing century, a great many things on the political scene changed as dramatically as they had in the 1760s and 1770s. Certainly, Republican-Democratic confrontation in the late 1850s had distinct and transforming societal and racial dimensions, a fact that both parties recognized in all that they said about themselves and about the other side.

But the style, structure, and overall substance of the partisan arguments offered in response to new issues and new fissures in the 1850s did not change from what had been the norm. The discourse of the new two-party structure continued to echo the familiar themes of the immediate past political generation. The discourse of the 1850s remained, at least in part, firmly embedded in the same continuum of rhetorical style and substantive concern that now stretched over a generation of conflict, whatever changes in the external social and political environment had occurred. Beyond the specific focus on slavery, the territories, and immigration, the debates among Democrats, Know Nothings, and Republicans reawakened and stressed the earlier arguments about power, liberty, and the nature and future of the Republic. As the Republicans became the new second party in the United States, building on the ruins of the Whigs and the failure of the Know Nothings, they brought forward much that echoed past anti-Democratic rhetoric. The Democrats, in turn, found virtue in their traditional arguments and discourse against the old Federalist threat to rend the Republic apart, under whatever name the heirs of the Hartford Convention adopted.

"A NATIONAL GOVERNMENT *OF UNITY AND STRENGTH*"

These continuities persisted into the Civil War era. During the war, familiar echoes from an earlier time were frequently heard and continued to comprise the basic structure of partisan discourse. The war itself was both transformative and restorative, as far as the American party battle was concerned. It unleashed a vast storm of political controversy because of the pressures, problems, and initiatives it created. It was transformative in that these new pressures on society led to an unprecedented expansion of the reach and responsibilities of the government, an expansion that ultimately included the end of slavery by legislative and executive action. The national state, out of necessity,

---

81. Bailyn, *Pamphlets of the American Revolution*, pp. 90–202.

came to the center of affairs during the Civil War. The power of the federal government reached far beyond any of its earlier boundaries, both in its action and in terms of existing notions of the use of federal power.[82]

At the same time, wartime political conflicts were restorative in that much of the electoral battles that occurred between the Democrats and the Republicans were cast in terms of the traditional basic issues of liberty, power, and legitimacy. The exigencies of wartime and the revolutionary policies culminating in slave emancipation called, in the minds of many, for a vast exercise of power. But, unsurprisingly, notions of a powerful government and its consequences for the Republic and its people still fiercely divided American society and therefore its political parties. Republicans generally welcomed the unprecedented expansion of federal power that took place after 1861. What then happened went far beyond anything the Democrats would accept.

The result was a rekindling of many of the old issues that had divided the parties in an atmosphere undergirded by violence and the pressures of war, conditions that promoted the most extreme rhetoric, especially during the regular election campaigns that continued to be held. Whatever claims there were to this being a new era, with new subjects, elements and conditions, Democrats and Republicans readily continued their great debate about the nature and solidity of the Union, the powers of government, and the consequences to the nation of too much or too little of that power being exercised.[83]

The issue of which party best defends the nation against its enemies and counters the internal threats to its existence was debated once again with the same focus on iniquity—but with the contestants now reversed. The Republicans, with their Whig roots—in Democratic eyes, the heirs of Hartford Convention federalism and of the debilitating opposition to the Mexican War—were now the militant nationalists, insisting that secession and war had created a very different political environment, one that justified certain policies. First, the war provided the Republicans with a renewed basis on which to argue the need for effective national power in order to defeat the rebellion and save the Union. They took their stance quite seriously, vigorously drawing on a variety of familiar themes to make their case. To further their aims, they denounced as dangerous to the republic's survival any opposition to

82. The title of this section is from Abraham Wakeman, "'Union' on Disunion Principles! The Chicago Platform, McClellan's Letter of Acceptance . . . A Speech . . . November 3, 1864" (New York, 1864), p. 3. For general background, see Joel H. Silbey, *A Respectable Minority: The Democratic Party in the Civil War, 1860–1868* (New York, 1978), and Richard Bensel, *Yankee Leviathan: The Origins of Central State Authority in America, 1859–1877* (Cambridge, 1990).

83. Allan G. Bogue, *The Earnest Men: Republicans of the Civil War Senate* (Ithaca, 1981); Eric Foner, *Reconstruction: America's Unfinished Revolution, 1863–1877* (New York, 1988).

their wartime policies. "The stake in this war is no less than our country"; therefore, there could no longer be "divided counsels and irrelevant controversies." The question was no longer one of politics but rather "one of patriotism." Everyone's commitment had to be, as the Republican publicist Francis Lieber entitled one of his pamphlets, "no party now but all for our country."[84]

But their opponents, "the Peace Democracy, alias the Copperheads," went out of their way to resist efforts to save and restore the Union.[85] "One of the most singular anomalies which meets us in the present canvass," Republican pamphlet writers repeatedly underscored, "is the sympathy professed by those who call themselves democrats, with the authors and abettors of the rebellion." Of course, one writer suggested, "the so-called Democratic party is not, at this time, without distinguished and powerful allies: Jeff. Davis in Richmond, Louis Napoleon in Paris, Maximilian in Mexico . . . [and] the British merchants whose incomes have been swelled by the destruction of our commerce" during the war.[86]

The Republicans understood why this was so. The history they recounted of American politics continued to emphasize, as it had in the 1850s, slavery's long-standing control of the Democratic party. "Alike in victory or defeat, the Democratic party had for twenty years bowed to the slave propagandists." Whoever their leaders were, they had always, and voluntarily, engaged in the "low bending of the knee to the dark spirit of slavery." The results of that were seen clearly in the 1860s. "In the beginning, the Democracy invited secession, and, to the end, it encouraged rebellion." Two parties were, of course, welcome and necessary in a republic, "but an Opposition which, in a rebellion, takes sides with insurgents, forfeits for the future all claim upon public confidence."[87]

All of this was repeated incessantly by Republicans throughout the Civil War, their rhetoric becoming especially intense in the most critical of the contests held during the war in the North, the presidential election of 1864. The Democrats at that time were seeking an armistice with the Confederacy,

84. "Address of the Union League Club of Philadelphia . . ." (Philadelphia, 1864), p. 3; "A Few Plain Words with the Rank and File of the Union Armies" (Washington, D.C., 1863), p. 16; Francis Lieber, "No Party Now but All for Our Country" (New York, 1863), title page and p. 8.

85. The title of a Republican pamphlet published in Washington, D. C., in 1863.

86. "The 'Only Alternative.' A Tract for the Times (Philadelphia, 1864), p. 17; "The Great Issue. An Address Delivered before the Union Campaign Club, of East Brooklyn, New York . . . by John Jay, Esquire," (New York, 1864), p. 12.

87. "The Republican and Democratic Parties; What They Have Done, and What They Propose to Do. Speech of Hon. Henry Wilson, at the Republican Mass Meeting at Bangor Me., August 27, 1868" (Washington, D.C., 1868), p. 1; Henry C. Lea, "The Record of the Democratic Party, 1860–1865," (n. p., 1866), pp. 16, 39.

Republicans charged, "only to let the rebels recuperate." In their platform and in their leadership Democrats demonstrated that their real "treasonable purposes" are "the disruption of the union." The people should not be unsure of what was at stake. "Every other election has been trivial, compared with this. The choice is to be made by each one of us whether we wish that the Nation—the Great Republic—shall live or die." Fortunately the Constitution, "fairly and liberally expounded . . . does invest the government with all the power necessary to preserve itself and the nation."[88]

Preserving the union justified, in Republican eyes, the most expansive use of national power yet seen. They expounded a theory of government power unabashedly put forward to the northern electorate and worth quoting for its breathtaking sweep. "The war has taught us some valuable lessons of constitutional law," the pamphleteers of the Republican-controlled Union League of Philadelphia argued in 1864, "which plain men who are not lawyers, can understand. It had taught us that the government must have power to save the nation; that whatever is necessary to that end is constitutional; that the people are the nation, and that the constitution exists for the people; that the constitution belongs to us, the people of 1864, and that *we have a right to modify it to suit our needs according to our will*."[89]

The Democrats were no more reticent about their position than were their adversaries. At first they were thrown off stride by the enormity of civil war and the insistent demands of their opponents that they forego political activity, but they recovered soon enough because their worst fears were, appallingly, coming true. The Democrats' distrust of national power and its consolidation at the center only grew as the Lincoln administration demonstrated how far it was willing to push to attain its ends. During the war the Republicans enacted an 1860s version of the old Whig program: a protective tariff, a central banking system, and government support for the building of extensive internal improvements. They instituted a military draft and engaged in wide-ranging efforts to control people's speech, political activities, and movements. Nothing any longer seemed beyond the reach of a vigorous and purposive central power.[90]

In the Civil War years, therefore, Democrats easily, if sorrowfully, articulated their familiar rhetoric to counter what they say as a renewed assault on

---

88. "Speech of Governor [John] Brough . . ." (Cincinnati, 1864), pp. 10, 12; Wakeman, "'Union' or Disunion," p. 31; "Address of the Union League Club of Philadelphia," p. 25.

89. "Address of the Union League Club of Philadelphia," p. 25. Italics added.

90. See Leonard P. Curry, *Blueprint for Modern America: Non-Military Legislation of the First Civil War Congress* (Nashville, 1968), and especially Phillip S. Paludan, *A People's Contest: The Union and the Civil War, 1861–1865* (New York, 1988).

the nation's values and liberties. They found unconscionable the abuses inherent in "the revolutionary policy of the [Lincoln] Administration," the threat to liberty and national survival it posed as it used its power to advance the most illegitimate and frightening ends. Federalism and its successors once more controlled the government and, as could have been predicted, their policies evinced that their main endeavor was going to be an assault on the liberty of all Americans, especially those who disagreed with them.[91]

The long-term results of four years of such Republican policies were clear to the Democrats. The Lincoln administration had "broken the Constitution shamefully and often." The Democrats believed that the Union was, once again (as the Republicans also insisted in their turn), in mortal danger. They expressed grave fears for its survival. As a consequence of Republican policies, the nation's present was despairing, and its future would be disastrous. "That the party of the Administration is both vicious and incapable, has been most abundantly proved." As a result, "we are literally drifting toward destruction." The Republicans' "odious policy" would extract its price, that is, "the liberty of the whole country," since "when did a ruler who had deprived his country of its liberties ever voluntarily restore them?"[92]

But there was more. According to the Democrats, the Republicans had gone beyond their claims to be only interested in restoring the Union. The Lincoln administration had reached even further, confirming Democratic fears about their opponents' unbridled appetite and uncontrolled determination to push beyond reason. "Representing radical and violent elements . . . among us," the Republicans had "changed the war into a humanitarian crusade outside of any constitutional or lawful object." The nation was now in the thrall of "Puritanism in politics." America was controlled by the social and political extremism of Puritan New England, with that region's incessant preaching of a "fratricidal hate" against its enemies. Its tenets had taken over the Republican party. The issue that the Democrats particularly connected to such extremism was race—that is, the emancipation of African slaves and the resolution of their eventual place in American society. Given Republican instincts, the Democrats were not surprised by their wartime efforts in this area, efforts that the Democrats greatly feared and stridently opposed.[93]

Lincoln and his congressional colleagues were following racial policies, the Democrats lamented, "which tend to social debasement and [the] pollution

91. "Congressional Address. By Members of the Thirty Eighth Congress, Politically Opposed to the Present Federal Administration . . ." (Washington, D.C., 1864), pp. 5, 11, 21.

92. Ibid., pp. 17, 18, 21, 27.

93. "Puritanism in Politics. Speech of Hon. S. S. Cox, of Ohio, before the Democratic Union Association, Jan. 13, 1863" (New York, 1863), p. 13.

of the people." The government was "established by white men and for white men and their posterity forever, and it is for the common advantage . . . that the exclusion of the inferior races from suffrage should be permanently continued." The races "should be kept distinct, socially . . . they should not blend together to their mutual corruption and destruction."[94] In its content, style, intensity, and savagery, such partisan political rhetoric infused the North's politics during the war in the same manner as its predecessors had in earlier years. To the Democrats, such discourse and resistance were necessary given what was at stake. To the Republicans, such Democratic behavior was to be expected, given the base and iniquitous desires of that party to resist what needed to be done to preserve the Union.

"A REVOLUTION IN OUR GOVERNMENT"

The debate between the parties that raged during the Civil War did not end with the defeat of the South in 1865. Democrats and Republicans violently disagreed over what was to follow the North's victory, both at home and in the surrendered Confederacy. Republican leaders saw the need to continue to use the federal government's authority with vigor and purpose to pursue a policy of reconstruction that included the advancement of the rights of the former slaves; the Democrats maintained their strenuous opposition to such authority and the purpose to which it was being put by the Republicans who were in control in Washington.[95]

In all that ensued in the election campaigns of the dozen years following the war, the focus and content of political discourse continued to be familiar. Republicans retraced the recent historical record to draw from it lessons and, particularly, warnings about their opponents. They began the postwar discourse by asking "is it not reasonable . . . to judge of the future of a political party as you should judge of the future of an individual—by its antecedent history?" They never let up on sounding the familiar warning: the danger to all Americans posed by the Democrats, given their record of support for slavery and the South before and during the Civil War. That party's history "recalls no inspiring ideas, no beneficent policies, no ennobling deeds for patriotism, for liberty, for justice, and for humanity. But it does recall images of slavery, . . . the slave power, . . . dark conspiracies, lawless rebellion, fields of blood . . . and the graves of the nation's dead."[96]

---

94. "Congressional Address . . . of the Thirty Eighth Congress," pp. 19–20, 22.

95. The best introduction to the Reconstruction era is Eric Foner, *Reconstruction: America's Unfinished Revolution, 1863–1877* (New York, 1988).

96. "Speech of George H. Williamson . . . San Francisco . . . 1868" (San Francisco, 1868), pp. 1, 8; "The Republican and Democratic Parties . . . Speech of Hon. Henry Wilson," p. 13.

The Democratic party remained "hostile in war and wrong in peace." One of the Republican pamphlets listed all of the "traitors" who had been in the last cabinet of a Democratic president and asserted that Democrats "justify and exult in the murder of Lincoln." As they organized for their presidential run in 1868, the Democrats were still "faithless and heartless," led by a "promoter and representative of disorder and anarchy" (former governor Horatio Seymour of New York) who was surrounded by similar "revolutionary and treasonable spirits." Voting for the Democratic candidates, Seymour and Blair, in 1868, Republican publicists warned, would open "the flood-gates of revolution and anarchy" in the United States. Such rhetoric, the Republicans believed, remained useful as a means of linking bad people with the Republic's recent experiences and its dangers.[97]

As to their own claims, the Republicans continued to make a strong case on behalf of national power, as they had done during the war. Their mission had not ended. Much remained to be done, especially in the South. As Republican senator Henry Wilson argued in 1868, the party had successfully developed "the nation's power" and advanced "its material interests" so that the United States now "stands on a higher plane than that of any political organization on the globe." And there could be no retreat from what they had done if the nation wished to maintain itself and what it has gained since 1861. The "unrepentant" South, allied with their Democratic colleagues, continued to resist the will of the nation. The danger, as always, was real. Southerners intended to restore themselves and their values to power as soon as they could so that "the malignant spirit of slavery and caste" could "rule again."[98]

The Democrats, of course, disagreed, using their familiar arguments of the danger to freedom and the desirability—the necessity—of limited government. Their "sordid and selfish opponents" had used the occasion of the war to take advantage "of the passions and delusions incident to the occasion" in order to impose their "views of finance, revenue, and the administration of government." In consequence, "a revolution in our government" had "been going on," whose tendency was "to vest in the General Government nearly every power that a government can possess over a people." The result was clear: Republicans had passed "repressive and not reconciliative" measures, measures that tended "to the destruction of the republic."[99]

97. "The Issues of the Day. Speech of Hon. Roscoe Conkling, at Utica . . . 1876" (New York, 1876), p. 15; "Treasonable Designs of the Democracy. The Issue before the People . . ." (Washington, D.C., 1868), pp. 3, 7, 8.

98. "The Republican and Democratic Parties . . . Speech of Henry Wilson," pp. 10, 13.

99. "Speech of S. S. Cox . . . August 30th, 1872" (n. p., 1872), pp. 7, 20; "The Principles and Policies of the Democratic Party . . ." (New York, 1875), p. 30; "Speech of Allen G. Thurman, at Cincinnati, Sept. 10,

Democrats devoted much of their rhetoric to the present and future condition of the emancipated slaves in the South and what (if anything) should be done by the federal government to help them in their transformation from slavery to freedom. As during the war, they were not happy about the direction and substance of their opponents' efforts. America was, no one should ever forget, "the country of the White race, given by the Almighty on which to build a great white nation." But the Republicans had opted to ignore this sacred trust in favor of their own policy of racial egalitarianism. The Democrats fiercely condemned Republicans' "malignant efforts to degrade the white inhabitants of the Southern states and place them at the mercy of an inferior race." Their policies would lead to the nation's "mongrelization" (a favorite Democratic word in the context of race issues in this era).[100]

"FOUNDATION OF OUR FAITH"

Reconstruction lasted until 1877, and its consequences were felt for a very long time thereafter. By the time President Rutherford B. Hayes ordered the last northern troops out of the South and presided over the final restoration of local control there, the parties had fully internalized the issues raised by the war and its aftermath and found ways to argue them that were infused with their previous approaches to American politics. In the 1870s, as before, although many of the specific details of American politics had changed over the past twenty years, the basic thrust of party warfare and tone of partisan rhetoric did not. Even with the rise of new issues in that decade, from civil service reform to monetary policies, neither party wavered in its basic course. The Democrats demanded that the government be reformed and restored, constantly reiterating their long-established commitment "to limit and localize government," which was now, as it was in the past, the "foundation of our faith." As they had been saying for a decade and more, "the necessities of war cannot be pleaded in a time of peace." It was time to restore the federal government to its previous limited role in national life.[101]

But there continued to be a serious problem. Under the Republicans, "the authors and abettors of administrative centralism," the federal government "is paternal, without limits and without well defined duties. It undertakes the

---

1870," (Washington, 1872), p. 1; "Speech of Hon. L. D. Campbell, at Delaware [Ohio] September 7, 1870, in Reply to Senator John Sherman" (Cincinnati [1877], p. 1.

100. *Illinois State Register,* Springfield, April 4, 1866; *Louisville Democrat,* November 20, 1867. This theme is discussed and analyzed in Forrest Wood, *Black Scare: The Racist Response to Emancipation and Reconstruction* (Berkeley, 1968).

101. *Official Proceedings of the National Democratic Convention . . . 1876* (St. Louis, 1876), p. 196.

care of the people—their morals, their industries, and their property . . . It legislates for every conceivable interest . . . It seeks to put a spy in every house and a constable at every elbow." As a result, Democrats continued to list the not unfamiliar issues of the day, from taxation, financial policy and the tariff, to radicalism, "republican disregard of the Constitution," the "Bayonet election law," and "our state governments belittled," among others, and ask, as they always had, whether faced by Federalists, Whigs, or Republicans, "Where is the old simplicity and purity" of the government?[102]

The time had come, the Democrats kept repeating, to reduce and reform the national government, and restore amicable relations between the sections. The election of 1876, August Belmont told the Democratic National Convention that year, "is a struggle between Democracy, representing union, progress and prosperity, and Republicanism, representing sectional strife, religious intolerance, and a continuation of financial and industrial prostration." The country remained endangered by the Republicans' control of national power. Only under the Democrats would the nation "return to the ark of the Constitution, to frugal expenditures, to the administrative purity of the founders of the Republic."[103]

The Democrats' opponents remained equally faithful to their existing discourse and ideological substance in the 1870s. Although "the cause of the Union and of freedom" had triumphed, the Republican publicists continued to point out that victory had come without the aid of the Democratic party. The latter, voters were once more reminded, was "debased by slavery and demoralized by Calhounism." Its members "had neither the courage, nor wisdom, nor patriotism to sustain the war which the nation waged in self-defense." Nothing had changed. In the 1870s, as in the past, the Democrats remained subservient "to the disloyal elements of the South," those who remained "unsubdued, defiant, hopeful, active and aggressive." The Democrats' presidential candidate in 1876, New York's Samuel J. Tilden, was "the man who did more than any other to precipitate the rebellion." He was "the most obnoxious person in the nation to all principles of order and good government."[104]

---

102. Ibid., p. 62; "The Danger and the Duty of the Democracy. A Letter to the Hon. Francis Kernan by Clarkson N. Potter of New York" (New York 1876), p. 9; "Peril of the Hour. Speech of General A. Saunders Piatt, Delivered at Mac-a-Check [Ohio], 18th September, 1876" (n. p., 1876), pp. 3, 15; "Speech of Hon. George Pendleton, at Loveland, O., August 22, 1871" (n. p., 1871), passim; "Grant or Greeley? Speech of S. S. Cox . . . 1872" (New York, 1872), p. 1.

103. *Official Proceedings of the . . . Democratic Convention . . . 1876*, p. 63.

104. "The Three Secession Movements in the United States" (Boston, 1876), pp. 17, 20, 24; "A Change to Democratic Rule; What It Means . . ." (n. p., 1876), pp. 6, 7, 8.

In contrast to the actions of their Democratic opponents, "the Republican party's deeds of usefulness, and acts of fidelity to the best interests of the people" were clear and positive, and, most important in the writer's view, were the proper policies for the nation. The Republicans' record was "no more to be compared to . . . [that] of the democratic party than light is to darkness, or loyalty to treason." And that record still counted although the war was over. Was the United States, Republican pamphlet writers asked, "sufficiently recovered from the effects of the war" so that it could "afford to put the high priest of secession at the head of the Government?"[105]

Through it all, the Republicans also continued to stress the power of the national government: "The nation not the states, is supreme," one writer argued, proceeding to underscore the theme of order and preservation through the use of federal power against the Democrats' disruptive degeneracy. The latter's "cry of 'centralism' is a mere fetch. The real danger is the other way. De-centralization, which means State Rights in the old pestilent secession sense is the real danger . . . 'Centralism' is a mere goblin . . . All the 'centralism' we have now, is a strong and stable government under which the nation prospers, with safety to property, labor, liberty, and life." In short, the Republicans' unrelenting message continued to be that "on one side [their own] is safe, tried, and stable government, peace with all nations, and prosperity at home, with business thriving, and debt and taxes melting away. On the other side [the Democrats], is a hybrid conglomeration made up of the crotchets, distempers, and personal aims, of restless and disappointed men. What ills might come of committing to them the affairs of the nation, no judgment can fathom, no prophecy can foretell."[106]

While the two major parties continued their warfare in the style and substance that had characterized them for half a century, there were glimmerings of new forces emerging onto the national scene in the 1870s. Most of these new impulses sought a home within the major parties.

Women had always played a role on the American political scene, but one that was largely informal, since they could not vote and were usually not encouraged to participate directly in nominating caucuses and other party activities. At the same time, women had repeatedly sought to expand their role, particularly by winning the right to vote. Like members of established political parties and proponents of various issues, women articulated their

105. "Address of the Republican State Convention Held at Little Rock, September 15, 1874" (Little Rock, 1874), p. 17; "The Three Secession Movements," p. 21.

106. "The Three Secession Movements," p. 24; "The Presidential Battle of 1872 . . . Speech of Hon. Roscoe Conkling at Cooper Institute, N. Y.,. . . 1872" (New York, 1872), pp. 36, 48.

perspective in pamphlets, adding their voice to the debates of the late 1860s and early 1870s. Like other reformers, they claimed to want to improve the Republic and enhance the freedoms of a significant part of the population within it. Leading suffragists, echoing the established style of political discourse, saw a clear distinction between the Republicans and their opponents. "We are willing," Massachusetts women argued in 1872, "to trust the Republican party" to follow through on the demand for voting rights by doing away with what the Republicans called restrictive "class" legislation, which defined suffrage in gendered terms.[107]

A powerful economic downturn in 1873, which seriously affected the whole country, provided the Democrats with an opportunity to break away from war-related issues and slash at their opponents along another familiar line of cleavage, the misbegotten economic policies of Federalist-Whig Republicanism. Although the Democrats, like their opponents, had significant internal differences over financial policy in the 1870s, specifically due to the vociferous demands of some Democrats that the government continue to accept paper money as legal tender and the resistance of others to what they thought was a dangerously inflationary policy, party leaders tried hard to play down their conflict and stress the basic differences between the parties over economic affairs.

To Democrats, the depression had been caused (unsurprisingly) by "the false policies of the Federal Government," with its "excessive" activities everywhere and the imposition of high taxes to pay for them. The period since the war "has been characterized by unsound public finances [and] . . . an extravagance in public and private expenditure." As a result, "labor finds scanty employment even at reduced wages. Incomes are lessened and fail altogether." Restoration of government frugality was an absolute neccesity. But it would never happen under a Republican Administration, as history abundantly demonstrated.[108]

The Republicans did not take the bait. They stated firmly that the real issues between the parties remained as they had been: the war, the preservation of the Union, the issues flowing from Democratic submission to the South, the Democrats' treasonable wartime behavior, and the inadequacy of

---

107. "Address of the Republican Women of Massachusetts" (Boston, 1872), p. 1. On the women's suffrage movement in this era, see Beverly Beeton, *Women Vote in the West: The Woman Suffrage Movement, 1869–1896* (New York, 1986).

108. "Governor Tilden's Letter of Acceptance, July 31, 1876," in *Official Proceedings of the . . . Democratic Convention . . . 1876*, p. 189; Samuel J. Tilden, "Finance, Taxation, and Reform" (Scarborough, Me., 1876), pp. 5,7.

that party's principles in every area. So far as the economic issues of the day were concerned, the Republicans blamed the Democrats for their succumbing to wild monetary panaceas that disrupted economic confidence. "It is my conviction," Rutherford B. Hayes wrote in his letter accepting the Republican party's presidential nomination, "that the feeling of uncertainty and insecurity from an irredeemable paper currency, with its fluctuations of value, is one of the great obstacles to a revival of confidence and business, and a return to prosperity." The longer such instability lasts, "the greater will be the injury inflicted upon our economic interests and all classes of society." The message was clear. The problem was, as always, the errors of the other side.[109]

This general pattern of blame and counterblame between the two major parties did not satisfy everyone. Some of the new participants who had appeared on the political scene challenged the hegemony of the major parties on behalf of their particular concerns. Some women's suffrage activists found both parties wanting and looked to third parties for redress. The economic distress of the early 1870s prompted vigorous third-party activity as well. A group of "independents," forerunners of what was to become the National Greenback Labor Party, joined the presidential contest in 1876 as the first of the third parties that were to become a prominent part of the political landscape in the last third of the nineteenth century. The Greenbackers argued for unorthodox financial policies, the issuance of paper money, and an income tax. They were forced to organize as an independent political movement, they said, because neither major party would do what needed to be done for the American economy.[110]

The Greenbackers' arguments echoed familiar themes and idioms that had long been heard in American political discourse. They, too, were in a "fight for the liberty of the American people" and, as a result, were engaged "in one of the greatest battles for reform that ever engaged the attention of man." American freedom was again in danger, this time from the concentration of economic power in the hands of a few, as well as "dangerously large fortunes," "foreign influence," and "corruption." Only through a Greenback victory at the polls would the wrongs perpetrated "against the rights and interests of the laboring, producing and commercial class" be corrected.[111]

<hr>

109. Reprinted in in Russell B. Conwell, *Life and Public Service of Gov. Rutherford B. Hayes* (Boston, 1876), p. 305.

110. A still very helpful introduction to the Greenback movement is Irwin Unger, *The Greenback Era* (Princeton, 1964).

111. "To the Independent Citizens of Ohio" (Cleveland [1871]), p. 1; "Address of the New York County Committee of the National Greenback Labor Party" (n. p., [1876]), pp. 1–2.

Despite the familiarity of their expression and its compatibility with the existing style of political confrontation, neither women's suffrage nor the class-conscious economic demands of the Greenbackers gained much political authority in these years in terms of support from party leaders or from voters, although their emergence signaled some compelling changes on the horizon for a political landscape that was still dominated by partisan warfare rooted in republican values and issues engendered by economic development, individual liberty, and the role of the national government. But those changes remained in the future. The familiar still held sway as the years of Civil War and Reconstruction came to a close in the late 1870s.

New York's Republican senator, Roscoe Conkling, nicely invoked the power of the continuing confrontation between the two major parties in an address to his party's state convention in 1878. "The mission of the Republican Party is not ended," he began. "It has done much. It has put down a vast rebellion, freed 4,000,000 slaves, made a free Constitution, united the fragments of a shattered empire, managed war and finance to the amazement of mankind; it has carried railroads over deserts and mountains . . . it has made harbors . . . ; it has secured to every man who will have it a homestead of 160 acres of fertile land; it has stood for free speech, free labor, and freemen always; it has upheld the public credit; and its aims have been those of humanity and right."[112]

The Democrats ended the era in equally vigorous—and familiar—fashion. "The time is ripe," Samuel J. Tilden argued in 1876, "to discard all memories of buried strifes, except as a warning against their renewal; to join altogether to build anew the solid foundations of American self-government." There was much to do after too long a time under the sway of extremism and too much central power. The American people carried tax and other burdens greater even than those imposed by the immense and elaborate governments of Europe due to the policies of the Republicans, who had commanded the nation since 1861. They had built up "a more costly machinery than the imperial governments of the two richest and most powerful monarchies of modern times." It was now time to "make governmental institutions simple, frugal,—meddling little with the private concerns of individuals,—aiming at fraternity among ourselves and peace abroad,—and trusting the people to work out their own prosperity and happiness."[113]

---

112. "Speech of Roscoe Conkling, as President of the Republican State Convention, at Saratoga, [N.Y.,] September 26, 1878," (n. p. [1878]), p. 6.

113. Tilden, "Finance, Taxation, Reform," pp. 10, 27, 28.

"Consider Well . . . the Platforms . . . of the Parties Now Asking Your Suffrage"

America's political parties produced a mountain of words in the campaign pamphlets they published from 1828 to 1876. Their political battles had an extraordinary harshness and bite as well. Throughout, the pamphlets etched sharp contrasts and sounded warnings to never let up in this inevitable and serious conflict. Each party demonized the other by attacking its policies, its leaders, and its intentions in the most threatening and colorful manner. American political discourse was always one of excess.[114]

But these rhetorical excesses did not mean that the parties were only playing hostile games with each other—or with American voters. The monsters that they created in every campaign season in their narratives of America's past and present touched real and recognizable elements in the nation's political culture. The parties successfully articulated the basic nature of American politics as partisan leaders and voters understood it. Party leaders knew their audience well. Americans were concerned about the security and state of their society, and they had strong prejudices, fears, aspirations, and agendas, all rooted in their many experiences. But they were not in agreement about any of these. This half century was characterized not only by two-party dominance but also by a range of ideas and policies that remained essentially divisive and, depending on which side one was on, either positive or threatening to the nation and to the people's liberties.

Some scholars have lately been inclined to dismiss much of this partisan discourse as only electorally driven and therefore suspect as expressions of what its authors really believed (or what the voters they addressed really thought). As stated earlier, however, party activists were in fact deadly serious about their beliefs and what they wrote and distributed. A great deal of evidence challenges such skepticism as a misreading of a truly divided political scene. The parties went beyond rhetoric and differed from one another at every level of political confrontation. The Whigs (later the Republicans) and the Democrats espoused significantly different worldviews and repeatedly acted on those distinctions.

To be sure, the nation's political discourse in this era, rich in its language of conflict and divisiveness, always remained within particular ideological boundaries. Most political arguments do so. Neither side moved outside of the general framework that defined their society in its broadest terms. But

114. The quotation in the heading of this section is from "The Republican and Democratic Parties . . . Speech of Hon. Henry Wilson," 1868), p. 14.

that hardly made the debates the parties engaged in consensual, except at the outer boundaries of their confrontation. It is very hard to find any level of consensus in the highly charged expressions of both parties, except that each claimed that they were trying to achieve the same thing: the security and future of the nation.

One is also struck by the continuities in the style, structure, and content of writings of the various parties; all were remarkably stable over time. The parties used history to frame their arguments, to draw out telling examples, and to recount the critical moments that gave shape and direction to the present. They both used the vocabulary of classical republicanism and focused their attention on the fragility of republics in a hostile world, especially because of always-present internal dangers. They paid constant attention to the needs and the future of their economy and their society. Most of all, each party intensely and clearly argued that it was battling for the soul, the future, even the survival of the American experiment. The parties touched on all they themes in clear-cut, straightforward terms.

This discourse, though commonplace in much of its content, gave order and direction to its society and its political system. After fifty years of such widespread partisan articulation, no one who had paid any attention could doubt where the parties stood on the issues of the day or could ignore how much was at stake in these battles; that each voter had better attend to what was being said and act for himself and for the future of the country. Democrats and their Republican opponents, as Jacksonians and Whigs before them, stood for different things and represented different interests.

In fact, one can argue that two very different political cultures inhabited the same nation throughout these years, and that these cultures had quite different notions of proper policy, the nature of authority, and the definition of legitimacy. The reality of those differences is what gave the parties' campaign pamphlets their power. Neither the Republicans, nor the Whigs before them, sought to tyrannize the people of the United States, nor to degrade or destroy the nation—though Democratic audiences were not convinced of this. Simultaneously, in a dynamic nation undergoing rapid growth and facing unprecedented change, Democratic policies may have been more old-fashioned than their opponents thought helpful, wise, or legitimate; but the policies that the Democrats advocated were not as foolish, nor as treasonous, as the National Republicans, Whigs, and Republicans suggested.

The result was the continuation, from the Jacksonian generation into the years of sectional strife and beyond, of powerful political disagreements on the American landscape—disagreements that were thoroughly canvassed in the nation's many election seasons. The parties' ideological differences led to intense and unyielding partisan warfare that was well marked out and artfully expressed in the pamphlet literature produced by the leaders of the two major political parties as well as by those of the minor parties that appeared more fleetingly on the scene, but who spoke with the same intensity as the Democrats, Whigs, and Republicans, despite their more limited chances of electoral victory.

PART THREE

New Issues and Parties: Americans, Republicans, and Divided Democrats 1854–1860

❧ 10 ❧

A Few Considerations for Reflecting Voters (New York, 1855?)

BETWEEN 1854 and 1856, the two-party dominance of the Whigs and the Democrats collapsed. In 1856, the still-powerful Democrats faced two successors to their Whig adversaries: the American party (the Know Nothings) and the Republican party. The leaders of the former echoed previous claims about the increasing obsolescence of the two major parties, particularly in the face of horrible new dangers to the American republic. "When the scum of European society . . . floats to our shores," New York City Know Nothings pointed out, neither our institutions nor our values could be sustained without a powerful counterattack. Of particular concern was the number of Catholics among the immigrant hordes because the Catholic church "is at heart a tyrant," determined to destroy America's Protestant republic. Only a new party with new aims could carry out the necessary defense against these dangers. This message proved to be so powerful to voters in the mid-fifties that for a time it seemed that the Know Nothings would replace the Whigs as the second major national party.

WHAT FOREIGNERS THINK OF US

New-York is a mosaic of nationalities. Our population speaks the language of every civilized nation, and exhibits almost every type of the human race. The great exodus of Europeans to our shores, which we have witnessed during the past few years, is indeed one of the most important events of the age in which we live. It surpasses, both in interest and in magnitude, those ancient migrations whereby the peoples of Asia transferred their home at once from Asiatic to European soil.

Great principles give rise to, and direct these nomadic tendencies. The Greeks, from the time of Alexander, inclined eastward toward the Euphrates, while the tide of Slavonic conquest has rolled in the direction of the Caucasus. In like manner, the Romans and the Teutonic nations of the north sought, from the first, to extend their influence westward. They met on the soil of western Europe. As the conquerors and the conquered learned from each other, there followed, to a certain extent, a blending of races and institutions. The Roman law, the equalizing influence of Christianity, and that barbaric love of independence which characterized the ancient Germans, were the chief elements of civilization that have contributed to the upbuilding of the central and western European States.

The East of Europe lies open to the surplus population of the West. The half starved millions of western Europe might find a near asylum on the uncultivated plains which border the lower Danube, and in the rich forests of European Turkey. In vain, however, does the Danube, that magnificent inundation hurrying for ever to the Euxine, invite the nations of Germany to return toward the soil of Asia, the ancient home of their race. In vain, or almost in vain, have the sovereigns of Austria and Russia encouraged emigration from the Germanic States to their wide and thinly populated domains. Nature has decreed otherwise, but from the weary and pent up millions of western Europe streams of emigration burst forth, like the fabled fountain of the sacred Aretheusa, and forcing their way through other channels, reach the shores of our western world, the home of a free people who love, and who have struggled, to be free. For political as well as physical reasons we can not, neither would we, check the tide of immigration constantly rolling toward us from the Old World, but it is for us to direct the same, for good or for evil both to ourselves and the myriads thus cast among us.

Our national character has impressed its mark upon this age. "Nothing is impossible to an American," has become a common saying in more than one language of continental Europe. Pompey said that the foot of a Roman soldier had but to touch the soil of the most distant region, and new institutions would spring forth as if spontaneous. We may justly boast of the same thing in reference to our countrymen.

Those who have grown up around the despotic thrones of Europe, and talk pompously of absolutism and the sword as the only panaceas for all social and political evils, look contemptuously upon our form of government as an experiment destined to fail. All the magnificent circumstances and surroundings of our national existence, and the gigantic proportions to which a marvelous growth has brought the confederacy, serve only to strengthen their conviction that the failure of our political system will be final and complete.

The *savans* and philosophers of the Old World, whose teachings, unfortunately, are not permitted to reach the level of its despotic thrones, regard our country as the great theater upon which civilization is destined to achieve her noblest triumphs. Political considerations, and especially the deductions of physical geography, lead to this conclusion.

The gigantic scale upon which everything is here exhibited, our great inland seas, our rivers thousands of miles in length, our almost boundless plains, and the magnificent distances which in general characterize our continent, would have discouraged the human race in its first efforts to overcome the forces of nature. But when man had learned to subdue these forces on the contracted theaters of the different European States, the discovery of America opened a *terrain* on which are to be achieved far mightier results than are possible in the Old World. What is embryonic there, will be developed here. That partial fusion of the Latin and Teutonic races which has taken place in western Europe will be completed here. Here will be exhibited a language and literature common to the teeming millions, who shall inhabit this continent, and here also a religious faith, varied in unimportant features, but common to all in having for its basis the cardinal truths of Christianity, will strengthen the foundations of law and promote national virtue and prosperity. This is the destiny for which nature has clearly marked out our country, and we, as a people, are determined that her great purposes shall not be defeated by those who would gladly see upon our soil an *apothesis* of the false systems and despotic institutions of the Old World.

The liberty loving of the Old World naturally regard our land as the Atlantis of their hopes and dreams. What visions of plenty and of happy repose are wafted across the ocean to the oppressed millions of Europe! It is they whom we welcome among us. Only the minority of them, however, are permitted to emigrate to our shores. Despotism has so successfully applied its chains that the great majority of those who hope for better things are compelled, like Sampson in the mill of the Philistines, to labor for the support of tyranny.

The prevalence of war in continental Europe as an institution, the slight restraints imposed by morality and religion, and the low propensities encouraged there by the "powers that be," for the purpose of drowning nobler aspirations in the direction of liberty, produce a state of society contrasting strangely with that of our Pilgrim forefathers. It is the glory of our Republic, that even in the lower class of native born citizens, there is a great amount of virtue as well as of intelligence. What the corresponding class in Europe think of us is of little moment; but when the scum of European society, ejected by its rotten institutions, or cast up by the surges of revolution, floats to our shores, and demands immediate baptism to the high honor of American citizenship, there arise questions worthy our maturest consideration.

Adventurers of every stamp look to America as the land where unbounded license prevails; where law puts few or no obstacles in the way of evil doing; and where vice and crime reap richer rewards than industry and virtue.

These false impressions are strengthened by what they see on their arrival in our midst. They behold none of the pomp and pride with which governmental authority is maintained abroad. They see no grand military preparations, no armed police in the streets to awe and intimidate. They witness no exhibition of brute force for the purpose of preventing popular outbreaks, or drying up individual drops of disaffection. All moves on quietly and calmly. They see no ponderous wheels of government, hear not the clash of its operation; and, unable to comprehend that man can restrain and rule himself, come to the conclusion that we are a people without government.

In like manner, the fact that we have no established Church, and the absence of imposing religious ceremonials, are apt to lead foreigners arriving in our midst to believe that we are a people without religion.

The Ballot Box is justly styled the Palladium of Liberty. Europeans, however, do not, in general, appreciate its importance or comprehend its workings as an institution, from the fact that they are not accustomed to the rule of the majority. They look upon the excitements and the *bella verborum* that attend our popular elections, as the incipient stages of revolution, but are surprised to see the agitation of the public mind subside after the vote has been given even more quickly than it rose, and the return of tranquillity and apparent contentment. The Frenchman, for instance, is not satisfied with merely an appeal to the Ballot Box, but finding himself in the minority, and not understanding the necessity of complying with the will of the majority, deems it necessary to make an appeal to the sabre and the musket. This is one of the great obstacles in the way of establishing a French Republic; and this utter ignorance of the nature and workings of republican institutions characterizes the inhabitants of continental Europe in general. They mistake the apparent for the real, the shadow for the substance.

Shortly after the election of General Jackson to the Presidency, many articles found their way into our prominent journals, reflecting severely upon the conduct of the Emperor of Russia. Some of them were republished in England, and reached the Czar himself. He was highly indignant, and protested against the same, through his Minister at Washington, to General Jackson. The previous political campaign had been exceedingly warm, and General Jackson cut from the public journals a few of the most pungent articles slandering and vilifying his own character and reputation. These were dispatched to the Czar of Russia, who made no further complaint. Nothing is, in fact, more natural than that Europeans in general should have a total misconception of us as a people, as well as of our institutions.

CIVILIZATION

Says Menexenus, "Neither a Pelops, nor a Danaus, nor a Cadmus, nor a Cecrops, nor any other, who, being originally a barbarian, has been naturalized among the Hellenes, has settled among us. We are of pure Hellenic blood—no mixed people; and hence the hatred of foreign manners and customs is especially implanted in our city."

It was for a long time customary to regard Grecian civilization as an importation from Egypt and Phœnicia. The best historians of our time have, however, discovered that it was of spontaneous origin, indigenous to Greece herself. Nothing, in fact, is more contrary to the teachings of history, than the common impression that the different types of civilization can be transplanted like exotics from country to country, and be made to flourish upon any and every soil. The elements of civilization are indeed thus transferable; but its peculiar and distinguishing type, the essential entity, must be a spontaneous development. Greece no doubt borrowed much from Egypt and Phœnicia, but her civilization was neither Egyptian nor Phœnician; it was Grecian. Rome, in turn, borrowed much from Greece, but her civilization was not Grecian; it was essentially Roman—notwithstanding the source from which its chief elements had been derived. The Persian, Turkish and Arabian types of civilization had also their distinguishing characteristics The attempt to civilize the Turks of to-day by exhibiting an *apothesis* of French manners along the Bosphorus, will prove a failure. The institutions of the West can not flourish under the ægis of Ottoman protection. The only way to regenerate Turkey is to develop a germ of civilization that is peculiarly Turkish. Foreign elements and foreign means may be employed with advantage, but the plant itself must be native, and not exotic.

As a people, we differ widely from all others. We boast of an Anglo-Saxon origin, of the language and literature of Shakespeare and Milton, and yet we differ from the English almost as widely as from the French and Germans. We have our national characteristics. Our innate love of Liberty, our intense hatred of aristocratical and monarchical institutions, our untiring activity, and the practical talent we possess for adapting means to procure results, render us unlike any other people on the globe. In other words, our type of civilization is American; a word which fully explains itself. It possesses an individuality. We do not say that it can not and will not be improved; but it is to its development in all of its essential points, that we look for great results in the future. It is not to be denied that the stream of immigration gives us new sinews of national strength, and imparts to us important elements of civilization. Could these be assimilated at once, all would be well. That, however, is not possible; and as a natural consequence, our national institutions are suffering therefrom.

Our national character rests upon a religious and moral basis. We do not believe that the faith handed down to us from our Pilgrim forefathers can be bettered by any association with the Jesuitism and Infidelity of the Old World. We are not of the opinion that the comparatively high standard of morality which characterizes us as a people, is to be improved by contact with the low morality and licentiousness of Europe. Nor can our strong instincts in favor of liberty be invigorated by the weak and fluctuating aspirations of the great mass of Europeans in the same direction. On the contrary, Jesuitism and Infidelity would gladly remove, and are seeking to remove, the pillars of our religious faith. The low morality and licentiousness peculiar to continental Europe are fast undermining our national virtue and infusing their poison into the life blood of our people. The instincts in favor of liberty so peculiar to our ancestors, and even strong with us, are fast being weakened and deteriorated by the influx of foreign ideas.

These things are fraught with peril to the institutions of our land. The elements of destruction are silently at work. Their influence is already apparent. The results which they are intended to produce will be none the less fatal from their being long deferred.

IMMIGRATION

Before describing the different classes of emigrants which reach our shores, and the various foreign agencies and influences which we oppose, it may be well to allude to the subject of immigration in a general way. From the year 1688 to 1775, namely, from the Revolution in England to the Declaration of Independence by the American Colonies, almost the entire emigration from Europe to this country was from the continent, chiefly the persecuted French and German Protestants.

It was during this period of almost one hundred years that the Anglo-American population acquired that ascendency which it has since maintained. During the twenty-five years following the Declaration of Independence, the immigration of foreigners was limited on account of the war and subsequent difficulties. It increased considerably during the first ten years of this century, to be checked again by the war with England. From 1820, however, it steadily advanced until it acquired its present magnitude and importance. Every nation of western and central Europe has been represented in the tide of emigration that has flowed toward our shores, and even the east of Europe has contributed a portion. China has also sent her thousands to California. These converging streams of immigration have brought with them the polluting heathenism of Asia and the worthless Christianity of Europe, the superstitions of Rome and the refined Infidelity of the German schools, false political systems and corrupt morality, not to mention the festering vice, the intense poverty, and the abject ignorance thus cast among us.

True, there has been a falling off in the number of immigrants the present season compared with the numbers of the two preceding years, but the source is by no means exhausted. On the contrary, did not France, the States of Germany, and especially Austria, place all possible obstacles in the way of emigration, the stream would enlarge from year to year. Millions look longingly to us from across the Atlantic, and the convulsions, which are destined to shake the European world, will yet cast myriads upon myriads of exiles and wanderers upon our shores.

Of the poverty of those who are thus thrown among us, we do not so much complain. We have a virgin soil, and there is room enough for all. Capital demands labor, and we can soon put the emigrants in our midst in the way of supporting themselves. Their ignorance, however, imposes enormous burdens upon us. That is especially the case in a religious point of view. Dr. Baird, in his Report on the progress and prospects of Christianity in the United States, read before the Evangelical Alliance during the great London Exhibition in 1851, says, that it is absolutely easier for us to provide for the spiritual wants of our entire native population than for those of the foreign. They are entirely unacquainted with our voluntary system. All who come from the continent, and many from the British isles, have been accustomed to look up to the State for everything that concerns the support of religion. We get but little help from them in that respect. They will in general submit to any toil and self-denial for the purpose of acquiring wealth, but they do next to nothing for the religious institutions of our country.

Two of the wealthiest men who ever lived in the United States were natives of France and Germany. They left behind millions of dollars, but many an American mechanic of moderate means has done more for the cause of Christianity than both of them.

There is another view of the case that must alarm every considerate citizen. These ignorant millions, for they are numbered by millions, are the willing instruments not only of our own political demagogues, but of the emissaries of foreign tyrants, who would gladly succeed in overthrowing our political and religious institutions.

CATHOLICISM

The Catholic Church maintains an absolute control over millions of subjects scattered over almost every region of the globe. Rome, in fact, illustrates the idea of the Church Universal, mutilated though it be. She boasts of an intimate connection with that vast spiritual brotherhood which has existed in all times and in all lands. She has embalmed the memory of the good and great of all ages; has enshrined the ancient chivalry of the faith; and realizes to her believing children, in a literature of legends and prayers, lively and beatified pictures of the saintliest virtues combined with the most heroic deeds.

It is not our purpose to describe the means whereby this ascendency and perpetuity are maintained. We can only refer to the splendor and antiquity of her chosen shrines; to her Cathedrals, gorgeous with pictorial and statuesque treasures; to that ancient ceremonial, rendered theatrical by the moving of solemn processions, by the dress and genuflections of the priests, and by all those other accidents of her worship which closely resemble the ever shifting scenes and changing characters that belong to the stage. She exhibits an imposing drama, where each one acts his part with distinguished skill.

This is the exterior which the Church of Rome presents. But she is leagued with despots, and is at heart a tyrant. Ambition has entered her soul, and converted the spiritual instruments of her ancient warfare into carnal weapons, which she wields unscrupulously in the struggle for wealth and power. True, she does not dictate to kings and princes in the haughty and imperious manner of former times, and in certain parts of Europe can only keep her head above the waves of revolution by clinging with the grasp of death to the bayonets of temporal power; but she still controls the policies of cabinets and courts, and from one shining center of power, exercises a mighty influence in every quarter of the globe. Her imposing pageantry is witnessed by the people of every clime, and her ritual chanted in almost every language spoken on the earth. The Catholic clergy of France alone numbers more than 40,000 souls, and the government of Louis Napoleon expends annually over a hundred millions of francs in support of the established religion, a tax imposed alike upon the sceptic and the believer, upon the Jew and the Protestant as well as upon the Roman Catholic.

Circumstances have compelled the Church of Rome to modify her external policy. Some of the harsher features have been softened or entirely removed, but at heart she remains the same. Ultramontane Romanism, by which we mean Romanism that would reinstate the fires of the Inquisition if it dared, and which does violently persecute wherever it can, is still Orthodox Romanism. She remains a foe to progress, an enemy to human society. She still proscribes the Bible as a book opposed to religion and morality, combats freedom of thought everywhere, and is the Upas tree whose breath poisons the noblest aspirations after liberty. In her worship she inculcates an apparent equality, but in reality makes a slave of the subject, and exhibits the refinement of cruelty, bigotry and tyranny.

This is the character of the Church of Rome in the Old World, and this is the dominion she would gladly establish in our midst. It is to procure such results, to overthrow our free institutions, to destroy the noblest temple of Liberty ever erected, raised by the toil and sacrifice of our fathers and cemented with their blood, that Jesuit emissaries are laboring in our midst.

When the Church of Rome confines herself to acting upon individuals she succeeds. Such, thus far, has been her policy with us, and hence her remarkable success. The Roman Catholics have now in the United States four Archbishops, thirty Bishops, 1,073 churches, 1,081 priests, thirteen colleges, and numerous male and female schools. The number of Roman Catholics was estimated by Archbishop Hughes to be, in 1850, 3,000,000. According to Dr. Baird, the communicants in the several evangelical branches of the Protestant Church, numbered, in the same year, only 3,292,322 souls, being a majority of less than 300,000 over the Catholic population. The Catholic clergy constantly receive large sums of money from abroad—from the Lyons Society for Propagating the Faith, from the Leopold Society in Vienna, as well as from other sources, which are expended with consummate skill in the business of proselyting.

But the Church of Rome can no more rest contented with her present achievements, than the victim can remain quiet to whose flesh is applied the red hot iron of torture. The ambition of her priests and Jesuits will urge her on to strivings after power and deeds of open violence.

Unfortunately our foreign population is, for the most part, made the instrument of designing emissaries. Those of them who come among us as Catholics, generally remain so to the day of their death.

> Cœlum
> Non animum mutant qui trans mare current.

And when we remember that the present Catholic population of the United States is as numerous and possesses almost as much wealth as did our entire population at the time of the Declaration of Independence, and the facility with which the right of suffrage can be obtained, we justly find cause for alarm.

Where the Ballot Box is the Palladium of Liberty, should not every possible safeguard be thrown around it? And what surer way for accomplishing the overthrow of our Republic than to grant this blood bought privilege to those who, from education and their foreign associations, have no conception of its value, and use it at the command of Jesuits or of native demagogues for purposes of destruction?

We do not advocate a proscriptive policy. The portals of our land are thrown open to the world. We invite to our shores the weary and oppressed of every clime; we grant to them the full measure of protection and freedom enjoyed by ourselves; but in view of the value of liberty to them as to us—to their offspring as well as to our own, and the necessity of preserving our free institutions, is it too much to ask that Americans should rule America?

Infidelity

The influence of Infidelity is not confined to individuals. It extends to them in their collective capacity, proves ruinous to social security, and destructive of the stability of governments. It is the enemy of order and justice, and tends to disorganize whatever of good there is in the construction of society. Infidelity promotes vice of every kind, in that it represents the practice of rectitude as an evidence of weakness, and removes every motive to a life of virtue. The saying of Talleyrand, the infidel Bishop of Auton, that "The very object of language is to conceal our thoughts," is a maxim of Infidelity. The declaration of Hume, that "Adultery, when not discovered, is no crime whatever," and that Spartan code of virtue, according to which injustice, imposture and deceit are regarded as commendable when craftily executed—these constitute the morality of Infidelity.

Who is not shocked by the written account of such men as Fouché and Machiavelli, Danton and Robespierre, Paine and Marat, all eminent in the ranks of Infidelity, and, be it added, equally eminent in the list of incarnate depravity? Let society be composed of such individuals, and Pandemonium itself could scarcely exhibit a more terrible condition of things.

We have an instance of one, and fortunately of but one infidel nation, ruled for a length of time by an infidel government. "There is no picture," remarks a celebrated writer, "more terrible in the history of the world than that of revolutionary France, the boasted land of elegance and refinement, the home of philosophy and fashion, of chivalry and glory. On the one hand we see her Sabbaths abolished, her churches turned into theaters, and her priesthood imprisoned and slain. We see the most sacred ties of nature despised and violated, distrust, selfishness and cruelty take the place of family affection, of friendship, and of all the ordinary sympathies of human existence. On the other hand, poverty and want become the promotives of universal licentiousness, whose fires are fed by the confluent resources of beauty, accomplishment and wit. The knowledge and fear of God are forgotten, and every base passion is allowed to run riot in boundless freedom. An infidel and blasphemous government makes league with the grave, and hurries its thousands to a violent death; the soil of France is deluged with the blood of her bravest and best citizens. The supremacy of hell in crime and was at last endangered by the scenes there enacted. Not only did death ravage the land, but such a sink of moral corruption and filth did France become; so completely was almost every religious institution and association removed; so wholly *heathenish* had that people become; and to such universal wretchedness and disaster did all these calamities lead, that, had this state of things continued for a few years, the whole social fabric would have dissolved in revolutionary ruin. France, even with all her vast resources, was rapidly verging toward this end; nothing produced it but the influence of Infidelity and its natural consequences; nothing prevented it but the return of Christianity, though even in a corrupted form."

Of old fashioned English Infidelity, characterized by a manly, open tone, and great vigor of thought in its defense, there is perhaps not so much in the United States as was the case half a century ago. In its place, however, we have French Infidelity, marked by keenness and frivolity, and that of the Germanus, a muddy stream of presumption, erudition and pedantry. The refined transcendentalism of Emerson and Parker, at present quite fashionable in a certain class of New England society, has not even the merit of originality, and is a bad imitation of German philosophy. The worst forms of Infidelity are brought to this country by French, German and Italian immigrants. There is no end to the variety and contradiction of different systems, but they all agree in one respect—in tending to undermine the foundations of society and of government, by the corruption of manners, virtue and religion, which they infallibly produce.

The German newspapers published in New-York and other cities, contain the vilest attacks upon Christianity. The hosts of German Infidels in our land regard Tom Paine, not Washington, as the greatest and noblest man ever produced in America, and celebrate his birth-day rather than that of the "Father of his Country." Societies are organized in our midst for the vile purpose of putting down Christianity. Infidel ideas, revolting in their character, terrible in their influence, and foreign in their origin, are propagated in our midst, not only from the pulpit, but by means of books, journals and magazines. They are put forth in the most seductive form, and operate ruinously upon our native social institutions. The consequence of this is, that society is fast becoming corrupt. Infidelity is becoming fashionable, especially with the young. This is not the tendency of the native American mind; it is a direction given it by foreign ideas, especially by German Infidelity. Our Pilgrim ancestors were God-fearing men. Religion was made the corner stone of the Republic which they founded.

And in view of the rapid spread of Infidelity in our midst, in view of its corrupting influence upon individuals, its disorganizing influence upon our family and social relations, and its tendency to undermine the foundations of our government, we ask, is it not time to return to the simple religious and political faith of our forefathers? Is it not time to oppose a stream of foreign influence which threatens to overwhelm our cherished institutions? Lastly, is it not time to cultivate truly American sentiments, sentiments which had their origin in a religious patriotism and love of liberty which tend to strengthen, and not to enervate?

Most of the crime and pauperism in our midst results from intemperance and a low state of morality, but to what class of population are these chiefly confined? Unquestionably to foreigners. Who in our midst pay the least regard to the institution of the Sabbath? Foreigners. Who desecrate that sacred day by pleasure trips, balls, scenes of drinking and debauch, and by the holding of political as well as anti-Christian meetings? Foreigners. Who in our midst propose to remove that ancient and venerated institution, the Trial by Jury, and advocate principles which tend to anarchy? Foreigners. Who especially keep, inhabit and patronize the houses of prostitution which corrupt and disgrace our cities? Foreigners. Who especially swell the armies of paupers and criminals that people our alms-houses and prisons? Foreigners. We do not refer to these things for the purpose of deprecating foreigners, as such, but as startling facts which need no presentation of statistical proof. Nor is it our fault that foreigners as a class fall far below our native society in morality, intelligence and respectability. In our country every class finds its own proper level, and foreigners are at the bottom simply because, under existing circumstances, they belong there. If they wish to occupy a higher position in society they must learn to be better, must seek to raise themselves up to our level, not attempt to drag us down to theirs. As before remarked, we do not complain of the burden thus imposed upon us. We gladly furnish schools for the education of their young, organize philanthropic societies for their benefit, and annually distribute thousands of dollars among them in the way of public and private charities. At the same time we do not believe that the condition of our foreign population is in the least improved by investing them so hastily with the high dignity of American citizenship. On the contrary, the very fact of their possessing the right of suffrage is a sufficient reason, on the part of demagogues and the emissaries of foreign tyrants, for keeping them, so far as possible, ignorant and debased. Let the foreigners among us become more industrious, more intelligent, more moral, and in every way more respectable; then their condition will be in reality ameliorated, their influence immensely increased, and they will render themselves worthy of taking a part in the direction of public affairs.

But the facility with which naturalization is at present effected, is of no benefit to those who are intended to be benefited by it, while on the other hand it is fraught with danger to the perpetuity of our free institutions.

In view of these things, should not Americans rule America? Can foreigners, can Americans object?

LIBERTY

The Frenchman looks upon Liberty as a capricious mistress; the German,

Fuddled by the profound philosophy of beer,

regards Liberty as he does the memory of the great grandmother whom he never saw; but the American loves Liberty as he loves his wife. No one can deny the fact—the instincts of the Europeans in favor of Liberty are by no means so strong and lively as our own. Were they, western Europe would have exhibited, ere this, a galaxy of Republics. The repeated mistakes and failures of the European republicans demonstrate the fact. The Germanic States unquestionably furnish us with the best class of emigrants from the Continent. They are the most temperate and industrious—appreciate best the blessings of Liberty, but are, at the same time, destitute of political education. The main principles upon which are founded the English *Magna Charta* and our own Constitution, had their origin in the forests of Germany; but compare the Germans of to-day with their Teutonic ancestry. So fallen are they, so stripped of all political rights by the despotism which they have suffered to grow up in their midst, that in reference to political sins, at least, we may say with the Russian adage, "God has sufficiently punished a man in permitting him to be born a German." German literature, like Sterne's wig, is both above and below criticism; above criticism in vigor of thought—below criticism in its despotic, anti-liberal tendency. Judging by results, what weak and puerile blows have the great German minds dealt upon the brazen shield of Tyranny! With them the golden smiles of Royalty

———— drink up the liberal sap,
The vegetating vigor of philosophy,
And leave it a mere husk.

We especially welcome the Germans to our shores. We invite them to a feast crowned with the blessings of Liberty, where they can enjoy as much as ourselves. All we ask is to remain "Master of Ceremonies." So much belongs to us, and on the part of foreigners it should be a matter of gratitude. We give our children a political education which requires years for its attainment, before permitting them to take an active part in public affairs. Is it too much to require a similar education from those who come to us from the Old World, bringing with them the associations of despotism, and equally ignorant of our free institutions?

Among the Athenians, the man who took no interest in political affairs was regarded not only as a blameless, but also as a useless person. With us, likewise, every citizen should take an active part in political matters. It is a duty which he owes to the State, but a duty whose performance in such a manner as to benefit the State, implies an amount of political knowledge which our foreign population do not in general possess. True, there may be high-minded individuals among them; men of intelligence and strong instincts in favor of Liberty. With the great majority of immigrants, however, it is different. Even the best instances of statesmanship afforded by our adopted citizens, are nothing of which Americans can be proud; while many of them have exercised a baneful influence, and brought upon us well merited reproach.

Let Americans, then, govern America. And while we, as a people, are growing great and powerful, let us remember, in the language of the Athenian orator, that "*it is not wealth and great possessions, it is not fleets and armies, that constitute the power of States; but it is* WATCHFULNESS."

Now, it is to develop our own type of civilization, to cultivate a national spirit that shall be purely and essentially American, to maintain the moral and religious institutions of our Pilgrim ancestors, and to preserve that inestimable boon of liberty which was purchased with the blood and treasures of our forefathers that the American Party was organized. The principles upon which it is based are nothing new. They are as old as civilization itself. To their development Greece owed her glory, Rome her colossal power. To their application, also, the great European powers are indebted for the strength and energy which they exhibit. In consideration of these principles, the framers of the federal Constitution declared that no adopted citizen could ever become President of the United States. A like sentiment was adopted by the citizens of this State, and till the late Convention for the amendment of the Constitution, it stood written that no person of foreign birth could be elected Governor of New-York. And could our patriot forefathers know, that we, who boast of the glory of belonging to "The Great Republic," of being "the foremost people" of the globe, have become the scavenger of nations, and that the honor of being an American citizen has become a bauble so cheap and worthless as to be given away even to the enemies of our liberties, surely "they would turn in their graves." They fought and bled for the Republic, and it was their intention that "Americans should govern America."

The ægis of our protection is destined to be extended over Mexico and Central America. The latter, in consequence of their own centripetal force, will ultimately fall into our constellation of States. But when that event occurs, as sooner or later it must, for good or for evil to ourselves, a vast population under Catholic influence will be admitted to share in the general government. In view of this fact, also, it becomes us, as a people, to cultivate a truly republican and national sentiment, to adopt, and act upon, the principles of the American Party.

The old political parties have been found wanting, and are passing away. Some of them are already extinct, others "are playing on the verge of fate." An organization, more patriotic in its objects and more national in its tendencies, is fast assuming their place.

To those of our citizens who ask for retrenchment and reform in the administration of our City Government, we commend the principles of the American Party. We commend them to young men who are interested in the welfare of their country. We commend them, finally, to all who hope for the preservation of our liberties and the perpetuity of our free institutions.

❧ II ❧

The Parties of the Day. Speech of William H. Seward at Auburn, October 21, 1856 (Washington, 1857)

THE DEMOCRATS claimed that the factionalism resulting from the new parties and their emphasis on particular issues was a temporary disruption of normal political activity. But William H. Seward (1801–1872), for more than twenty years the leading Whig figure in New York state, and national, politics, powerfully argues in this 1856 speech that a new political agenda has emerged, dividing the forces of liberty from those of slavery. This new agenda demanded new parties that would reflect this new cleavage. While loyal to the memory of the Whig party, which was once his home, Seward argued to his political friends in his home town that the Whigs had failed because they would not face up to the new problems confronting the country and had tried to avoid dealing with them. The Democrats, he argued, were hopelessly indifferent to the danger that slavery and its expansion posed to the Republic. Whatever the Democrats' claims, the Republican party was needed, and was here to stay.

Fellow-citizens: We are neighbors and friends. We know each other well. I know that you are sincere, and you know, as I trust, that I am not a man of ungrateful disposition. We have a common memory of many political storms through which we have passed, not altogether without occasional alienations and separations. You therefore can readily conceive, without the use of amplification on my part, how profoundly gratifying it is to me now to see not only a general brightening of the skies, auspicious of the triumph of the political principals which I have cherished through so many trials, but also troops and crowds and clouds of friends, more numerous, more earnest, and more confiding, than those by whom I was surrounded in the most successful and happiest periods of my life.

If politics were indeed, as many seem to suppose, merely an uncertain sea, bounded by rich ports and havens, tempting private adventure, I should not be one of those who, standing on the beach, would be inciting my fellow-citizens to embark on board of this craft or of the other. If politics were, as others seem to think, merely a game cunningly compounded of courage, accident, and skill, in which prizes or crowns were to be won by the victors for their own glory and gratification, I certainly should not be found among the heralds of the contestants on either side. If, again, politics were only a forum in which social theories, without immediate bearing on the welfare and safety of the country, were discussed, I might then by a listener, but I should not be a disputant.

But, although politics present these aspects to superficial observers, they are nevertheless far more serious and practical. They are in reality the regulation and direction of the actual life of the American people. How much of individual, domestic, and social happiness depends on the regulation and conduct of only one single human life! How much more of human happiness depends, then, on the regulation and conduct of this whole nation's thousand-fold longer life!

Since I have come before you on this occasion influenced by these sentiments, you will not expect from me either humorous, exaggerated, passionate, or prejudiced speech, but will calculate on an examination of the merits of candidates for public favor, and of the parties by whom those candidates are respectively sustained.

It is not my habit to speak largely of candidates; I refrain for two reasons. First, because, being necessarily brought into personal combination or conflict with public men, my judgment concerning them is liable to the biases of partiality and jealousy. Secondly, because it is not a habit of parties in our country to select unfit, unworthy, or unreliable men, to be their representatives. Whatever may be the personal merits or demerits of a candidate, he cannot act otherwise, if he be chosen, than as an agent of the majority to whom he owes his place. The real question, therefore, in every canvass, is, What are the merits of the party by whom a candidate is preferred? And inquiries concerning the personal characters, dispositions, and conduct of candidates, are wasted on a false and delusive issue. You can try the truth of this position at once, by inquiring of whomsoever assails the character of the candidate of your choice, whether he would give his support to that candidate, abandoning his own, if all his personal objections could at once be removed. Your opponent, if a candid man, would probably answer in the negative.

But the case is quite different with political parties or masses of citizens. A nation acts at any one time through the consent and activity, not of all its members, but of only a majority, who determine what shall be done, not only for themselves, but for all other citizens. By our individual suffrages, we express our choice, whether one class of citizens, with a specific policy and peculiar principles, shall rule the country, directing it in a course of their own; or whether a different class, with different policy and principles, shall conduct it in a contrary direction. I shall therefore discuss existing parties freely. You shall judge whether I perform this duty with moderation and candor.

In the first place, I must ask you to notice the fact that American society is now in a transition state, so far as political parties are concerned. Two or three years ago, the American People were divided into two well-defined, distinct, and organized parties, the Whigs and the Democrats. To-day, instead of those two parties, we see three masses, uncertainly defined, and apparently at least quite unorganized—namely, Americans, Democrats, and Republicans; and we see portions of each of these easily detached, and passing over to the others, while a very considerable number of citizens stand hesitating whether to join one or the other, or to stand aloof still longer from all.

Such a transition stage, although unusual, is not unnatural. Established parties are built on certain policies and principles, and they will remain so long as those policies and principles are of paramount importance. They must break asunder and dissolve when new exigencies bring up new and different policies and principles, and the transition stage will last until the paramount importance of these new policies and principles shall be generally felt and confessed.

In a healthy and vigorous Republic, the transition stage I have described cannot last long, because, in the absence of a firm and decided majority to direct its course, it would fall under the management of feeble and corrupt factions, under whose sway it would rapidly decline and speedily perish. Our Republic, God be thanked, is yet healthy and vigorous, and we already see that society is passing out of the transition stage, to the ancient and proper condition. This condition is one which tolerates two firm and enduring parties—no less, and no more. There must be two parties, because at every stage of national life some one question of national conduct, paramount to all others, presents itself to be decided. Such a question always has two sides, a right side and a wrong side, but no third or middle side. The right side unites a party. The wrong side attracts a party. All masses which affect neutrality, as well as all masses which seek to stand independently on questions which have already passed and become obsolete, or which have not yet attained paramount importance, are crowded and crushed in the conflicts between the two parties which occupy for the time being the whole field of contest.

If such an emergency has now occurred, presenting a vital question, on which society must divide into two parties, and if those parties are actually found in the political arena, then we are now individually to decide whether to identify ourselves with a mass which will exist uselessly for a short period, or unite with one of two parties which will be enduring, and on whose conflict depends the welfare of the Republic; and as between these parties, whether we shall attach ourselves to the party which will maintain the wrong, and perish with it, or that which shall maintain the right, and immediately or ultimately triumph with it.

You yourselves shall prove by your responses that that emergency has occurred, and that question is upon us. What has produced the disorganization and confusion which we have all seen and wondered at, involving the dissolution of the Whig party, and the disorganization of the Democratic party, and given room and verge for the American or Know Nothing party? You all answer, the agitation of Slavery. And you answer truly. Answer again. What shall I discourse upon? The contest of the American Colonies with Great Britain, and the characters of the Whigs and Tories? No; these are themes for the Fourth of July. The adoption of the Constitution, and the disputes between Federalists and Republicans? No; let them sleep. The Tariff, National Bank, and Internal Improvements, and the controversies of the Whigs and Democarts? No; they are past and gone. What, then, of Kansas—the admission of Kansas as a free State or a slave State, the extension of Slavery in the territories of the United States? Ah, yes; that is the theme—the extension of Slavery, and nothing else. What are the Americans in the North and in the South discussing in their secret councils, so far as their debates are suffered to transpire? The abrogation and restoration of the Missouri Compromise, and nothing else. The Democrats also, in the North and South—they talk of nothing else but saving the Union from destruction, by suppressing this discussion about the extension of Slavery.

Is this question about the extension of Slavery new, unreal, and imaginary—the mere caprice of an hour? Is it a wind that "bloweth where it listeth, and thou hearest the sound thereof, but cannot tell whence it cometh and whither it goeth?" No; it is an ancient and eternal conflict between two entirely antagonistic systems of human labor combined with American society, and not unequal in their forces; a conflict for not merely toleration, but absolute political sway in the Republic; between the system of free labor, with equal and universal suffrage, free speech, free thought, and free action, and the system of slave labor, with unequal franchises secured by arbitrary, oppressive, and tyrannical laws. It is as old as the Republic itself, although it has never ripened before. It presented itself when the Constitution was adopted, and was then only temporarily repressed by a compromise, which allowed to slaveholding communities three votes for every five slaves, while it provided at the same time for the abolition of the African slave trade. It presented itself in the Constitutional Congress of 1787, and was then put aside only by the passage of the Ordinance of 1787, dedicating all the Northwest Territory to free labor. It occurred again in 1820, threatening to distract the Union, and was then again put to rest by another compromise, which relinquished Missouri to slave labor, and gave over the Territory which now constitutes Kansas and Nebraska to free labor. It occurred again in 1844, when Texas was annexed, and was put to sleep for only a short space by the division of Texas—very unequally, indeed,—into slave soil and free soil. It arose again during the war with Mexico, and was quieted by the memorable Compromise of 1850, whose details I need not repeat. It occurred again in 1854, on the opening of Kansas and Nebraska Territories to civilization, and was put to sleep once more by the adoption in Congress of the specious delusion of popular sovereignty. The question, that is so old, that has presented itself so often, and never without disturbing, as it seemed, the very foundations of society, and that has deranged and disorganized all the political combinations of the country, fortified as they were by so many interests, ambitions, and traditions, must be confessed to be a real and enduring, if not a vital, question. But a moment's examination will serve to satisfy you that it is also a vital question. It is really one in which the parties are a sectional, local class of slaveholders, standing on the unnatural principle of property in human beings on the one side, and the greater mass of society on the other, who, whether from choice or necessity, are not, cannot, and will not be, either slaves or the owners of slaves. A small minority, which cannot even maintain itself, except by means of continually-increasing concessions and new and more liberal guaranties, against a majority that could never have been induced to grant any guaranties whatever except by threats of disunion, and that can expect no return for new and further concessions and guaranties, but increasing exactions and ultimate aggressions or secessions. The slaveholders can never be content without dominion, which abridges the freedom as well as circumscribes the domain of the non-slaveholding freemen. Non-slaveholding freemen can never permanently submit to such dominion. Nor can the competition or contention cease, for the reason that the general conscience of mankind throws its weight on the side of Freedom, and presses the resistants onward to oppose the schemes and aggressions of the slaveholding class. Heretofore, opposing political combinations, long established, and firmly intrenched in traditions and popular affections, have concurred in the policy of suppressing this great and important question; but they have succumbed under it at last. Henceforth, the antagonistical elements will be left to clash without hindrance. Heretofore, the broad field of the national Territories allowed each of the contending interests ample room, without coming into direct conflict with the other. Henceforth, the two interests will be found contending for common ground claimed by both, and which can be occupied by only one of them.

One other condition remains to be settled—namely, that this great question is imminent and urgent; in other words, that it must be settled and determined, without further postponement or delay. How can it be further postponed? If it could be postponed at all, it could be only by the same means which have been used for that purpose heretofore—namely, compromise. Where are the agents necessary to make new compromises? The agents of the past compromises are gone. Although they sleep in honored graves, and the mourners over them have not yet quitted the streets, yet no new compromisers arise to occupy their places. A compromise involves mutual equivalents— something to give, and something to take in exchange. Will Slavery give you anything? No; it insists on a free range over all the Territories. What have you to give in exchange? When you have given up Kansas, you will have relinquished all the Territories; for the principle of the relinquishment is, that Slavery may constitutionally take them all. When compromise is exhausted, what follows? Dispute, contention, contest, conflict.

Again, the question is imminent, and must be met now. Kansas, at the last session of Congress, voluntarily offered itself as a free State, and demanded to be admitted into the Union, and was rejected. Since that time, the Territory has been subjugated by slaveholders; and they, having usurped its sovereignty, are organizing a slave State there, which will offer itself for admission into the Union at the next session of Congress. Utah, already organized as a slave State, with her incestuous social system, is lying concealed and waiting, ready to demand admission so soon as Kansas shall have been received into the Union. The adoption of both, or even one of these States, will bear heavily, perhaps conclusively, on the fortunes of the entire conflict between Freedom and Slavery.

Insomuch as the question, that is henceforth to divide society into two parties, is thus seen to be a vital and imminent one, let us fully possess ourselves of its magnitude. We have a sluggish, turbid, and desolating stream of slave labor, issuing from fifteen slave States. We have ever-increasing and commingled volumes of free labor, issuing from sixteen free States, swollen by a stream scarcely less full from European and Asiatic fountains. These two variant floods cannot be combined, but one necessarily repels and excludes the other. We have half a continent yet to be opened to the flow of the one or of the other. Shall we diffuse Slavery over the new region, to react upon and destroy ourselves, or shall we extend Freedom over it, and spread happiness throughout all its mountains and plains, and thus forever establish our own safety and welfare?

If this great question were disembarrassed of all personal and partisan interests and prejudices, the universal voice of the American people would be pronounced for Freedom, and against Slavery. Freedom is nothing more than equality of political right or power among all the members of a State. It is natural, just, useful, and beneficent. All men instinctively choose the side on which these advantages lie. How true this is, you may infer from the fact that every one of the banners, borne to this field by one of the great contending masses, wears, as its inscription, a tribute to Freedom, while no banner, borne by either of the other parties, is ever defiled with homages to Slavery.

Nevertheless, while all avow themselves favorable to Freedom, we have to choose, between the three existing masses, the ones which will effectually secure its predominance in the Republic.

Shall we join ourselves to the Know Nothing or American organization? What are its creed and its policy? Its creed is, that the political franchises of alien immigrants and Roman Catholics in our country are too great, and its policy is to abridge them.

Now I might, for argument sake, concede that this creed and this policy were just and wise; still I could not unite with the Know Nothings, even in that case, because their movement is out of season and out of place. The question of the day is not about natives and foreigners, nor about Protestants and Roman Catholics, but about freemen and slaves. The practical and immediately urgent question is, Shall Kansas be admitted into the Union as a free State, or shall she be made a slave State, and so admitted? What have the franchises of alien immigrants and Roman Catholics to do with that? If the American people declare for Freedom, Kansas will be free. If the American people declare for Slavery, Kansas will be a slave State. If the American people divide, and one portion, being a minority, declare for Freedom, while another portion, being also a minority, declare against foreigners and Catholics, and a third, larger than either, declare for Slavery, nothing is obtained against foreigners and Catholics, and nothing against Slavery, and Kansas becomes a slave State. Thus it is apparent that the issue raised by the Know Nothings, whatever is its merit, is an immaterial irrelevant, and false issue. A false issue always tends to divert and mislead the people from the true one, and, of course, to prejudice the judgment to be rendered upon it. I do not accuse the Know Nothings of designing so to mislead, because, first, I know nothing of the motives of others; and, secondly, because the question is not upon motives, but upon effects. What have been the effects thus far? The Know Nothing members of Congress divided between the advocates of Freedom in the Territories and its opponents. Their votes, combined with either, would have given it a complete triumph. Those votes reserved, and cast as some peculiar interest dictated, have left the question of Freedom in Kansas to the ordeal of the sword.

What is the effect in the present canvass, on which depends the question of the admission on Kansas and of Utah, as slave States, in the next Congress? Distraction of the public mind. Such effects are inevitable. Whoever seeks to interpose an unreal or false issue, must necessarily, in order to gain even a hearing, affect neutrality on the real one. At the same time, no party can practice neutrality on a vital issue with fairness. It will necessarily sympathize with the weaker of the two contestants, and, in some degree, co-operate with it to overthrow the stronger, which is the common adversary of both. Of course, as the two great contestants possess unequal strength in different States, the neutral will favor one in some of the States, and favor the other in other States. By virtue of a law that is irresistible, it will, sooner or later, betray each party, when its own peculiar ends require that course. The experience of the Whig and Democratic parties has proved how impossible it is to practice neutrality on the great question of Slavery. The former has broken into pieces, and perished in the effort. The latter has been crowded from a neutral position, and, with crumbled ranks, has taken that of the extension and for-tification of Slavery. The Know Nothing mass can expect no better success. The effort will cost its life. Crowded and jostled between the two combatants, it will and must dissolve, giving up portions of its host here to Freedom, and there to Slavery, but not until it is too late to secure the triumph of Freedom. Thus you see that the Know Nothing mass is not really a political party. It is only an ephemeral and evanescent faction, as useless and injurious as a third blade in the shears, or a third stone which an ignorant artisan might attempt to gear in between the upper and the nether millstone.

By another sign you shall know it to be not a party, but a faction. From the days of the landing of the Pilgrims at Plymouth, until now, every one of the great parties, which has been engaged in directing the life of the American people, has recognised, from necessity, the fact that the political system which exists and which must continue to exist here is a Republican one, and is based on the principle of the rightful political equality of all the members of the State; and has confessed that directness, publicity, and equality of voices, are necessary in the conduct of affairs. The Know Nothings reject these princi-ples, and seek to exclude a large and considerable portion of the members of the State from all participation in the conduct of its affairs; and to obtain control and carry on the operations of the Government of all, by secret machinery, inconsistent with the Constitution of a Republic, and appropriate only to a conspiracy either for or against despotism. It will, I think, be hereafter regarded as one of the caprices of politics, that a system of combination so puerile was ever attempted in the United States. The absurdity of the attempt is rendered still more glaring, when it is considered that the grounds of persecution, assumed against the class to be excluded, are those of nativity and religious belief—grounds directly in conflict with that elementary truth announced by the Declaration of Independence, that all men are created equal, and are by nature endowed with certain inalienable rights, to secure which Governments are instituted among men; and with that other fundamental article of the Constitution, which declares that no system of religion shall ever be established.

Who, then, will choose to enroll himself under the banner of an ephemeral, evanescent, and injurious faction, like this, to be compromised in its frauds for a day or a year, or two years, and then to be left by it to the pity and scorn of the nation whose confidence it has sought to abuse? Certainly no one who values at its just worth the great interests of Freedom and Humanity, which are staked on the present contest, nor even any one who values at its just worth his own influence, or even his own vote, or his own character as a citizen.

Our choice between parties, fellow-citizens, is thus confined to the Democratic and Republican parties. On what principle could we attach ourselves to the Democratic party? Let us look the actual state of things full in the face. Seven years ago, when I entered Congress as a Senator from this State, there was not one acre of soil within the national domain from which Slavery was not excluded by law. It was excluded from Minnesota by the Ordinance of 1787, which was then of fully acknowledged obligation and effect. It was excluded from Kansas and Nebraska by the Missouri Compromise restriction, which also was then in full effect. It was equally excluded from California, including New Mexico and Utah, by Mexican laws, which had never been impaired, and were of confessed obligation. It was excluded from Oregon by the organic law of that Territory. Now, there is not an acre of the public domain which Congress has not opened to the entrance of Slavery. It has expressly abrogated the Missouri Compromise, on the ground that it was void, for want of power in Congress under the Constitution to exclude Slavery, and also on the ground that the Compromise of 1850 had already settled its invalidity. This legislation, if acquiesced in by the people, will henceforth be irresistibly claimed as abrogating alike the Ordinance of 1787, the Missouri Compromise restriction, and the Mexican laws. Thus, the whole of the Territories have been already lost to Freedom by the legislation of the last seven years; and the controversy before us is one not to save, but to reclaim. During the first six years of the period I have named, there were only two parties—the Democratic and Whig parties—in Congress and in the country. During the last year, there were three—the Democratic, Know Nothing, and Republican parties. Every one will at once acquit the Republican party, and those who now constitute it, of all agency in the betrayal and surrender of Freedom, which have thus been made. The responsibility for them, therefore, belongs to the Democratic party and to the Whig party. Now, you may divide this responsibility between the Democratic and Whig parties, just as you like. The Whig party has perished under its weight, but a still greater responsibility lies upon the Democratic party. It was the Democratic party that refused to admit California, without condition or compromise, in 1850; that forced on the Whig party the Compromise of that year, and adopted it as its own permanent policy, and elected Franklin Pierce the present President of the United States. It was the Democratic party that invented the new, plausible, deceptive, and ruinous policy of abnegation of Federal authority over Slavery in the Territories, and the substitution of the theory of Popular Sovereignty; and it was the Democratic party that, with the co-operation of a portion of the Know Nothings, rejected the appeal of oppressed and subjugated Kansas for relief and restoration to Freedom by admission into the Union as a free State. The Democratic party did indeed, in some of its Conventions in Northern States, for a time hesitate to commit itself to the policy of Slavery Propagandism, by a breach of public faith, and by fraud and force, but it has finally renounced all opposition, and it now stands boldly forth, avowing its entire approval of that policy, and a determination to carry it through to its end, whatever that end may be.

Nor will any candid person claim that anything better is to be hoped from the Democratic party in the future. It is a party essentially built on the interests of the slaveholding class. Deprived of that support, it would instantly cease to exist. The principle of this class is, that property in man is sanctioned by the Constitution of the United States, and is inviolate. All that has been won by this class from Freedom has been won on that principle. The decisions of Judge Kane and other Federal Judges, and the odious and tyrannical laws of the usurpers in Kansas, are legitimate fruits of that principle. To that principle the Democratic party must adhere or perish, and it accepts it as the least fearful of two alternatives. But the principle, when established in the Territories, will then be with equal plausibility extended to the States, and thenceforth we shall have to contend for the right of the free States to exclude Slavery within their own borders.

If these arguments be sound, we are shut up to the necessity of giving our support to the Republican party, as the only means of maintaining the cause of Freedom and Humanity. Why, then, shall we stand aloof from it, in this election, or for a day or an hour? I will review the arguments urged from all quarters, and you shall see, in the first place, that every one of them is frivolous and puerile; and, secondly, that it involves nothing less than a surrender of the entire question in issue, and acquiesces in the unrestricted domination of Slavery.

First. We are conjured, by those who, in Boston, New York, and elsewhere, call themselves Straight-out Whigs, to wait for a re-organization of the National Whig party, to rescue the cause of Freedom. But is it written, in any book of political revelation, that a resurrection awaits parties which have fulfilled the course of nature?

Secondly. The Whig party perished through a lack of virtue to maintain the cause of Freedom. Amongst all of those who are waiting and praying for its resurrection, there is not one that to-day yields his support to that cause. What, then, but new betrayals can be expected, if it is destined to a resurrection?

We are told, on all sides, that the Republican party is new and partially organized, and merely experimental. It is indeed new, and as yet imperfectly organized. But so once was the ancient Whig party, that gave to the country its Independence. So once was the Federal party, that gave to the country its Constitution. So once was the ancient Republican party, that gave to the country a complete emancipation of the masses from the combination of classes. So once was the Whig and the Democratic party. It is the destiny of associations of men to have a beginning and an end. If an association is born of an enduring political necessity, it will continue and wax in vigor and power until it supplants other and superfluous, though more aged combinations. That such is to be the case with the Republican party, is seen in the fact that all existing combinations are uniting against it, on the ground that such a union is necessary to prevent its immediate and overwhelming ascendency. This union is an effective answer to the common argument, that the Republican party is an ephemeral and evanescent one.

Thirdly. We are favored with criticisms, by the Democrats and Know Nothings, on the course of the Republican members of the House of Representatives, in voting for Mr. Dunn's bill, to restore the Missouri Compromise, and against Mr. Toombs's bill, for pacifying Kansas; which votes, it is said, prove the Republicans insincere in their devotion to Freedom! These are of the same class of arguments with those which are urged by infidels against the Christian Church, on the ground of the short-comings of its members.

Suppose we abandon the Republican party for its short-comings, will Freedom then have any party left; and if so, what party, and where shall we find it? Certainly no other party but the Democratic Party, of which Franklin Pierce and Stephen A. Douglas are the Apostles. But that is the party of Slavery.

Fourthly. We are warned that Mr. Fremont is an improper man to represent the Republican Party; that his accounts with the Government are wrong; that he is a Roman Catholic; and that otherwise he was improperly chosen as a candidate. Now, these accusations are newly trumped up, and have been already a thousand times disproved. Nevertheless, neither Democrats, nor Know Nothings, nor Straight-out Whigs, have become any the more Republicans on that account, nor would they, were Mr. Fremont proved to be an angel descended from above, to rescue the cause of Freedom. Suppose, on the other hand, that we should give up Fremont upon these cavils, what would follow but the ascendency of the American party, which substitutes a false issue for the true one, and so betrays the cause of Freedom; or that of the Democratic party, which is the party of Slavery?

Fellow-citizens: I have discussed parties without asperity and with no partiality—for I know that masses and individuals are alike honest, well meaning, and patriotic. I have no animosities and no griefs. While I have tried to pursue always one steady course which my conscience has approved, friends have often been alienated, and adversaries have become friends. The charity of judgment to which I feel that I am entitled—that is the charity I extend to others.

I do not predict the times and seasons when one or other of the contending political elements shall prevail. I know this—that this State, this nation, and this earth, are to be the abode and happy home of free men. Everywhere the hills and valleys are to be fields of free labor, free thought, and free suffrages. That consummation will come when society shall be prepared for it. My labors are devoted to that preparation. I leave others to cling to obsolete traditions, and perish with them, if they must; but, in politics as in religion, I desire to be with that portion of my fellow-men who hold fast to pure truth and equal justice with hope and confidence, enduring through all trials in their ultimate and eternal triumph.

12

The Conspiracy to Break Up the Union. The Plot and Its Development. Breckinridge and Lane the Candidates of a Disunion Party (Washington, 1860)

THE DEMOCRATIC PARTY split in two in 1860. This pamphlet, issued by the National Democratic club in Washington, D.C., embodies the argument of its northern wing, the Douglas Democracy, which hoped to keep the party united by focusing on the disastrous course of the southern, or Breckinridge, Democrats. The latter was a "disunion party" intent on breaking up the United States by guaranteeing the election of the destructive Republicans and thus uniting the South against remaining part of the United States. In the style of many of these pamphlets, it consists of extracts from speeches, newspaper editorials, and so forth in support of its charge that "a preconcerted, deliberately planned and organized scheme to break up the Union" was behind the candidacy of John C. Breckinridge. Variations of such charges against other candidates had been heard many times before in partisan warfare. This time, the appeal failed to reunite the Democrats behind a single candidate.

Let the Masses Read and Ponder

FROM THE NASHVILLE (TENN.) PATRIOT

The first serious attempt to dissolve the Union and revolutionize the Government of this Republic was made by the State of South Carolina in 1832–'33. It met with no sympathy outside of that State, and Gen. JACKSON, then President, gave it an effectual quietus. The advocates of secession, at that day, and in that State, were forced to retire from the unequal contest in disgrace, or surrender their position, and to address themselves to the correction of what they conceived to be evil and injustice in a constitutional way. Hence we heard but little more of secession and disunion for nearly twenty years.

In 1850–'51, however, the agitation of the question of slavery growing out of the acquisition of territory from Mexico, gave rise to a state of feeling between the North and the South, which was fearfully violent. There was, before that time, a latent spirit of enmity toward the Union, lurking in the breasts of a *few* discontented and restless spirits—of which it is sufficient evidence to recite the course of Mr. WILLIAM L. YANCEY in an effort to break up the Baltimore Democratic Convention of 1848. The agitation of 1850 was disposed of by the series of acts passed by Congress during that year, familiarly known to the country as the "Compromise Measures." Upon the passage of these the small disunion faction suddenly rose to an importance which it had never attained before. In several of the southern States, in elections following, the issue was made of submission to those measures, or dissolution of the Union. The question was discussed before the people, and every effort made to fire the public mind, to arouse the popular passions, and to bring about a violent disruption of the Government. It was at this time that Hon. JEFFERSON DAVIS, now the leading secessionist in the national legislature, declared that "he was for resistance, and would never submit to the stain of degradation" which those measures, in his estimation, imposed. He ran as a candidate for governor of Mississippi on that issue, and was defeated before the people. In other States similar issues were made, and the people throughout the South placed the seal of their condemnation upon the enemies of the Union at the ballot-box. While this excited feeling was at its highest pitch, a southern convention was called to convene in this city, to extend the spirit of disunion, and to make it paramount in the southern States. It also resulted in an ignomonious failure. Wherever, and in whatever shape the issue was presented to the people, it was rejected with scorn and indignation.

Thus covered with defeat, baffled at every point, rejected, spurned, and driven from place and the hope of place, the disunionists retired from the contest in humiliation and shame. In 1852, they, with the same hypocritical solemnity which distinguishes their present professions of love, and admiration, and friendship for the Union, met with the Democracy in National Convention, and proclaimed that the "Compromise Measures" of 1850, were a just and final settlement of the slavery question. They gave their adhesion to the Union, as they now pretend to do, and declared they would shed their blood in its defence. We heard no more of injustice, aggression, and unconstitutional enactments. But now the spirit of treason and discussion is again abroad in our land. It now has no congressional compromise as a point of attack, as a rallying cry. But the enemies of the Union have what they imagine will serve their purpose equally as well. They now hold that the election of a

Black Republican to the Presidency, is a just cause for secession, disunion, and revolution. They have cultivated this idea for several years—not the people, for such a thing has scarcely been seriously considered by them, but the leaders. It is the inception of this idea and the means to be used to bring that contingency about, that is the purpose of this article, and to present the evidence of a preconcerted, cold-blooded, deliberate, heartless conspiracy to break up the union of these United States. We propose to present such an array of facts, as will satisfy all that it is the purpose of certain of the leaders of the Baltimore secession movement which nominated BRECKINRIDGE for the Presidency, to overthrow and terminate the existing government of the United States.

We begin this array by citing a fact, which was disclosed for the first time in Knoxville, in this State, on the occasion of a Union meeting held in that city in the month of January last. Judge BAILEY, who was a citizen of Georgia, until within a short time previous to that time, delivered a speech on that occasion, in which, according to the Knoxville *Whig:*

> He said, that during the Presidential contest, Governor WISE had addressed letters to all the southern governors—and that the one to the governor of Florida, had been shown to him,—in which WISE said that *he had an army in readiness to prevent Fremont from taking his seat, if elected,* and asking the co-operation of those to whom he wrote!*

*NOTE.—The following letter of GOV. WISE to GOV. LIGON is a copy of the letter addressed to the Governors of certain southern States, in 1856:

RICHMOND, VA, *Sept.* 15, 1856.

DEAR SIR: Events are approaching which address themselves to your responsibilities and to mine as chief executives of slaveholding States. Contingencies may soon happen which would require preparation for the worst of evils to the people. Ought we not to admonish ourselves by joint counsel of the extraordinary duties which may devolve upon us from the dangers which so palpably threaten our common peace and safety? When, how, or to what extent may we act, separately or unitedly, to ward off dangers if we can, to meet them most effectually if we must?

I propose that, as early as convenient, the Governors of Maryland, Virginia, North Carolina, South Carolina, Georgia, Florida, Alabama, Louisiana, Texas, Arkansas, Mississippi, and Tennessee, shall assemble at Raleigh, N.C., for the purpose generally of consultation upon the state of the country, upon the best means of preserving its peace, and especially of protecting the honor and interests of the slaveholding States. I have addressed the States only having Democratic Executives, for obvious reasons.

This should be done as early as possible, before the Presidential election, and I would suggest Monday, the 18th of October next. Will you please give me an early answer, and oblige.

Yours, most truly and respectfully,
HENRY A. WISE.

His Excellency Thomas W. Ligon,
Governor of Maryland.

Here we have the fact that it has been in contemplation from the first national struggle after the organization of the Republican party, to resist the inauguration of a member of that party as President of the United States, though he were elected fairly by the people, under the sanctions and all the forms prescribed by the Federal Constitution, WITHOUT AWAITING ANY HOSTILE DEMONSTRATION, OR ANY OVERT ACT *which should justify a resort to such extremities.*

We next trace the course of WILLIAM L. YANCEY, of Alabama, who is now the recognized leader in the secession movements in the Charleston and Baltimore Democratic Conventions, which eventuated in the nomination of Mr. BRECKINRIDGE for the Presidency. Though a disorganizer in 1848, and a disunionist in 1850–'51, we begin our quotations from his outgivings with the 10th of May, 1858, as it was only then that he began to prepare actively to consummate the aim which had a partial fruition at Baltimore. On that day, the Southern Convention met in the city of Montgomery. At the opening of that Convention, he delivered an address of welcome to the delegates, of which the subjoined is an extract:

> I must be allowed, at least on my own behalf, to welcome you too, as but the foreshadowing of that far more important body; important as you evidently will be, that if injustice and wrong shall continue to rule the hour and councils of the dominant section of the country, must, ere long, assemble upon southern soil for the purpose of devising some measure by which not only your industrial, but your social and political relations shall be placed upon the basis of an *independent sovereignty,* which will have within itself a unity of climate, a unity of soul, a unity of production, and a unity of social relations; that unity which alone can be the basis of a successful and permanent government.

At that session the chief topic of discussion in the convention was the reopening of the American slave trade, and a general exposition of the supposed wrongs of the South. Mr. Yancey had a good opportunity of conferring with the ultraists of other southern States, on the subject of secession and disunion, which, we are led to believe, he industriously improved. For within about a month afterward he addressed a letter to Mr. JAS. S. SLAUGHTER, dated June 15th, 1858, which is as follows:

> MONTGOMERY, *June* 15, 1860.

> DEAR SIR: Your kind letter of the 15th inst. is received. I hardly agree with you that a general movement can be made that will clean out the Augean stable. If the Democracy were overthrown, it would result in giving place to a

greater and hungrier swarm of flies. The remedy of the South is not such a process. It is in a diligent organization of her true men, for prompt resistance to the next aggression. It must come in the nature of things. *No national party can save us; no sectional party can do it. But if we could do as our fathers did, organize committees of safety all over the cotton States, (and it is only in them that we can hope for any effective movement) we shall fire the southern heart—instruct the southern mind—give courage to each other, and at the proper moment, by one organized concerted action, we can precipitate the cotton States into a revolution.*

The idea has been shadowed forth in the South by Mr. Ruffin—has been taken up and recommended in the *Advertiser,* under the name of 'League of United Southerners,' who, keeping up their old party relations on all other questions, will hold the southern issue paramount, and will influence parties, legislatures, and statesmen. I have no time to enlarge, but suggest merely.

In haste, yours, &c.,
W. L. YANCEY.

To Jos. S. SLAUGHTER, Esq.,
Atlanta, Georgia.

He had evidently now pretty well matured his scheme, but still held himself open to friendly suggestions. So far as the plot had gone, its diabolical excellence was never surpassed. Mr. RUFFIN had agreed to it, and the Montgomery *Advertiser* had taken it up and recommended it. The masses of the people who were to second and sustain the treason, were to retain their party relations on other questions—they were to give their entire faith to their leaders, have their passions duly aroused by fiery appeals, and at "the proper moment, *we* (the leaders) can precipitate the cotton States into a revolution." Mr. YANCEY lost no time in setting on foot the proposed organization, and to enlist the masses under his disunion and revolutionary banner. On the 10th of July following, he repaired to the country, and at Bethel church, in the county of Montgomery, delivered an address to the people who had assembled to hear him. His theme, of course, was the wrongs and oppressions of the South. At the conclusion of his speech a "League" was formed, under the following Constitution, as a basis of organization:

1. The members of this organization shall be known as the "*Leaguers of the South;*" and *our motto shall be,* A SOUTHERN REPUBLIC IS OUR ONLY SAFETY.

2. There shall be primary leagues, State leagues, and a league of the southern States.

*　　*　　*　　*　　*　　*

12. No league shall ever nominate a candidate for any office of profit or of honor under the Federal or any State government; *but each league shall vote according to his own conscience, remembering always his duty to the South.*

Thus was the Organization set on foot among the masses, which was to "control parties, legislature, and statesmen." To what extent and how rapidly it succeeded, we have no means of knowing; but subsequent events would indicate that Mr. Yancey thought the plot had grown to be wide and strong enough to warrant a bold attempt to sectionalize the country in the present presidential campaign. In the meantime, the revolutionary letter to Mr. Slaughter having been published in the newspapers, and being severely criticised by the Richmond *South,* Mr. YANCEY wrote a letter to the editor, Mr. RODGER A. PRYOR, of Virginia, by way of defence and explanation, in the course of which he says:

It is equally true that I do not expect Virginia to take any initiative steps toward a dissolution of the Union, when that exigency shall be forced upon the South. Her position as a border State and *a well-considered southern policy (a policy which has been digested and understood and approved by the ablest men in Virginia, as you yourself must be aware,)* would seem to demand that, when such a movement takes place by any inconsiderable number of southern States, Virginia and the other border States should remain in the Union, where, by their position and their counsels, they could prove more effective friends than by moving out of the Union, and thus giving the southern confederacy a long abolition, hostile border to watch. In the event of the movement being successful, in time Virginia, and the other border States that desired it, could join the southern confederacy, and be protected by the power of its affirmance and its diplomacy.

Here we have the important disclosure that the scheme had been submitted to, understood and approved by, the ablest men in Virginia, and that Mr. PRYOR was also then in the secret. In publishing this extract on the 9th of September, 1858, in the columns of the *Patriot,* we asked Mr. Pryor the question, "who are these ablest men in Virginia who had digested, understood, and approved" this well considered southern policy! And though we exchanged with the *South,* and doubtless it was cognizant of the question, he failed to answer. Undoubtedly Gov. WISE was one of the men referred to, as a circumstance presently to be mentioned will more fully show.

The foregoing completely demonstrates that a preconcerted, deliberately planned and organized scheme to break up the Union of the States was concocted, taking its shape from secret consultations held by men from various southern States, during the sitting of the southern convention at Montgomery, Alabama, in 1858. It also shows that WILLIAM L. YANCEY, the head and front of the BRECKINRIDGE party at the South, was the leading spirit in the wicked and traitorous proceeding. It also proves, beyond question, that the entire design, plot, and aim, rested, in its inception, on no ground other than cold-blooded enmity to the Union, and the pretence that disunion *per se,* of itself and without cause, would be of advantage to the South. But no one ever suspected Mr. YANCEY of a lack of sense. He well knew that the whole conspiracy would fail, and that he and his coadjutors would be overwhelmed with disgrace unless the people could be brought up to its support. The plan was all perfect, except that it had no immediate pretext. He had introduced into the southern convention at Montgomery, or procured to be introduced, resolutions in favor of reopening the African slave trade; but it was soon found that such a pretext alone would not meet the popular acceptance and approval, and that it could not be relied on to answer the purpose. Another, more directly affecting the people, was absolutely necessary. Fortunately for Mr. YANCEY and his fellow conspirators, one, supposed to be suitable in all respects, was found in the idea of congressional protection to slavery in the Territories.—About the 10th of September, 1858, the New Orleans *Delta,* a well known disunion paper, cautiously put forward the doctrine of congressional protection.

It was shortly taken up by other journals, and in the first days of January, 1858, it was formally promulgated by the Richmond *Enquirer.* Here the finger of Gov. WISE is plainly discernible. But a short time previous he had approved the course of Mr. DOUGLAS in his split with the Administration, and the sudden change of front by his organ shows an undoubted understanding that the doctrine of congressional protection was to be made, for the first time, an *issue in party politics.*

The parties of this disunion intrigue perfectly well knew that the proposition was impracticable—that there was no reasonable hope of bringing Congress, under existing circumstances, to grant the demand. They knew, also, that it would inevitably create a division of the Democratic party, whereby it would be demoralized and denationalized. At the time they did not know, however, that the present Union movement would be so successfully brought forward. The calculation was to break up the Democratic party (as Mr. YANCEY intimated in his "Slaughter Letter") to excite violent sectional antagonism, to unite the North against the South, and the South against the North, and thus insure the election of the Republican candidate. Upon this event, thus designedly effected, the programme was and is to resist his inauguration and bring on the final catastrophe. At this juncture, JEFFERSON

DAVIS appears upon the stage to play his part in the infamous drama. In the autumn of 1858, on his return from a tour of through the northern and eastern States, he delivered an address at Jackson, Mississippi, in which he broached the idea of a disunion in the event of the election of a Republican. This was the first declaration of this purpose by a leading man. He thus stated it:

> If an abolitionist be chosen President of the United States, you will have presented to you the question of whether you will permit the Government to pass into the hands of your avowed and implacable enemies? Without pausing for your answer, I will state my own position to be that such *a result would be a species of revolution by which the purposes of the Government would be destroyed, and the observance of its mere forms entitled to no respect. In that event, in such manner as should be most expedient, I should deem it your duty* TO PROVIDE FOR YOUR SAFETY OUTSIDE OF THE UNION, with those who have already shown the will and would have acquired the power, to deprive you of your birthright, and to reduce you to worse than the colonial dependences of your fathers.

The next step was to go actively into the work of indoctrinating the masses with the idea of Congressional protection in slavery in the Territories, and to enforce the propriety of resistance to the inauguration of a Republican President; and to this the year 1859 and a portion of this were industriously devoted. In the early part of the year 1859, the newspapers began to prepare the public mind for the issues concocted, in the manner above recited, and to be enforced by the leaders during the then approaching summer campaign. We now group a few expressions from that source:

From the Mobile Mercury, April, 1859

The times are now ripe for the organization of a political movement in the slave-holding States, irrespective, of course, of all old party designations; and there are peculiar reasons why such a movement should be undertaken now and here. Indeed, we are credibly informed that conferences have already been held by leading patriotic gentlemen of this city, of all parties, and the *plans of a southern organization have been set on foot and almost matured, preparatory to action. We earnestly hope the good work may go on, and speedily.*

The country, we repeat, is ripe for the movement, and if judiciously inaugurated, it will sweep over the land with a force that no opposition will be able to check. We therefore caution our friends in the country everywhere, to be prepared for it, and to keep themselves from all entangling alliancies which may hinder them from joining in it untrammeled.

The Charleston *Mercury*, in April, 1859, said of the Democratic Presidential convention of the present year, "*Unless it is limited exclusively to delegates from the South, it will be no convention of the Democratic party.*" How truly it spoke the disunion sentiment late events have fully shown.

From the New Orleans Delta, April, 1859

In 1860 the South and the North are to be arrayed in deadly content; *the battle of the sections is then to be fought for the last time,* and its issue is to be decisive of our fate.

From the Montgomery Advertiser, March, 1859

It is important that we should send such men to represent us (in Congress) as possess the ability to combat the approaches of Republicanism, and the nerve to *secede from Washington in case abolitionism should instal one of its leaders in the Executive mansion of the nation.* It is important to the South also, that her delegation should present a united front of State-rights Democrats, for in the principles and the doctrines of the State-rights Democracy *rest the hope of the South, in the Union* OR OUT OF IT.

From the Eufala (Ala.) Gazette, March, 1859

Could we all think and feel alike; were our interests identical and our occupations similar, we might adopt a common government without detriment to either; *but, as we are different in all these, it becomes us to prepare for an immediate withdrawal from the alliance which has hitherto held us together;* and we hold it to be the first duty, as it should be the first object of southern statesmen and the southern press, *to inaugurate a southern confederacy* AND THEREBY ESTABLISH SOUTHERN INDEPENDENCE.

From the Washington Correspondent of the Charleston Mercury, March, 1859

There are of the members of Congress from the different States of the South, a number of staunch State-rights men. *As the Democratic party goes to pieces,* these will form the nucleus of a *southern organization which must be formed* to meet the aggressions of northern consolidation through the general Government. * * There can be no doubt that the politicians, no less than the people of the South are strengthening in the opinion that nothing is left but taking their destinies in their own keeping. Yet there is a great reluctance to acknowledge the truth, and men hide their eyes to it as long as possible. By the end of the next session we may look to be out of the woods. When the Democratic party is resolved into its northern and southern elements, now incongruously joined for the sake of the spoils, *then* the South will wheel into line for the defence of her rights on the positions occupied by the State-rights men.

From the Eufala Spirit of the South, March, 1859

The North and South agreeing about some things and differing about others, made a Union for their benefit and a Constitution for their common government. The Supreme Court, who, according to the established creed of the North, are the final expounders of that Constitution, say that by its provisions slavery is protected in the Territories, but the greater portion of the North denounces that decision openly, while the remainder covertly repudiate it. What remains, then, but to do that which has been done in all ages and countries, by sensible and right-minded people, who have the misfortune to differ irreconcilably—TO SEPARATE.

From the Charleston Mercury, May, 1859

A revolution is, therefore, inevitable. Submission or resistance will alike establish it. The old Union—the Union of the Constitution, of equal rights between sovereign States is abolished. It is gone forever; strangled by consolidation, and now the instrument of centralism, to establish an irresponsible despotism of the North over the South. To break up the present Union and establish another of the South alone, is no greater revolution than that which now exists. In fact it will be a lesser change. Let the struggle come when it may, the South, to achieve her safety, will have to trample down a Union party in the track of her political emancipation.

The above extract from the Washington correspondent of the Charleston *Mercury,* so clearly foreshadows the very events which have since transpired, that the conclusion is almost irresistable that there was a junta of these disunionists in the city of Washington, who had, at that early day, arranged the entire course to be pursued. The newspapers were promptly and vigorously seconded by the leaders. Below we subjoin outgivings of a portion of those leaders, to indicate the progress of the work of perfecting an organization which should "control parties, legislatures and statesmen."

On the 18th April, 1859, Judge H. S. BENNETT, a very prominent man in North Mississippi, in a letter to the editor of the Grenada *Locomotive,* says:

Since 1850, it has been my opinion, and recent events have more than confirmed this opinion, that we have but little hope in looking to a Federal Congress for the protection of our rights. In every combat we have lost ground; in every argument our forces have been weakened; in every compromise we have been the dupes of northern fanaticism. If we ask for the application of the doctrine of non-intervention, we are presented with the hideous ghost of squatter sovereignty. If we ask for the protection of our slaves in the Territories, we are told we can have none save what a lawless rubble in the Territories may see proper to give us.

It may, then, be asked, to whom can we appeal? If to the guarantees of the Constitution, we are insulted and told the North has yielded to us the fugitive slave bill, and with that we should be contented. If we demand the rendition of our fugitive slaves, we are pointed to their statute books, to laws nullifying the laws of Congress.

With a full knowledge of all these facts, I appeal to every fair minded man in the South, if it is not time to cease this idle talk, and let our demand be made known in language that cannot be misunderstood, demanding congressional legislation for the protection of slaves in the Territories, as being in unison with the plainest principles of justice, equal rights, common sense and the mandates of the Constitution.

This being refused, us our common right under the compact, in the Union; then let us seek equality outside of the compact of Union, where the laws of God, the rights of man, and the feelings of free men counsel us unerringly that we should seek our redress.

And having, as I do, but the faintest hope that this reasonable demand will be granted, may I not justly conclude that it is futile to fix our hopes upon Congress for protection and aid? I answer, to ourselves, to the means within our reach, to the proper organization of our own State.

Hon. JOHN J. PETTUS, the present Governor of Mississippi, during his canvass for that office last year, delivered speeches in all sections in the State, in each of which he declared that in the event of the election of a Republican to the Presidency, he was for a dissolution of the Union. The Vicksburg *Whig*, having been informed that Gov. PETTUS had stated "that in the event of his election to the Governorship, and a Republican should be elected to the office of President of the United States, *he would await some hostile demonstration towards the South* before advising resistance," the Jackson *Mississippian* replied:

The informant of the *Whig* is clearly in error. Col. PETTUS, at all times and places, in his public speeches and private conversations, in his open declarations to the people at the hustings and in his councils with his friends, declares, without reservation or qualification, his approval of the platform that nominated him, pledging the State to resistance in the event of the election of a Black-Republican to the Presidency, upon the avowed purposes of the anti-slavery organization. In his speech at Scooba, in his own county, on the 6th inst., (August,) he went so far as to declare, according to the DeKalb *Democrat,* whose editor was present and reported his remarks, that, "although he now held, as it were, the chief magistracy of the State in his hands, he would freely give it up and retire from the canvass, if he thought the people would not sustain him IN STRONG RESISTANCE TO THE INAUGURATION OF A BLACK REPUBLICAN PRESIDENT.

In July, 1859, the following questions were propounded to Hon. L. P. WALKER, of Alabama, one of the seceders at Charleston and Baltimore, by the editor of the Huntsville *Advocate:*

1. Is it the duty of Congress to intervene for the protection of slavery in the Territories of the United States?

2. Are you in favor of a repeal of the laws of Congress which declare the foreign slave trade piracy?

3. What position should the southern Democracy assume in the Charleston Convention?

The first two he answered in the affirmative, and to the third replied:

We should insist upon adopting a platform *before* making the nomination. This platform *must* embody the first of the foregoing propositions, and should embrace, in principle, the second also. If the first of these propositions—viz: protection to slavery in the territories—is not adopted, the South should withdraw from the convention and make its own nominations, and enunciate a platform of principles consistent with the dignity of sovereign States and the great right of self-protection. * * * * We have a mission to fulfill, *"ennobled by its danger and purified by its isolation."*

> With this spirit let the crisis come!
> Be bold, united, firmly set,
> Nor flinch in word or tone;
> *We'll be a glorious people yet—*
> *Redeemed—erect—alone!*

On the 9th of May, 1859, the Southern Convention—an institution which figures conspicuously in this treasonable business—met at Vicksburg, Mississippi. Ex-Governor McRAE, ex-Senator and present member of Congress from that State, being ill and unable to attend, gave it his encouragement by sending to it a letter of regret, in which he enclosed a series of resolutions, of which the following touches the main matter in in hand:

> *Resolved, That the success of the Republican party in the election of a President of the United States by a sectional majority in 1860 upon the principles above declared will be a virtual dissolution of the compact of the existing Union of the States; and* in that event this convention recommends to the people of the slave holding States to meet immediately in connection to determine the mode and measure of upholding the constitutional government as it at present exists, *by preventing the installation into office of a Republican President and the inauguration of the Republican party in power; or, failing in that, to resolve the slave-holding States into a separate independent organization,* with such constitutional form of government as will best secure their safety, their honor, their rights and institutions, and make them a power of the earth.

On another occasion he said:

> If the Douglas construction of the Cincinnati platform prevailed at Charleston, I, for one, *would not submit.* I AM FOR INDEPENDENCE OUT OF THE UNION IN PREFERENCE TO DISHONOR IT.

Again, on the eve of his departure for Washington, on the 19th of November, he spoke at Jackson, Mississippi—which the *Mississippian* reported thus:

> With his accustomed candor, Ex-Governor MCRAE avowed himself in favor of the repeal of the Federal and State laws branding as an ignominious crime the purchase of slaves in Africa, thereby constituting a system of legislation unfriendly to southern institutions, and detrimental to southern interests. In the event of the election of a Black-Republican to the Presidency, the speaker argued that *Mississippi separately, or in concert with other Southern States, as she might elect ought at once to discontinue her connection with the Abolition States.*

Hon. R. BARNWELL RHETT, of South Carolina also lent his helping hand, the same who said shortly after the election of Mr. BUCHANAN: "All true statesmanship in the South consists in forming combinations and shaping events so as *to bring about a dissolution of the present Union and the establishment of a southern confederacy.* He made a speech on the 4th July, 1859, at Grahamville, S. C., which was a masterly appeal to the passions of the South, on the questions of congressional protection and disunion. He had found at last, that those combinations were forming and that events were being so shaped as to justify his estimate of true statesmanship in the South, and such as to bring about the desired southern confederacy. He was unusually hopeful, and the success which he contemplated inspired him with unusual strength and vigor. The speech was in all respects conformable to the conclusion, which alone we quote, at this time. Said Mr. RHETT:

> Should the public regard, after I am gone, ever reach my humble services, let it be remembered that, after twenty years of earnest effort to preserve the Union, by keeping it within the limitations of the Constitution, and arresting its fatal tendency to despotism. I turned at last to the salvation of my native land (the South,) and in my latter years did all I could *to dissolve her connection with the North, and* TO ESTABLISH FOR HER A SOUTHERN CONFEDERACY.

During the year 1859, Mr. YANCEY was not an idle spectator of the work he set on foot; he wrote letters and made speeches on various occasions. JEFFERSON DAVIS, his greatest and most powerful coadjutor, was also active and zealous. We give an extract from a speech of the latter at Jackson, Miss., on the 6th July, 1859. He said:

> The success of such a party would indeed produce an "irrepressible conflict." To you would be presented the question, will you allow the constitutional Union to be changed into the despotism of a majority? will you become the subjects of a hostile government, or will you outside of the Union, assert the equality, the liberty and sovereignty to which you were born! For myself, I say, as I said on a former occasion, in the contingency of the election of a President on the platform of Mr. Seward's Rochester speech, *let the Union be dissolved. Let the "great, but not the greatest of evils" come.* For as did the great and good Calhoun, from whom is drawn that expression of value. I love and venerate the Union of these States—but I love liberty and Mississippi more.

From the newspapers and the hustings the cry of disunion and revolution rose to State Legislatures and to Congress. Here the evidence of a purpose to dissolve the Union and to revolutionize the Government are so abundant that we have space for comparatively few. Governor GIST, of South Carolina, in his message to the Legislature of that State, November 28, 1859, uses the following language:

> With a united South our course would be clear, and our future glorious; we could enforce equality in the Union, or maintain our independence out of it. If, as *I solemnly believe, we can no longer live in peace and harmony in the Union*—notwithstanding the associations of the past, and the remembrance of our common triumph, (being treated as enemies and aliens, rather than brethren of the same family, and heirs of the same inheritance, by the North,) we can form a confederacy with ability to protect itself against any enemy, and command the

respect and admiration of the world. * * *The election of a Black Republican President will settle the question of our safety in the Union;* and although the forms of the Constitution may be complied with, its vital principle will be extinguished, and the South must consent to occupy an inferior and degrading position, or seek new safeguards for her future security.

Gov. PERRY, of Florida, about the same time, in a like "State paper," said:

True, Florida, as the youngest and least populous of the southern sovereignties, can only follow in action the lead of her sisters, yet this constitutes no reason why, at a time demanding the freest conference and frankest expression among those joined by a common destiny, she should remain silent. I believe that her voice should be heard in "tones not loud but deep," IN FAVOR OF AN ETERNAL SEPARATION from those whose wickedness and fanaticism forbid us longer to live with peace and safety. There are good grounds for the hope *that most of the southern States will not consent to see the General Government pass into hands avowedly hostile to the South.* If such is their purpose, it is not unlikely that they will prepare for the emergency of the approaching Presidential election.

Gov. McWILLIE, of Mississippi, responded in pretty much the same spirit for that State. And in due time, the Senate of South Carolina, on the 19th December, passed the following preamble and resolution, which were concurred in in the House, with very slight, if any, alteration:

Whereas, the State of South Carolina, by her ordinance of 1852, affirmed her right to secede from the Confederacy whenever the occasion should arrive justifying her, in her own judgment, in taking that step; and in the resolution adopted by her convention, declared that she forbore the immediate exercise of that right in deference to her sister States; and whereas more than seven years have elapsed since that convention adjourned, and in the intervening time, the assaults upon the institution of slavery, and upon the rights and equality of the southern States, have unceasingly continued with increasing violence, and in new and more alarming forms, *South Carolina still deferring to her southern sisters, nevertheless respectfully announces to them that, in her judgment,* THE SAFETY AND HONOR OF THE SLAVEHOLDING STATES IMPERATIVELY DEMAND A SPEEDY SEPARATION FROM THE FREE-SOIL STATES OF THE CONFEDERACY, *and earnestly inspires and urges her sister States of the South to originate the movement of southern separation in which she pledges herself promptly to unite.*

Resolved, That the State of South Carolina owes it to her own citizens to protect them and their property from every enemy, and that for the purpose of military preparation for any emergency, the sum of $100,000 be appropriated for military contingencies.

Mississippi and Alabama promptly responded, and passed resolutions PLEDGING THEMSELVES TO GO OUT OF THE UNION IN THE EVENT OF THE ELECTION OF A REPUBLICAN PRESIDENT. They stand solemnly pledged to day to that course. In Congress, during the last session, we had similar expressions from various southern members, of which the following are but mere specimens:

Mr. GARNETT, of Virginia, said:

You must go home to your people, and must put down this abolition spirit. You must repeal the laws with which you have polluted your statute-books, to nullify that provision of the Constitution which protects the value of our slave property along the border, for we do not mean to stay in the Union until you have converted the border States into free States, and so demoralized and enervated our strength. You must pass laws at home, condemning and subjecting to the hands of justice the men who advise and the men who plot and the men who engage in these insurrectionary attempts. You must do for us what we do for foreign nations, and what they do for every country with which they are at peace. Unless you do pass such laws, unless you do put down this spirit of abolitionism, the Union will be short.

Mr. DEJARNETTE, of Virginia, said:

You may elect him President of the North; but of the South never. Whatever the event may be, others may differ, but Virginia, in view of her ancient renown, in view of her illustrious dead, in view of her *sic semper tyrannis,* will resist his authority.

Mr. MOORE, of Alabama, said:

I do not concur with the declaration made yesterday by the gentleman from Tennessee, that the election of a Black Republican to the Presidency was not cause for a dissolution of the Union. Whenever a President is elected by a fanatical majority at the North, those whom I represent, as I believe, and the gallant State which I in part represent, are ready, let the consequences be what they may, to fall back on their reserved rights and say, "As to this Union, we have no longer any lot or part in it."

Mr. PUGH, of Alabama, said:

If, with the character of the Government well defined, and **the** rights and privileges of the parties to the compact clearly asserted by the Democratic party, the Black Republicans get possession of the Government, then the question is fully presented, whether the southern States will remain in the Union, as subject and degraded colonies, or will they withdraw and establish a southern confederacy of coequal homogeneous sovereigns?

In my judgment the latter is the only course compatible with the honor, equality, and safety of the South, and the sooner it is known and acted upon, the better for all parties to the compact.

Mr. CURRY, of Alabama, said:

However distasteful it may be to my friend from New York, (Mr. CLARK,) however much it may revolt the public sentiment or conscience of this country, I am not ashamed or afraid publicly to avow that the election of William H. Seward or Salmon P. Chase, or any other such representative of the Republican party upon a sectional platform, ought to be resisted to the disruption of every tie that binds this Confederacy together.

Mr. GARTRELL, of Georgia, said:

I need not tell what I, as a southern man, will do—I think I may safely speak for the masses of the people of Georgia—that, when that event (the election of a Republican President) happens, they, in my judgment, will consider it an overt act, a declaration of war, and meet immediately in convention to take into consideration the mode and measure of redress. That is my position; and if that be treason to the Government, make the most of it.

Mr. CRAWFORD, of Georgia, said:

Now with regard to the election of a Black Republican President, I have this to say, and I speak the sentiment of every Democrat on this floor from the State of Georgia; we will never submit to the inauguration of a Black Republican President. I repeat it sir—and I have authority to say—that no Democratic representative from Georgia on this floor will ever submit to the inauguration of a Black Republican President.

Mr. BONHAM, of South Carolina, said:

As to disunion, upon the election of a Black Republican, I can speak for no one but myself and those I have here the honor to represent; and I say, without hesitation that, upon the election of Mr. Seward, or any other man who indorses and proclaims the doctrines held by him and his party—call him by what name you please—I am in favor of an immediate dissolution of the Union.—And, sir, I think I speak the sentiments of my own constituents, and the State of South Carolina, when I say so.

Mr. KEITT, of South Carolina, said:

Should the Republican party succeed in the next presidential election, my advice to the South is to snap the cords of the Union at once and forever.

Mr. SINGLETON, of Mississippi, said:

You ask me when will the time come; when will the South be united? It will be when you elect a Black Republican—Hale, Seward, or Chase—President of the United States. Whenever you undertake to elect such a man to preside over the destinies of the South, you may expect to see us undivided and indivisible friends, and see all parties of the South arrayed to resist his inauguration.

Mr. REUBEN DAVIS, of Mississippi, said:

Gentlemen of the Republican party, I warn you. Present your sectional candidate for 1860; elect him as the representative of your system of labor; take possession of the Government, as the instrument of your power in this contest of "irrepressible conflict," and we of the South will tear the Constitution in pieces and look to our guns for justice and right against aggression and wrong.

We have now seen how this southern organization, set on foot by Mr. YANCEY in May, 1858, has extended its influence over "legislatures and statesmen," as he vauntingly declared it would and should, in his letter to SLAUGHTER. It only now remains to show that the same influence has extended over and broken up the Democratic party. For in that letter let it not be forgotten that Mr. Yancey said of the power of this organization, it "WILL HOLD THE SOUTHERN ISSUE PARAMOUNT, AND WILL INFLUENCE PARTIES, LEGISLATURES, AND STATESMEN." Having asserted its influence, as we have undeniably shown, over legislatures and statesmen, a few words will serve to exhibit how it has affected the Democratic party. It was indispensable to the success of the scheme, that the Democracy should be broken up—that the southern wing should dissolve its connection with that of the North. And that necessity was successfully met and accomplished. As early as October, 1859, the Charleston *Mercury* put forth the following programme, by which the thing could be done:

1. Let the Legislatures of the southern States, at their next meetings, distinctly declare the rights of the South, as plainly deducible from the Dred Scott case, accompanied with a resolution that they will vote for no one for the Presidency or Vice Presidency of the United States who does not plainly and distinctly affirm and support them without non-committalism, dodging, or equivocation.

2. Should the Charleston Convention declare and affirm these rights, and nominate candidates for the Presidency and Vice Presidency who distinctly support them, then the southern States will support such candidates; and should they be elected, proof will be afforded that the South may continue with safety in the Confederacy.

3. But should the candidates for the Presidency and Vice Presidency, thus fairly nominated by the Charleston Convention, be defeated in the presidential election, and the Republican or Abolition party succeed in electing their candidates, then the southern Legislatures, as soon thereafter as they shall successively assemble together, should recall their Senators and Representatives from the Congress of the United States, and invite the co-operation of their sister southern States to devise means for their common safety.

4. But should the Charleston Convention refuse to declare and affirm the rights of the South, as deducible from the Dred Scott case, or nominate candidates who will not affirm and support them, then let the southern States nominate and support candidates of their own, plain and faithfully reflecting and supporting their rights.

5. Should the southern States succeed in electing the sectional candidate, thus nominated, of course they will deem it a sufficient proof for the present of their safety in the Union.

6. But should the southern States fail in electing the sectional candidates thus nominated, then let the safe course be pursued as has been suggested in case the Democratic party be defeated with a candidate standing on the rights of the South, and the Black Republican or Abolition candidates be elected

This programme was accepted and acted upon. The January, 1860, convention of Alabama which appointed delegates to Charleston, was blessed with the presence of Mr. YANCEY. Indeed, he was always to be found wherever his presence would likely prove most effective. He was in the Alabama convention, was the leading and controlling spirit in it, and he thus laid down the law to his followers:

To obtain the aid of the Democracy in this contest, it is necessary to make a contest in its Charleston Convention. In that body, Douglas adherents will press his doctrines to a decision. If the State-rights men keep out of this convention, that decision must inevitably be against the South, and that, either in direct favor of the Douglas doctrine, or by the indorsement of the Cincinnati platforms, under which Douglas claims shelter for his principles. The State-rights men should present in that convention their demand for a decision, and they will obtain an indorsement of their demands, or a denial of these demands. If indorsed, we shall have a greater hope of triumph within the Union. If denied, in my opinion, the State-rights wing should secede from the convention, and appeal to the whole people of the South, without distinction of parties, and organize another convention upon the basis of their principles, and go into the election with a candidate nominated by it, as a grand constitutional party. But in the presidential contest a Black Republican may be elected. If this dire event should happen, in my opinion, the only hope of safety for the South is in a withdrawal from the Union before he shall be inaugurated before the sword and the treasury of the Federal Government shall be placed in the keeping of that party. I would suggest that the several State Legislatures should by law, require the Governor, when it shall be made manifest that the Black Republican candidate for the Presidency shall receive a majority of the electoral vote, to call a convention of the people of the State to assemble in time to provide for their safety before the 4th of March 1861. If, however, a Black Republican should not be elected, then, in pursuance of the policy of making this contest within the Union, we should initiate measures for Congress which should lead to a repeal of all the unconstitutional acts against slavery. If we should fail to obtain so just a system of legislation, then the South should seek her independence out of the Union.

We beg of the reader to turn and read again that passage, and to imagine it to be printed in capital letters. We beg of him to read it a third time, and then run over in his mind the events at Charleston and Baltimore. The programme of a school examination, a theatrical performance, or a Fourth of July celebration, was never more exactly fulfilled. Here the unholy intrigue was to salute bright-eyed Success, or fall into the embrace of scowling Despair. At Charleston the demand was not granted, and the Alabama delegation, led *personally* by Mr. YANCEY, who was in the Convention for *that purpose,* went out of it, and were followed by those States which were in the secrets and sympathies of "the movement." The Alabama delegation were the first to set up the standard of rebellion to the party. The Alabama delegation were, in the hands of Mr. YANCEY, clay in the hands of the potter. Other "cotton States" followed, as it was intended from the first they should do. On the very night of this secession from the Convention, on the night of the 30th April, at Charleston, Mr. Yancey addressed a crowd, in which he is thus reported in a Charleston journal:

Mr. YANCEY appeared, and was proud and happy to see the South taking so proud a position in favor of her constitutional rights. He spoke of the seceding delegates as about to form the "constitutional Democratic convention," and the delegates who remained, as composing the "rump convention." He said this rump convention would speedily be in fact a sectional convention, and would represent only a faction of the free-soil sentiment of the North. He said the South must come up as a unit, and vindicate its constitutional rights. Every ultra sentiment was applauded with mad enthusiasm. *Yancey said that perhaps even now the pen of the historian was nibbed to write the story of a new revolution.* At this, some one in the crowd cried 'three cheers for the independent southern republic.' They were given with a will.

Further Developments of the Conspiracy against the Union

The Nashville *Patriot,* from which the foregoing history of the times is selected, has traced with a masterly hand the inception, progress, and development, down to the secession from the Democratic National Convention at Charleston, of the "conspiracy to break up the Union." It has shown by indisputable evidence, that the main reliance for the success of that conspiracy is the disruption of the Democratic party, and the sequence, as the plotters and disorganizers hope, of the election of a Black Republican to the Presidency, in which event they are solemnly pledged "*to snap the cords of the Union* at once and forever." We propose to take up the history of the conspiracy where the *Patriot* left off, to trace its progress to the present period, and supply further proofs that the end and aim of leading southern supporters of Breckinridge and Lane is—Disunion.

Upon their withdrawal from the Convention at Charleston the Secessionists assembled in St. Andrews' Hall. Let us briefly narrate their proceedings. Mr. john c. preston, of South Carolina, was called to the chair and made a short address. The following is an extract:

> We only know that the institutions of our country are imperilled, and we are here to preserve our rights and redress our wrongs. If we had submitted, we would have done that which would have driven us from the land of our forefathers, and deprived us of the liberty they fought for, and ultimately would have driven us from the spot on which their sacred ashes repose.

Mr. Yancey, of Alabama, said:

> We were sent to the National Democratic Convention as delegates, but our mission has been fulfilled and we return as mere citizens from the late National

Convention, which is now a mere sectional gathering. A few southern delegates still remain there, it is true, but it is in the hope of inducing others to forego their Black Republican purposes. He proposed that they should take no action, but to remain here and watch the proceedings of the Convention. If Douglas is nominated, it would then become their duty to present and recommend to the people of the United States candidates for President and Vice President, and on a national and constitutional basis, and therefore, a Southern basis. He thought no steps should be taken by the Seceding Convention until the proper time.

Mr. MEEK, of the same State, said:

Any southern man that shall go into the Baltimore Convention would go there an approver of Squatter Sovereignty. The resolutions adopted at their adjournment invites the southern States to fill up the vacancies occasioned by our secession, declaring our seats vacant.

Mr. YANCEY, said:

He approved the proposition of Judge Meek for appointing a committee to prepare an Address. He did not think it would either save or break the Union. The delegate from Georgia, in predicting a disunion movement by disunion leaders, looked to the Georgia delegation, but declined to name who and what he meant.

Another delegate seemed to charge him (Yancey) with singing pæans to the Union."
Mr. JACKSON, of Georgia, in reply, said:

I certainly never intimated that the gentleman from Alabama sang pæans to the Union. Certainly no one will ever charge him with any such an offence. My remarks were directed rather to my colleague, who, I thought, was placing Georgia in a wrong position. He did not wish Georgia to be placed in the position of singing pæans to the Union.

Mr. HOOKER, of Mississippi, said:

We are no longer delegates to the other Convention. We separated from them on principle, and he was unwilling that they should carry them to Baltimore as an adjournment to that Convention. If we adjourn without doing anything or saying anything, we will stullify ourselves; and if we follow them to Baltimore, we shall lose all the moral effect of this movement. Make our nominations now, manfully and boldly. We are here for an object and purpose, and if we go home without action we will be merely denounced.

The Convention, as it was styled, finally adjourned, without any definite action, to meet at Richmond, on the 11th day of May. It is apparent from the proceedings at St. Andrews' Hall, of which we have given enough for a clear understanding of the whole, that the Seceders considered their connection with the Democratic National Convention permanently dissolved. As Mr. YANCEY pointedly said, they considered that their "mission had been fulfilled." In the language of Mr. HOOKER, of Mississippi, they were "no longer delegates to the *other* Convention"—that from which they seceded. They had no intention of following the Convention to Baltimore, until the address of the "Immortal Nineteen" southern Senators and Representatives, inviting and urging them to resume their seats in the Convention which should re-assemble on the 18th of May, was issued. That celebrated paper held out to the Seceders the inducement, for which its signers had no authority whatever, that the "platform" would be modified at Baltimore to meet their demands. And, "if your demands be not complied with," said the address to the Seceders, "you can secede again." Subsequent events justify the belief that the real purpose connected with the appearance of the Seceders at Baltimore, was to effect a larger secession from the Convention—a secession extending, if possible to all the southern States, and to such of the delegates from the North as held office under the Federal Administration. Of these office-holders there were some fifteen or twenty.

The Seceders at the appointed time, on the 11th of May, came together again at Richmond, to which Convention, as well as to Baltimore, all of them had been accredited, meanwhile, some regularly, and others irregularly, except the delegations from Florida and South Carolina, whose commissions confined them to Richmond alone. They adjourned over on the second day, until the 23d of May, and repaired to Baltimore—all of them who held "roving commissions"—to demand the seats in the adjourned Convention which they had vacated at Charleston. They demanded admission into a body which their leader, Mr. YANCEY, had denounced in St. Andrews' Hall, at Charleston, as "a mere sectional gathering, and contemptuously termed "*the late National Convention.*" They demanded seats in the Convention, with this same Mr. YANCEY at their head, although he had declared, but a few weeks before, at Montgomery, in a public speech, that, "the seceding States could not be represented, and at the same time *preserve their honor untarnished and not have their high moral position demoralized and degraded.*"

Why the Seceders Demanded Admission at Baltimore

It was mysteriously given out, about the time the Seceders met at Richmond, that if they would seek admission at Baltimore, and should be refused, Virginia, and a majority of the other southern States that had not seceded at Charleston, would unite in the bolt. And there was a further assurance, it was said, that a like result would occur, if the "platform" was not reconstructed to suit the wishes of the Secessionists. At all events, it was apparent early at Baltimore, that upon one or the other of these pretexts, a further secession was inevitable. It came, as was anticipated, on the pretext that "bogus delegates" were admitted from Alabama and Louisiana, whereas in truth it was premeditated and prearranged, and had no other or better justification than the refusal of the Convention to admit the Seceders from those States who had no shadow of authority to seek admission. *They* were in fact the "bogus delegates," and were rightly rejected.

The Maryland Institute Nominations

The Seceders, with their number increased by the fresh secession at Baltimore, instigated by the Administration, acting upon its office-holders, and by candidates for the Presidency whose weakness had been made manifest at Charleston, assembled at the Maryland Institute, and nominated John C. Breckinridge for the Presidency, and Joseph Lane, for the Vice Presidency. Of the original seceders all were present but South Carolina; and there were a number present who were mere political waifs. However, for want of space, we shall not go into these details. It is sufficient to say, it was an assemblage of bolters, disorganizers, and disunionists, whose acts are entitled to no respect whatever, and *with whom no National Democrat can hold* Fellowship or Communion. Subsequently, a portion of the seceders from the South returned to Richmond, where their Convention had been adjourned from day to day from the 18th of June, and Breckinridge and Lane were nominated again.

Disunion Supporters of Breckinridge and Lane

We continue the proof which the article from the Nashville Patriot presents in part, that Breckinridge and Lane are the candidates of the Disunionists. The record is readily made up.

Mr. IVERSON, of Georgia, in the Senate, on the 6th of January 1859, said:

The election of a northern President, upon a sectional and anti-slavery issue, will be considered cause enough to justify secession. Let the Senator from New York (Mr. Seward) or any other man avowing the sentiments and policy enunciated by him in his Rochester speech, be elected President of the United States, and, in my opinion, there are more than one of the southern States that would take *immediate steps* towards separation. And, sir, I am free to declare here, in the Senate, that whenever such an event shall occur, for one, *I shall be for disunion,* and shall, if alive, exert all the powers I may have in urging upon the people of my State the necessity and propriety of an *immediate separation.*

Mr. TOOMBS, the colleague of Mr. IVERSON, in the Senate, on the 14th of February, 1860, said:

When that time comes, freemen of Georgia, redeem your pledge: I am ready to redeem mine. *Your honor is involved, your faith is plighted.* I know you feel a stain as a wound: your peace, your social system, your firesides, are involved. Never permit this Federal Government to pass into the traitorous hands of the Black Republican party. It has already declared war against you and your institutions. It every day commits acts of war against you: it has already compelled you to arm for your defence. Listen to "no vain babblings," to no treacherous jargon about "overt acts;" they have already been committed. Defend yourselves: the enemy is at your door; wait not to meet him at the hearthstone— meet him at the door-sill, and drive him from the temple of liberty, or pull down its pillars and involve him in a common ruin.

Capt. B. H. RUTLEDGE, at the BRECKINRIDGE and LANE ratification meeting in Charleston, South Carolina, said:

The operation of the Richmond Convention has set on foot a movement in which the whole South joins; so far, at least, the South appears united. Let us hope, let us pray to God, that it will continue united, one and inseparable, upon the vital issue which will come upon us if Lincoln is elected. This would be the last insult which could be offered to a free people.

*　　*　　*　　*　　*　　*　　*

Upon such an event, every operation of the Federal Government ought to be made to stop within the limits of every Southern State. No judge should administer Federal justice; no collector should collect Federal customs throughout the whole South. No Southern man should consent to hold office under a commission signed by an Abolition President; and it will be for the people of the South to say whether any Northern man shall be permitted to enter any of the State lines with such intent.

Gen. W. E. MARTIN, a South Carolina delegate to the Richmond Convention, at the same meeting, said:

> The South, I am sure, is not more divided than were the American colonies in the Revolution. The great feeling with us, antagonistic to resistance, is love of the Union. Yet, deplorable as I consider this sentiment, in this aspect, it is not more powerful for mischief than was the loyalty of our ancestors to the British Crown. We see, however, that they who entered the struggle with no view to separation from the mother country, yet happily attained that end; and so it may be, and I trust will be, with the South. Circumstances of late have enabled me to judge of the state of sentiment in the Southern States. If the delegations from Alabama, Mississippi, Florida, Texas, Louisiana and Georgia reflect the opinion of the people—and it is but fair to think they do—then there is much hope for the South.

Mr. R. BARNWELL RHETT, at the same meeting, said:

> Now, my friends, this consolidation is culminating into the Presidential election. We have now going on a struggle: we have now, at last got the two sections of the Union pitted against each other.
>
>   *   *   *   *   *   *   *
>
> If we are successful, there is a trust, at least, of happy and better days.
>
> If, on the contrary, the Black Republicans succeed in electing Lincoln and Hamlin, who will openly advocate that slavery be abolished throughout the whole world, then we have to look to ourselves. * * I am very chary of seeing the South pass resolutions. I am sick at heart of vain attempts to hold out the olive branch, when *we should grasp the sword.*

Hon. W. PORCHER MILES, the Representative in Congress of the Charleston district, at the same meeting, spoke as follows:

> We said Douglas' notions of squatter sovereignty are unconstitutional, and the South could not accept him as their standard-bearer. Yet it was Douglas or nobody; Douglas or defeat; and so it is, the great Democratic party has been disbanded. I do not regret it. Great as that party has been; great as its triumphs; worthy as its services, when that party, or any great party, becomes subservient to the will of the mobocracy, and will tear away constitutional principles for the purpose of transient success. I say perish such party, no matter what may be the result.

How do we stand now? The South stands upon her own platform, dependent upon her own strong arm for support. We have determined to support two men who have cordially and heartily indorsed the platform with a Southern code. In that respect, we will have, for the first time, the South standing together in solid phalunx. I know both these gentlemen who are our candidates. They are both able, and I believe them both to be sound.

The resolutions of the meeting were not less significant than the speeches. We have space for one only, which shows that the South Carolina disunionists support BRECKINRIDGE and LANE as the candidates of the Junta which met at Richmond. Here it is:

> *Resolved,* That we heartily approve of the proceedings of the Richmond Convention, and will uphold the principles that Convention has announced, and the candidates it has nominated for the Presidency and Vice Presidency of the United States.

Gen. JOHN MCQUEEN, a representative in Congress from South Carolina, made a speech on the 4th of July, at Bennettsville, in that State, of which a sketch is given in the local paper—*Son of Temperance.* It says:

> He reviewed the Federal politics of the day, cordially indorsed the nomination of Breckinridge and Lane for the Presidency and Vice Presidency—said they were good and true men for the South to support, and would maintain the constitutional rights of the Confederacy, and should be supported by every Southern man. * * * If they submit, and permit Lincoln to be inaugurated President, without resistance and seceding from the Union, in such an event be, for one, believed that we were a degraded people, and a thousand times more than the Colonies were under Great Britain. He counseled secession of the South from the Union, if a Black Republican was elected President of the Government, for it would be an open declaration of an irrepressible conflict against our peculiar institutions, which are as dear to us as our lives.

Hon. LAWRENCE M. KEITT, another representative in Congress from South Carolina, in a recent letter, said:

> But, should the Black Republican party obtain power, and the South remain passive—what then? While I invoke co-operation—while I appeal to the States around me to be sure to their honor—yet, if these fail, I will counsel this State alone, if necessary, and at all hazards, to secede from this Union.
>
>   *   *   *   *   *   *   *
>
> This Union is just as travelers tell us many Eastern habitations are; a palace to look upon; all fair on its outside, and presenting the appearance of a house

that should last for generations; but the master puts his walking-stick or his boot heel through the rafters, and he finds that the white ants have eaten all the substance out of the timbers, and that all that he sees about him is a coating of paint, which an intrusive blow may disperse in a cloud of dust. The skirting boards have already perished, the rafters are now ready to tumble in.

Ex-Governor HUBBARD, of Alabama, one of the seceders at Charleston, recently said:

Resistance! Resistance! to death, against the Government is what we want now.

MR. BRECKINRIDGE COUNSELS RESISTANCE

We have reached the culminating point in this history; we have to present the evidence now that JOHN C. BRECKINRIDGE sympathizes with his disunion supporters, and counsels resistance in the event of the election of LINCOLN to the Presidency. Hear him in his speech at Frankfort, his home in Kentucky, on the 21st of December, 1859:

I have seen the growing evidences for the last few years, culminating recently into proof, of the determination of the Republicans to take possession, if possible, of the Government, for the purpose I have described. And I have seen in the representatives of the lower southern States a most resolute and determined spirit of resistance. In the meantime I perceive a sensible loss of that spirit of brotherhood, that feeling of love for a common country, that favor of loyalty, which is at last the surest cement of the Union; so that in the present unhappy state of affairs. I was almost tempted to exclaim that we are DISSOLVING, week by week and month by month. The threads are gradually fretting themselves asunder; and a stranger visiting Washington might imagine that the Executive of the United States was the President of two hostile Republics.

     *   *   *   *   *   *   *

Resistance in some form is inevitable. Some members of the Confederacy may contemplate it in the form of a separate political organization. Kentucky, while a single ray of hope penetrates the thick darkness, will resist under the Constitution and within the Union. Resistance, I repeat, is certain.

We cannot delude ourselves with the thought that the dangers that menace us are afar off, nor should others delude themselves with the thought that there will be no resistance. Constitutional resistance we contemplate to the latest moment, even against unconstitutional attacks. But when the subject of contest reaches the homes and firesides of a people, who is wise enough to predict or control the progress of events?

Perhaps the most imminent danger springs from the possible action of certain members of the Confederacy. The representatives from South Carolina, Georgia, Alabama, and Mississippi, not to mention other southern States, say that they represent their constituents—nay, that they scarcely go so far as their constituents—and most of them declare that they are ready at any moment for a separate organization. Some of the southern Legislatures have passed resolves of this character, and we may safely assume that is the true feeling of the people.

That speech pledges Mr. BRECKINRIDGE as fully as R. BARNWELL RHETT, or WILLIAM L. YANCEY is pledged to resistance. Unless he "meanly deserts his friends," Mr. BRECKINRIDGE like Mr. TOOMBS, will "*listen to no vain babblings, to no treacherous jargon* about 'overt acts,'" if the Republicans elect their candidate. No, he will counsel Kentucky then, as Mr. TOOMBS has counseled the people of Georgia to defend themselves, to drive the enemy from the temple of liberty, "or pull down its pillars, and involve him in a common ruin." What will that be but treason,—treason against the Union, and treason against the Constitution which in "his high office" Mr. BRECKINRIDGE has sworn to support. He should ponder well, the burning denunciation which HENRY CLAY pronounced against R. BARNWELL RHETT, of South Carolina, in the Senate, in 1850. Said *the* Great Kentuckian on that occasion,—"If he, (Mr. RHETT) pronounced the sentiment attributed to him of *raising the standard of disunion and of resistance to the common Government,* whatever he has been, if he follows up that declaration by corresponding overt acts, *he will be a traitor, and I hope he will meet the fate of a traitor.*" Let Mr. BRECKINRIDGE take warning in time.

It was that Frankfort speech which commended him to the Southern Secessionists. It was that speech which made him the leader of the column which would have been headed otherwise by JEFFERSON DAVIS, or WILLIAM L. YANCEY. Listen to the testimony of Gen. W. E. MARTIN, of South Carolina, a delegate to the Richmond Convention, from whose speech at the ratification meeting we have already had occasion to cite. Speaking of Mr. BRECKINRIDGE he said:

Having read carefully his speech delivered at Frankfort, Kentucky, when he could not have expected a nomination, I am now better satisfied that he is a State-rights man of the strictest school—more satisfied than I was when I gave him my vote at Richmond. In that speech he lays down a broad ground—a ground that I will close my remarks with, and save me a great deal of what I intended otherwise to say. He tells his people that the Democratic party was a very good thing in itself, but they were not to rely upon the Democratic party or any party. They were to rely upon themselves. THE SOUTH MUST RELY

UPON ITS OWN STRONG ARM, and be prepared for any and every emergency.

An extract or two from Southern newspapers in the interest of the Secessionists, and we shall close the disunion record, forever, we hope.

From the Camden (Ala.) Democrat

We run up our flag to-day for BRECKINRIDGE and LANE, the Democratic nominees for President and Vice-President of the United States. We have unwaveringly contended for the last ten years that it would be better (for all concerned) to make two or more distinct governments of the territory comprising the United States of America—and that such will ultimately be done, there can be no sort of doubt; but it should be done with fairness and justice to every section of the Union; and believing that the party to which we belong is the only reliable one to carry out this measure, and secure to our own section all her rights, we intend to battle for its principles to the fullest extent of our ability.

From the Montgomery (Ala.) Mail

Run three Presidential tickets against Lincoln, thereby giving Lincoln the best chance for election. After Lincoln is elected, some Southern communities—most of them, perhaps—will refuse to let a Postmaster, appointed under his Administration, take possession of the office. Then the United States authorities will be interposed to 'enforce the laws.' Then the United States authorities will either be shot down, or they will shoot somebody down. Then the people of the community will rise up against the United States Government, and will be sustained by neighboring communities, until civil war, with all its horrible butcheries, envelops the land in a shroud of blood and carnage.

From the Cahawba (Ala.) Slaveholder

THE SOUTHERN TICKET.—We hoist to-day, as our choice of nominated candidates for the Presidency and Vice-Presidency, the names of John C. Breckinridge, of Kentucky, and Joe Lane, of Oregon.

Our selection is made with special reference to the principles we have heretofore advocated, the most prominent, controlling of which is an union of the Southern people for the protection of our Southern institutions.

Such are the doctrines inculcated by the leading supporters of BRECKINRIDGE and LANE. What are they but open, rank disunion, and whither do they tend but to the destruction of the Constitution, and the desolation of the country! What friend of the Union, what lover of constitutional liberty can read this dark catalogue of treason without a shudder! "Dissolve the Union, tear the Constitution in pieces, and look to our guns for justice," exclaim the southern supporters of BRECKINRIDGE and LANE, if LINCOLN be elected! And yet, they counselled secession at Charleston, forced further secession at Baltimore, disrupted the Democratic party, and set up a sectional organization, all of which increases and multiplies LINCOLN's chances of election.—What for? To wage war upon a mere abstraction. To crush out, if possible, the choice of three-fourths of the Democracy of the Union—STEPHEN A. DOUGLAS, for whom the South, with the same opinions then for which the Secessionists so bitterly denounce him to-day, on the last ballot that his name was before the Cincinnati Convention, cast *seventy three* of their one hundred and twenty votes. That was the ostensible cause of the secession. But with the deep designing leaders who planned and plotted from the beginning for discord and disorganization in the Democratic ranks, disunion, and a southern confederacy were and are the prospects ahead. Let the masses ponder these things well.

Thank God no disunionists sustain STEPHEN A. DOUGLAS and HERSCHEL V. JOHNSON. Not one that we know. Instinctively they have banded together as one man under the flag of BRECKINRIDGE and LANE. Why? They could control BRECKINRIDGE, if he were elected, and mould him to their purposes, and they know it. Defeated, they have assurance, that BRECKINRIDGE and LANE will either aid them, or oppose no obstacle to *"the disruption of every tie that binds this Confederacy together,"* in the event of LINCOLN's election. To support such a ticket is therefore, to league with disunionists, and countenance treason. Where is the Democrat who reveres the memory of JACKSON, and remembers the lofty stand which he maintained against the nullifiers of South Carolina, who will so degrade himself as to become the tool of the crafty plotters in the conspiracy, which has been tracked step by step, to break up the Union? Where is the Old Line Whig, who honors the grave of HENRY CLAY—the man whose life was made up of sacrifices for his country—who will insult his ashes by uniting with the enemies of the glorious Union which he loved so well? There should be, can be, must be no hesitation with such men. The path of duty and honor is straight before them. They must tread it with an unfaltering step. They must bear aloft the flag of their country, and stand fast by the noble sentiment of DOUGLAS' letter of acceptance: "THE UNION MUST BE PRESERVED. THE CONSTITUTION MUST BE MAINTAINED INVIOLATE IN ALL ITS PARTS." Thus, only can a well-regulated, conservative government be maintained, and the rights of every section upheld. Let all, then, who value the Union which is coeval with our political existence, and are ready to defend it, bury old animosities, forget past prejudices, and rally around the MAN OF THE PEOPLE, in this the hour of the country's peril. Clansmen of the Constitution, be firm, vigilant, and united in action, that you may scatter its enemies, and preserve it inviolate from the ruthless assaults of northern fanatics as well as southern disunionists.

❧ 13 ❧

Salient Points of the Campaign.
A Tract Issued by the Ill[inois]
Republican State Central Committee
(Springfield, 1860)

To the supporters of the growing Republican political tide in the northern states, the Democrats had too long been in power, embarked on policies that had promoted the spread of slavery, with its threat to the North, American free labor, and the Union itself. Someone had to end their malevolent reign and restore the balance between sections in the nation. At the same time, the Democrats had ignored other needs of the nation, such as the Pacific railroad, because of their deep preoccupation with the territorial question and their eagerness to promote southern interests. The only hope for the country on all of these matters lay in the Republican party and their candidates, Abraham Lincoln and Hannibal Hamlin. To their opponents, the Republicans were disruptive revolutionaries, a threat to the Union. The Republicans themselves, however, suggested stability, conservatism, restoration, and therefore, progress, as their central ideological tenets. As the conservative former Whig Edward Bates, of Missouri, wrote: "*I consider* Mr. Lincoln *a sound, safe, national man.*"

Chapter I
Judge Bates' Letter in Support of Lincoln and Hamlin

St. Louis, June 11, 1860.

O. H. Browning, Esq., Quincy, Illinois.

Dear Sir:—When I received your letter of May 22d, I had no thought that the answer would be so long delayed; but, waiving all excuses, I proceed to answer it now.

Under the circumstances of the case, it ought not to have been doubted that I would give Mr. Lincoln's nomination a cordial and hearty support.

But in declaring my intention to do so, it is due to myself to state some of the facts and reasons, which have a controlling influence over my mind, and which I think ought to be persuasive arguments with some other men, whose political opinions and antecedents are, in some important particulars, like my own.

There was no good ground for supposing that I felt any pique or dissatisfaction because the Chicago Convention failed to nominate me. I had no such feeling. On party grounds, I had no right to expect the nomination. I had no claims upon the Republicans as a party, for I have never been a member of any party, so as to be bound by its dogmas and subject to its discipline, except only the Whig party, which is now broken up and its materials, for the most part, absorbed into other organizations. And thus I am left, alone and powerless indeed, but perfectly free to follow the dictates of my own judgment and to take such part in current politics as my own sense of duty and patriotism may require. Many Republicans, and among them, I think, some of the most moderate and patriotic of that party, honored me with their confidence, and desired to make me their candidate. For this favor I was indebted to the fact that between them and me there was a coincidence of opinion upon certain important questions of government. They and I agreed in believing that the national government has sovereign power over the Territories, and that it would be impolite and unwise to use that power for the propagation of negro slavery, by planting it in free territory. Some of them believed also, that my nomination, while it would tend to soften the tone of the Republican party, without any abandonment of its principles, might tend also to generalize its character and attract the friendship and support of many, especially in the border States, who, like me, had never been members of their party, but concurred with them in opinion about the government of the Territories. Those are the grounds, and I think the only grounds, upon which I was supported at all at Chicago.

As to the platform put forth by the Chicago Convention, I have little to say, because whether good or bad, that will not constitute the ground of my support of Mr. Lincoln. I have no great respect for party platforms in general. They are commonly made in times of high excitement, under a pressure of circumstances, and with the view to conciliate present support, rather than to establish a permanent system of principles and line of policy for the future good government of the country. The conventions which form them are transient in their nature; their power and influence are consumed in the using leaving no continuing obligation upon their respective parties. And hence we need not wonder that platforms so made, are hardly ever acted out in practice. I shall not discuss their relative merits, but content myself with saying that this Republican Platform, though in several particulars it does not conform to my views, is still far better than any published creed, past or present, of the Democrats. And as to the new party, it has not chosen to promulgate any platform at all, except two or three broad generalities which are common to the professions of faith of all parties in the country. No party, indeed, dare ask the confidence of the nation, while openly denying the obligation to support the Union and the Constitution, and to enforce the laws. That is a common duty, binding upon every citizen, and the failure to perform it is a crime.

To me it is plain that the approaching contest must be between the Democratic and Republican parties; and, between them, I prefer the latter.

The Democratic party, by the long possession and abuse of power, has grown wanton and reckless; has corrupted itself and perverted the principles of the Government; has set itself openly against the great home interests of the people, by neglecting to protect their industry, and by refusing to improve and keep in order the highways and depots of commerce; and even now is urging a measure in Congress to abdicate the constitutional power and duty to regulate commerce among the States, and to grant to the States the discretionary power to levy tonnage duties upon all our commerce, under the pretence of improving harbors, rivers and lakes; has changed the status of the negro slave by making him no longer mere property, but a politician—an antagonist power in the State; a power to which all other powers are required to yield, under penalty of a dissolution of the Union; has directed its energies to a gratification of its lusts of foreign domain, as manifested in its persistent efforts to seize upon tropical regions, not because those countries and their incongruous people are necessary, or even desirable, to be incorporated into our nation, but for the mere purpose of making slave States, in order to advance the political power of the party in the Senate and in the choice of the President, so as effectually to transfer the chief powers of the government from the many to the few; has in various instances endangered the equality of the co-ordinate branches of the government, by urgent efforts to enlarge the powers of the Executive at the expense of the legislative department; has attempted to discredit and degrade the Judiciary, by affecting to make it, at first, the arbiter of party quarrels, *to become soon and inevitably the passive registrar of party decrees.*

In most if not all these particulars, I understand the Republican party (judging it by its acts and by the known opinions of many of its leading men) to be the exact opposite of the Democratic party; and that is the ground of my preference of the one party over the other. And that alone would be a sufficient reason, if I had no other good reason, for supporting Mr. Lincoln against any man who may be put forward by the Democratic party as the exponent of its principles and the agent to work out, in practice, its dangerous politics.

The third party, which, by its very formation, has destroyed the organization of the American and Whig parties, has nominated two most excellent men. I know them well, as sound statesmen and true patriots. More than thirty years ago I served with them both in Congress, and from that time to this I have always held them in respect and honor. But what can the third party do towards the election of even such worthy men as these against the two great parties which are now in actual contest for the power to rule the nation? It is made up entirely of portions of the disintegrated elements of the late Whig and American parties—good materials, in the main, I admit, but quite too weak to elect any man or establish any principle. The most it can do is, here and there in particular localities, to make a division in favor of the Democrats. In 1856, the Whig and American parties (not forming a new party but united as allies), with entire unanimity and some zeal, supported Mr. Fillmore for the Presidency, and with what results? We made a miserable failure, carrying no State but gallant little Maryland. And surely, the united Whigs and Americans of that day had a far greater show of strength, and far better prospects of success than any which belong to the Constitutional Union party now. In fact, I see no possibility of success for the third party, except in one contingency: the destruction of the Democratic party. That is a contingency not likely to happen this year, for, badly as I think of many of the acts and policies of that party, its cup is not yet full—the day has not yet come when it must dissolve in its own corruptions; but the day is coming, and is not far off. The party has made itself entirely sectional; it has concentrated its very being into one single idea: *negro slavery has control of all its faculties, and it can see and hear nothing else*—"one stern, tyrannic thought, that makes all other thoughts its slaves!"

But the Democratic party still lives; and while it lives, it and the Republican party are the only real antagonistic powers in the nation, and for the present I must choose between them. I choose the latter, as wiser, purer, younger, and less corrupted by time and self-indulgence.

The candidates nominated at Chicago are both men who, as individuals and politicians, rank with the formost of the country. I have heard no objection to Mr. Hamlin, personally, but only to his geographical position, which is thought by some to be too far North and East to allow his personal good qualities to exercise their proper influence over the nation at large. But the nomination for the Presidency is the great controlling act. Mr. LINCOLN, his character, talents, opinions and history, will be criticised by thousands, while the candidate for the Vice Presidency will be passed over in comparative silence.

Mr. LINCOLN's nomination took the public by surprise, because, until just before the event, it was unexpected. But really it ought not to have excited any surprise, for such unforeseen nominations are common in our political history. Polk and Pierce by the Democrats, and Harrison and Taylor by the Whigs, were all nominated in this extemporaneous manner—all of them were elected. I have known Mr. LINCOLN for more than twenty years, and therefore have a right to speak of him with some confidence. As an individual he has earned a high reputation for truth, courage, candor, morals and amiability, so that, as a man, he is most trustworthy. And in this particular, he is more entitled to our esteem than some other men, his equals who had far better opportunities and aids in early life. His talents and the will to use them to the best advantage, are unquestionable; and the proof is found in the fact that in every position in life, from his humble beginning to his present well-earned elevation, he has more than fulfilled the best hopes of his friends. And now, in the full vigor of his manhood, and in the honest pride of making himself what he is, he is the peer of the first men of the nation, well able to sustain himself and advance his cause against any adversary, and in any field where mind and knowledge are the weapons used.

In politics he has but acted out the principles of his own moral and intellectual character. He has not concealed his thoughts nor hidden his light under a bushel. With the boldness of conscious rectitude, and frankness of down-right honesty, he has not failed to avow his opinions of public affairs upon all fitting occasions.

This I know may subject him to the carping censure of that class of politicians who mistake cunning for wisdom and falsehood for ingenuity; but such men as LINCOLN must act in keeping with their own characters, and hope for success only by advancing the truth prudently and maintaining it bravely. All his old political antecedents are, in my judgement, exactly right, being square up to the old Whig standard. And as to his views about "the pestilent negro question," I am not aware that he has gone one step beyond the doctrine publicly and habitually avowed by the great lights of the Whig party, Clay, Webster, and their fellows, and, indeed, sustained and carried out by the Democrats themselves, in their wiser and better days.

The following, I suppose, are in brief his opinions upon that subject:
1. Slavery is a domestic institution within the States which choose to have it,

and exists within these States beyond the control of Congress. 2. Congress has supreme legislative power over all the Territories, and may, at its discretion, allow or forbid the existence of slavery within them. 3. Congress, in wisdom and sound policy, ought not so to exercise its power, *directly or indirectly,* as to plant and establish slavery in any Territory heretofore free. 4. And that it is unwise and impolitic in the government of the United States to acquire tropical regions for the mere purpose of converting them into slave States.

These, I believe, are Mr. LINCOLN's opinions upon the matter of slavery in the Territories, and I concur in them. They are no new inventions, made to suit the exigencies of the hour, but have come down to us, as the Declaration of Independence and the Constitution have, sanctioned by the venerable authority of the wise and good men who established our institutions. They are comformable to law, principle and wise policy, and their utility is proven in practice by the as yet unbroken current of our political history. They will prevail, not only because they are right in themselves, but also because a great and growing majority of the people believe them to be right, and the sooner they are allowed to prevail in peace and harmony, the better for all concerned, as well those who are against them as those who are for them.

I am aware that small partisans, in their little warfare against opposing leaders, do sometimes assail them by the trick of tearing from their contexts some particular, objectionable phrases, penned, perhaps, in the hurry of composition, or spoken in the heat of oral debate, and holding them up as the leading doctrines of the persons assailed, and drawing from them their own uncharitable inferences. That line of attack betrays a little mind conscious of its weakness, for the falsity of its logic is not more apparent than the injustice of its design. No public man can stand that ordeal, and, however willing men may be to see it applied to their adversaries, all flinch from the torture when applied to themselves. In fact, the man who never said a foolish thing, will hardly be able to prove that he ever said many wise ones.

I consider Mr. LINCOLN *a sound, safe, national man.* He could not be sectional if he tried. His birth, his education, the habits of his life, and his geographical position, compel him to be national. All his feelings and interests are identified with the great valley of the Mississippi, near whose center he has spent his whole life. That Valley is not a section, but, conspicuously, the body of the nation, and, large as it is, it is not capable of being divided into sections, for the great river cannot be divided. It is one and indivisible, and the North and the South are alike necessary to its comfort and prosperity. Its people, too, in all their interests and affections, are as broad and general as the regions they inhabit. They are emigrants—a mixed multitude—coming from every State in the Union, and from most countries in Europe; they are unwilling, therefore, to submit to any one petty local standard. They love the nation as a whole, and they love all its parts, for they are bound to them all, not only by a feeling of common interest and mutual dependence, but also by the recollections of childhood and youth, by blood and friendship, and by all those social and domestic charities which sweeten life, and make this world worth living in. The Valley is beginning to feel its power, and will soon be strong enough to dictate the law of the land. Whenever that state of things shall come to pass, it will be most fortunate for the nation to find the powers of government lodged in the hands of men whose habits of thought, whose position and surrounding circumstances constrain them to use those powers for general and not sectional ends.

I give my opinion freely in favor of Mr. LINCOLN, and hope that, for the good of the whole country, he may be elected. But it is not my intention to take any active part in the canvass. For many years past I have had little to do with public affairs, and have aspired to no political office; and now, in view of the mad excitement which convulses the country, and the general disruption and disorder of parties and the elements which compose them, I am more than ever assured that for me, personally, there is no political future, and I accept the condition with cheerful satisfaction. Still, I cannot discharge myself from the life-long duty to watch the conduct of men in power, and to resist, so far as a mere private man may, the fearful progress of official corruption, which for several years past, has sadly marred and defiled the fair fabric of our government.

If Mr. LINCOLN should be elected, coming in as a new man, at the head of a young party, never before in power, he may render a great service to his country, which no Democrat could render. He can march straight forward in the discharge of his high duties, guided only by his own good judgment and honest purposes, without any necessity to temporize with established abuses, to wink at the delinquencies of old party friends or to unlearn and discard the bad official habits that have grown up under the misgovernment of his Democratic predecessors. In short, he can be an honest and bold reformer on easier and cheaper terms than any Democratic President can be, for, in proceeding in the good work of cleaning and purifying the administrative departments, he will have no occasion to expose the vices, assail the interests, or thwart the ambition of his political friends.

Begging your pardon for the length of this letter, I remain, with the greatest respect,

Your friend and obedient servant,
EDWARD BATES.

Chapter II
The Three Platforms

NATIONAL REPUBLICAN PLATFORM, ADOPTED BY THE CHICAGO
CONVENTION, MAY 17, 1860

Resolved, That we, the delegated representatives of the Republican electors of the United States, in Convention assembled, in discharge of the duty we owe to our constituents and our country, unite in the following declarations:

The Republican Party

1. That the history of the nation during the last four years, has fully established the propriety and necessity of the organization and perpetuation of the Republican party, and that the causes which called it into existence are permanent in their nature, and now, more than ever before, demand its peaceful and constitutional triumph.

Its Fundamental Principles

2. That the maintenance of the principles promulgated in the Declaration of Independence and embodied in the Federal Constitution, "That all men are created equal; that they are endowed by their Creator with certain inalienable rights; that among these are life, liberty, and the pursuit of happiness; that to secure these rights, governments are instituted among men, deriving their just power from the consent of the governed"—is essential to the preservation of our Republican institutions; and that the Federal Constitution, the Rights of the States, and the Union of the States, must and shall be preserved.

True to the Union

3. That to the Union of the States, this nation owes its unprecedented increase of population; its surprising development of material resources; its rapid augmentation of wealth; its happiness at home and its honor abroad: and we hold in abhorrence all schemes for Disunion, come from whatever source they may. And we congratulate the country that no Republican member of Congress has uttered or countenanced the threats of Disunion so often made by Democratic members, without rebuke and with applause from their political associates; and we denounce those threats of Disunion, in case of a popular overthrow of their ascendancy, as denying the vital principles of a free government, and as an avowal of contemplated treason, which it is the imperative duty of an indignant people sternly to rebuke and forever silence.

State Sovereignty

4. That the maintenance, inviolate, of the Rights of the States, and especially the right of each State to order and control its own domestic institutions according to its own judgment exclusively, is essential to that balance of power on which the perfection and endurance of our political fabric depends; and we denounce the lawless invasion by armed force, of the soil of any State or Territory, no matter under what pretext, as among the gravest of crimes.

Sectionalism of the Democracy

5. That the present Democratic Administration has far exceeded our worst apprehensions, in its measureless subserviency to the exactions of a sectional interest, as especially evinced in its desperate exertions to force the infamous Lecompton Constitution upon the protesting people of Kansas; in construing the personal relation between master and servant to involve an unqualified property in persons; in its attempted enforcement everywhere, on land and sea, through the intervention of Congress and of the Federal Courts, of the extreme pretensions of a purely local interest; and in its general and unvarying abuse of power entrusted to it by a confiding people.

Its Extravagance and Corruption

6. That the people justly view with alarm the reckless extravagance which pervades every department of the Federal Government; that a return to rigid economy and accountability is indispensible to arrest the systematic plunder of the public treasury by favored partisans; while the recent startling developments of frauds and corruptions at the Federal Metropolis, show that an entire change of administration is imperatively demanded.

A Dangerous Political Heresy

7. That the new dogma that the Constitution, of its own force, carries Slavery into any of all of the Territories of the United States, is a dangerous political heresy, at variance with the explicit provisions of that instrument itself, with cotemporaneous exposition, and with legislative and judicial precedent; is revolutionary in its tendency, and subversive of the peace and harmony of the country.

Freedom, the Normal Condition of Territories

8. That the normal condition of all the territory of the United States is that of Freedom: That as our Republican fathers, when they had abolished slavery in all our national territory, ordained that "no person should be deprived of life,

liberty or property, without due process of law," it becomes our duty, by legislation, whenever such legislation is necessary, to maintain this provision of the Constitution against all attempts to violate it; and we deny the authority of Congress, of a territorial legislature, or of any individuals, to give legal existance to slavery in any territory in the United States.

The African Slave Trade

9. That we brand the recent re-opening of the African Slave Trade, under the cover of our national flag, aided by perversions of judicial power, as a crime against humanity, and a burning shame to our country and age; and we call upon Congress to take prompt and efficient measures for the total and final suppression of that execrable traffic.

Democratic Popular Sovereignty

10. That in the recent vetoes, by their Federal Governors, of the acts of the legislatures of Kansas and Nebraska, prohibiting Slavery in those Territories, we find a practical illustration of the boasted Democratic principle of Non-Intervention and Popular Sovereignty embodied in the Kansas-Nebraska Bill, and a demonstration of the deception and fraud involved therein.

Admission of Kansas

11. That Kansas should, of right, be immediately admitted as a State under the Constitution recently formed and adopted by her people, and accepted by the House of Representatives.

Encouragement of American Industry

12. That, while providing revenue for the support of the general government by duties upon imports, sound policy requires such an adjustment of these imports as to encourage the development of the industrial interests of the whole country; and we commend that policy of national exchanges, which secures to the working men liberal wages; to agriculture, remunerating prices; to mechanics and manufacturers, an adequate reward for their skill, labor and enterprise; and to the nation, commercial prosperity and independence.

Free Homesteads

13. That we protest against any sale or alienation to others of the Public Lands held by actual settlers, and against any view of the Free Homestead policy which regards the settlers as paupers or suppliants for public bounty; and we demand the passage by Congress of the complete and satisfactory Homestead Measure which has already passed the House.

Rights of Citizenship

14. That the Republican party is opposed to any change in our Naturalization Laws or any State Legislation by which the rights of citizenship hitherto accorded to emigrants from foreign lands shall be abridged or impaired; and in favor of giving a full and efficient protection to the rights of all classes of citizens, whether native or naturalized, both at home and abroad.

River and Harbor Improvements

15. The appropriations by Congress for River and Harbor improvements of a National character, required for the accommodation and security of an existing commerce, are authorized by the Constitution, and justified by the obligation of Government to protect the lives and property of its citizens.

A Pacific Railroad

16. That a Railroad to the Pacific Ocean is imperatively demanded by the interests of the whole country; that the Federal Government ought to render immediate and efficient aid in its construction; and that, as preliminary thereto, a daily Overland Mail should be promptly established.

Co-operation Invited

17. Finally, having thus set forth our distinctive principles and views, we invite the co-operation of all citizens, however differing on other questions, who substantially agree with us in their affirmance and support.

PLATFORM OF THE DOUGLAS FACTION OF THE DEMOCRACY, ADOPTED AT BALTIMORE, JUNE 23, 1860

Resolved, That we, the Democracy of the Union, in Convention assembled, hereby declare our affirmation of the resolutions unanimously adopted and declared as a platform of principles by the Democratic Convention at Cincinnati, in the year 1856, believing that Democratic principles are unchangable in their nature when applied to the same subject matter.

Resolved, That it is the duty of the United States to afford ample and complete protection to all its citizens, at home or abroad, and whether native or foreign born.

Resolved, That one of the necessities of the age, in a military, commercial and postal point of view, is speedy communication between the Atlantic and Pacific States, and the Democratic party pledge such constitutional enactment as will insure the construction of a railroad to the Pacific coast at the earliest practicable period.

Resolved, That the Democratic party are in favor of the acquisition of the Island of Cuba, on such terms as shall be honorable to ourselves and just to Spain.

Resolved, That the enactments of State Legislatures to defeat the faithful execution of the Fugitive Slave law are hostile in character, subversive of the Constitution and revolutionary in their effect.

Resolved, That it is in accordance with the Cincinnati Platform, that during the existence of Territorial Governments the measure of restriction, whatever it may be, imposed by the Federal Constitution on the power of the Territorial Legislature over the subject of the domestic relations, *as the same has been or shall hereafter be decided by the Supreme Court of the United States,* should be respected by all good citizens, and enforced with promptness and fidelity *by every branch of the General Government.*

PLATFORM OF THE BRECKINRIDGE FACTION OF THE DEMOCRACY, ADOPTED AT BALTIMORE, JUNE 23, 1860

Resolved, That the platform adopted by the Democratic party at Cincinnati be affirmed, with the following explanatory resolutions:

1. That the government of the Territory organized by an act of Congress is provisional and temporary, and during its existence all citizens of the United States have an equal right to settle with their property in the Territory, without their rights, either of person or property, being destroyed or injured by Congressional or Territorial legislation.

2. That it is the duty of the Federal Government, in all its departments, to protect the rights of persons and property in the Territories, and wherever else its constitutional authority extends.

3. That when the settlers in a Territory having an adequate population to form a State constitution, the right of sovereignty commences, and being consummated by their admission into the Union, they stand on an equality with the people of other States, and a State thus organized ought to be admitted into the Federal Union, whether its constitution prohibits or recognises the institution of slavery.

Resolved, That the Democratic party are in favor of the acquisition of the Island of Cuba, on such terms as shall be honorable to ourselves and just to Spain, at the earliest practicable moment.

Resolved, That the enactments of State Legislatures to defeat the faithful execution of the Fugitive Slave law are hostile in character, subversive of the Constitution, and revolutionary in their effect.

Resolved, That the Democracy of the United States recognize it as the imperative duty of this government to protect the naturalized citizen in all his rights, whether at home or in foreign lands, to the same extent as its native born citizens.

Whereas, One of the greatest necessities of the age, in a political, commercial, postal and military point of view, is a speedy communication between the Pacific and Atlantic coasts, therefore, be it

Resolved, That the National Democratic party do hereby pledge themselves to use every means in their power to secure the passage of some bill, to the extent of their constitutional authority, by Congress, for the construction of a Pacific Railroad from the Mississippi River to the Pacific Ocean, at the earliest practicable moment.

Chapter III
The Wickliffe Resolution

The concluding resolution of the Douglas Platform should be carefully examined by every voter in the North. It was offered just after Mr. Douglas was declared nominated, by Mr. Wickliffe, of Louisiana, who stated in open Convention, that its adoption "would give Douglas 40,000 votes in Louisiana." Whereupon, on motion of Mr. Payne, of Ohio, it was *adopted unanimously* in the following words:

> *Resolved,* That it is in accordance with the Cincinnati platform, that during the existence of Territorial Governments, the measure of restriction, whatever it may be, imposed by the Federal Constitution on the power of the Territorial Legislature over the subject of the domestic relations, *as the same has been or shall hereafter be decided by the Supreme Court of the United States,* should be respected by all good citizens, and enforced with promptness and fidelity *by every branch of the General Government.*

The question naturally and properly arises, *What does this resolution mean? Why was it adopted?* If it means nothing, why is it there? If it means something, what is that something? It was avowedly introduced to give Douglas 40,000 votes in Louisiana! At Freeport Mr. Douglas said: "It matters not what way the Supreme Court may hereafter decide as to the abstract question whether slavery may or may not go into a Territory under the Constitution, the people have the lawful means to introduce or to exclude it as they please." But now his platform says that as the aforesaid question has been or may hereafter be decided by the Supreme Court, it should be "enforced with promptness and fidelity *by every branch of the general government!*" Is not Congress one branch of the general government; and if the Supreme Court has already, or shall hereafter, decide that Territorial Legislatures cannot exclude slavery, or that slaves, being property under the Constitution, may be held as such in the Territories, is not the Douglas party, as well as the Breckinridge party, committed *to a Congressional slave code?* It happens that the whole quarrel in the Democratic ranks, so far as any principle is involved in it, has grown out of the fact that the Supreme Court *have already decided the question.* In the Dred Scott case, the Court, after deciding that Congress had no power to prohibit slavery in a Territory, proceeded as follows:

The powers over person and property of which we speak are not only not granted to Congress, but are in express terms denied, and they are forbidden to exercise them. And this prohibition is not confined to the States, but the words are general, and extend to the whole territory over which the Constitution gives it power to legislate, including those portions of it remaining under Territorial Government, as well as that covered by States. It is a total absence of power everywhere within the dominion of the United States, and places the citizens of a Territory, so far as these rights are concerned, on the same footing with citizens of the States, and guards them as firmly and plainly against any inroads which the General Government might attempt, under the plea of implied or incidental powers. And if Congress itself cannot do this—if it is beyond the powers conferred on the Federal Government—*it will be admitted, we presume, that it could not authorize a Territorial Government to exercise them. It could confer no power on any local government established by its authority, to violate the provisions of the Constitution.*

It seems, however, to be supposed that there is a difference between property in a slave and other property, and that different rules may be applied to it in expounding the Constitution of the United States. And the laws and usages of nations, and the writings of eminent jurists upon the relation of master and slave, and their mutual rights and duties, and the powers which governments may exercise over it, have been dwelt upon in the argument.

But in considering the question before us, it must be borne in mind that there is no law of nations standing between the people of the United States and their government, and interfering with their relation to each other. The powers of the government, and the rights of the citizen under it, are positive and practical regulations plainly written down. The people of the United States have delegated to it certain enumerated powers, and forbidden it to exercise others. It has no power over the person or property of a citizen but what the citizens of the United States have granted. And no laws or usages of other nations, or reasoning of statesmen or jurists upon the relation of master and slave, can enlarge the powers of the government, or take from the citizens the rights they have reserved. And if the Constitution recognizes the right of property of the master in a slave, and makes no distinction between that description of property and other property owned by a citizen, *no tribunal, acting under the authority of the United States, whether it be Legislative, executive or judicial, has a right to draw such a distinction, or deny to it the benefit of the provisions and guarantees which have been provided for the protection of private property against the encroachments of the government.*

Now, as we have already said in an earlier part of this opinion, upon a different point, *the right of property in a slave is distinctly and expressly affirmed in the Constitution.* The right to traffic in it, like an ordinary article of merchandise and property, was guaranteed to the citizens of the United States in every State that might desire it, for twenty years. And the Government in express terms is pledged to protect it in all future time, if the slave escapes from his owner. This is done in plain words, too plain to be misunderstood. And no word can be found in the Constitution which gives Congress a greater power over slave property, or which entitles property of that kind to less protection than property of any other description. *The only power conferred is the power, coupled with the duty, of guarding and protecting the owner in his rights.*

Now here is a plain logical proposition, which no man can fail to understand: 1. The Supreme Court have decided that neither Congress nor a Territorial Legislature can prohibit slavery in a Territory; 2. The Douglas platform says that the opinion of the Court on this point "as it has been or shall hereafter be decided," must be enforced "by every branch of the general government;" 3. Therefore Congress, as a branch of the general government, should enforce the doctrine that a Territorial Legislature cannot exclude slavery, by promptly repealing every law which may be enacted prohibiting slavery. If anyone is so purblind as not to see, that the Supreme Court have already decided the question adversely to "squatter sovereignty," let him read the above quotation from the Dred Scott decision, and ask himself what the Court will *hereafter* decide when the question shall come distinctly before them. The Wickliffe resolution is worded to accommodate both those who believe that the question has been already decided and those who believe it is "hereafter" to be decided. If it be admitted that the question is not yet decided, *then will it be decided* when it comes up again? Let the fair minded reader scan the decision *which has been made,* and frame the answer for himself. It is submitted to all candid persons that the Wickliffe resolution was adopted for the purpose of cheating somebody. If it is to be carried out in good faith to Mr. Wickliffe and his friends in Louisiana, its obvious purpose is to cheat the Democracy of Illinois. If it is to be nullified after the campaign is over, of course Wickliffe & Co., are to be cheated in like manner. Fraud is stamped upon every letter of it. But Wickliffe & Co., have taken good care that *they* shall not be cheated. They have got their resolution *into the platform,* and they have got the Dred Scott decision behind it. They know, if there is a controversy in the party as to what the Court did actually decide, the Court will "hereafter" decide in their favor. Who then is to be cheated? Douglas Democrat of the North, it is *you!* Some of your leaders are honest enough to admit that the Supreme Court have really decided against you. John W. Forney, of Pennsylvania, is one of these. In an "address to the People of Pennsylvania," published July 11, 1859, signed "John W. Forney, Chairman, Democratic State Rights Committee," he says:

> It will be observed that when Mr. Buchanan wrote, and when Mr. Cobb spoke, and when the entire Democratic party stood squarely united upon the honest construction of the Kansas-Nebraska bill, the odious theory advanced by this Pennsylvania National Democratic committee was not a novelty, nor was the subsequent *obiter dictum, as it is, of the Supreme Court, an unanticipated event.* But it was notorious that every conservative, Union-loving statesman in Congress, from Henry Clay, in the South, to Lewis Cass, in the North, had denounced the idea of an Executive or Congressional protection for the Territories, on the subject of slavery, as unworthy of the consideration of a free country, and that more than one eminent Southern leader had declared *that the political opinion of no court, high or low, could be wielded against the sacred and inalienable franchises of the people,* when they came to exercise their highest acts of sovereignty in regard to this very question of slavery.

Is it not a plain and palpable inference from this language, that Col. Forney admits the Southern construction,—the Wickliffe construction—of the Dred Scott decision to be correct, and that he proposes to repudiate it as the only proper way to save "popular sovereignty"? He calls it an *obiter dictum*—a "decision out of the way," that is, a declaration of law apart from the case before the Court, and therefore having no binding force. But Mr. Douglas does not consider it an *obiter dictum*. He says:

> The Court did not attempt to avoid responsibility by disposing of the case upon technical points without touching the merits, nor did they go out of their way to decide questions not properly before them and directly presented by the record. *Like honest and conscientious judges, as they are,* they met and decided each point as it arose, and faithfully performed their whole duty and nothing

but their duty to the country *by determining all the questions in the case,* and nothing but what was essential to the decision of the case upon its merits.— [Douglas' Springfield Grand Jury Speech, June 12th, 1857,—as published in the *State Register.*]

Hence he (Douglas), is bound to construe the decision *as law,* and he is bound by the Platform of his party to frame the territorial policy of the government "as the same has been, *or shall hereafter be,* decided by the Supreme Court." Are there not *two* slave-code parties in the field?

CHAPTER IV
HERSCHEL V. JOHNSON'S RECORD

It was fitting that the Douglas Democracy, after putting a slave code plank in their platform, should nominate *the original slave code man of the South,* as their candidate for Vice-President. That man is Herschel V. Johnson, of Georgia. The nomination of Fitzpatrick, who voted for the Lecompton bill, in all its stages, and who actually supported Jeff. Davis' slave code resolutions in the Senate, was bad enough; but the nomination of Johnson was, if possible, still worse. For the purpose of showing the Douglas Democracy of the Northwest the sentiments of *their* candidate for the Vice-Presidency, we quote from his speech delivered in the United States Senate, on the 7th of July, 1848, commencing on page 887 of the Appendix to the *Congressional Globe* for that year:

Protection of Slavery in the Territories.

It remains now to consider the question involved in the amendment proposed by the Senator from Mississippi. [Mr. Davis.] That question is, whether it is *the duty of Congress to guarantee* to the slaveholder who shall remove his slaves into the territory of the United States *the undisputed enjoyment of his property in them, so long as it continues to be a Territory.* Or, *in other words,* whether the inhabitants of a Territory, *during their territorial condition,* have the right to prohibit slavery therein.

No Power Whatever can Exclude Slavery from the Territories.

For the purpose of this question, it matters not where the power of legislating for the Territory resides—whether exclusively in Congress, or jointly in Congress and the inhabitants, **or** exclusively in the inhabitants of the Territory; the power is precisely the same—no greater in the hands of one than the other. *In no event, can the slaveholder of the South be excluded from settling in such Territory* WITH HIS PROPERTY OF EVERY DESCRIPTION.

Squatter Sovereignty Squelched.

But suppose that Congress have the right to establish a Territorial Government only, and that then, all further governmental control ceases: can the Territorial Legislature *pass an act prohibiting slavery? Surely not.* For the moment you admit the right to organize a Territorial Government to exist in Congress, you admit necessarily the subordination of the people of the Territory—their dependence on this Government for an organic law, to give them political existence. Hence, all the legislation must be in conformity with the organic law, they can pass no act in violation of it—none but such as it permits. Since, therefore, Congress has no power, as I have shown, to prohibit Slavery, *they cannot delegate such a power to the inhabitants of the Territory;* they cannot authorize the Territorial Legislature to do that which they have no power to do. The stream cannot rise higher than its source.

Absolute Congressional Sovereignty vs. Non-Intervention.

It is idle, however, to discuss this question in this form. For if Congress posesses the power to organize temporary governments, it must then possess the power to legislate for the Territories. If they may perform the greater, they may the less; the major includes the minor proposition. Hence, Congress has, in all cases since the foundation of our government, reserved a veto upon the legislation of the Territorial Governments: *it is absolutely necessary,* in order to restrain them from violations of the Constitution, and infringements of the rights of the States, as joint owners of the public lands. If, therefore, an act of the Territorial Government, prohibiting Slavery, should be sent up to Congress for approval, *they would be bound to withhold it, upon the ground of its being an act which Congress themselves could not pass.*

The People cannot Exclude Slavery from a Territory.

But suppose the right of legislation for the Territory be in its inhabitants, can they prohibit Slavery? *Surely not;* and for reasons similar to those which show that Congress cannot.

He demands a Slave Code.

It is urged that slavery does not exist in New Mexico and California; that they are free Territories; and although we deny to Congress any jurisdiction over the subject, *yet we ask Congress by this amendment to establish slavery therein.* Upon the execution of the treaty, all political regulations of the United States were extended over the Territories, *and the institution of slavery being political in its character, it now exists, in legal intendment, as absolutely in New Mexico and California as it does in Virginia and Georgia.*

Popular Sovereignty is Ridiculous and Absurd.

If you assert the broad proposition that the inhabitants of the Territory, by *virtue of the right of self-government,* have the right to exclude slavery therein the question arises, how many inhabitants shall there be to enable them to do this? Shall it be five hundred, or ten or twenty thousand? Shall a few thousand people in Oregon—a vast territory out of which five or six States may be carved—determine that question for all future generations, and fix their destiny for all time to come? Shall a few thousand half civilized Mexicans, inhabiting the Territories of California and New Mexico decide what institutions shall exist there? *The idea is ridiculous and absurd.*

The institution of Slavery is *guaranteed* by the Constitution of the United States, and it has *the same protection* thrown around it, which guards our citizens against the granting of titles of nobility, or the establishment of religion; *therefore Congress would be as much bound* to veto an act of Territorial legislation prohibiting it, as an act violating these rights of every citizen of the Republic.

A Disunion Tirade.

But suppose Mr. President, you have the right to prohibit Slavery in the Territories of the United States, what high political consideration requires you to exercise it? All must see that it cannot be affected without producing *a popular convulsion which will probably dissolve the Union.*

These were Mr. Johnson's sentiments in 1848. Let us see what they are in 1860. To show that he has not yet changed his mind on the matter in issue between the two wings of the pro-slavery party, we reprint from the *Southerner and Advertiser,* a Douglas paper, published at Rome, Ga., (an authority, therefore, that cannot be disputed,) the proceedings of the Democratic State Convention, held at Milledgeville, June 4th, called to take action in regard to the secession of most of the Georgia delegates at Charleston. It seems that a Business Committee of twenty-four was appointed, of which Herschel V. Johnson was one. This Committee disagreed as to the propriety of appointing new delegates to Baltimore, the friends of the seceders opposing, and a few who preferred to see Douglas elected to a dissolution of the party, favored that step; and the consequence was, that two reports were presented—a majority one by twenty members of the Committee, and a minority one by *four* members, which latter division included Herschel V. Johnson, who, as Chairman, introduced the minority report which was as follows:

> *Resolved,* That we re-affirm the Cincinnati platform, with the following additional propositions:
>
> 1st. That the citizens of the United States have an equal right to settle with *their property of any kind,* in the organized Territories of the United States, and that under the decision of the Supreme Court of the United States in the case of Dred Scott, which we recognize as the correct exposition of the Constitution in this particular, slave property stands on the same footing as all other descriptions of property, and that neither the General Government, NOR ANY TERRITORIAL GOVERNMENT, can destroy or impair the right to slave property; that property of all kinds, slaves as well as any other species of property, in the Territories, stand upon the same equal and broad Constitutional basis, and subject to like principles of recognition and PROTECTION in the LEGISLATIVE, judicial and executive departments of the Government.
>
> 2d. That we will support any man who may be nominated by the Baltimore Convention, for the Presidency, who holds the principles set forth in the foregoing proposition, and who will give them his endorsement, and we will not hold ourselves bound to support any man, who may be the nominee, who entertains principles inconsistent with those set forth in the above propositions, or who denies that slave property in the Territories does stand on an equal footing and on the same Constitutional basis of other descriptions of property.
>
> In view of the fact that a large majority of the delegates from Georgia felt it to be their duty to withdraw from the late Democratic Convention, thereby depriving this State of her vote therein, according to the decision of said Convention.
>
> *Resolved,* That this Convention will appoint twenty delegates—four from the State at large, and two from each Congressional District— to represent the Democratic party of Georgia, in the adjourned Convention at Baltimore, on the 18th inst., and that the delegates be and are hereby instructed to present the foregoing propositions, and ask their adoption by the National Democratic Convention.
>
>
>
> HERSCHEL V. JOHNSON,
> THOS. P. SAFFORD,
> H. K. McCAY,
> H. COLVARD.
>
>

But this is not all, nor is it the worst. Mr. Johnson believes that capital should own its labor, irrespective of color or condition. In a public speech delivered in Philadelphia on the 15th of September, 1856, he said:

We believe that capital should own labor; is there any doubt that there must be a laboring class everywhere? In all countries and under every form of social organization there must be a laboring class—a class of men who get their living by the sweat of their brow; and then there must be another class that controls and directs the capital of the country.

Chapter V
Opinions of Another Douglas Man in Georgia

This is perhaps as suitable a place as we can find to reprint the sentiments of another Douglas man—Mr. Gaulden, a delegate from Georgia in the Baltimore Convention. Mr. Gaulden was an enthusiastic advocate of "non-intervention" as will be seen from the following remarks which be made in the Convention on the

Re-opening of the Slave Trade

I say I go for non-intervention in the broadest sense of the term. I say that this whole thing should be taken out of the hands of the General Government. I say it is all wrong to be spending two or three millions of dollars annually from our pockets, and sacrificing thousands of lives upon the coast of Africa, in that terrible clime, to prevent our going there to get a few negroes. *If it is right for us to go to Virginia and buy a negro and pay $2,000 for him, it is equally right for us to go to Africa, where we can get them for $50.* [Applause and laughter.] Here is the condition we are placed in, and you may as well come to your senses and face the music.

There are 2,000 of our negroes now down at Key West, begging and pleading not to be sent back. If they should be sent back, what would be the result? One-half of them would die before they got there, and the other half would be turned upon the coast of Africa—upon the coast of Liberia, among strangers, to be eaten up by the cannibals, or caught and sold again, or die of starvation; and this you call humanity! I say it is piracy; I say that our Government is acting against right and reason in this matter; and if the Southern men had the spunk and spirit to come right up and face the North, I believe the Northern Democracy at least, would come to the true doctrine of popular sovereignty and non-intervention. [Applause and laughter.]

Think of it: two thousand of these poor barbarians from Africa, caught within the last four weeks, and kept upon the miserable Island of Key West, dying there from disease and starvation; and what do not die are to be sent back by our Government at an expense of one or two millions, though they are begging not to be sent back, and landed upon the coast of Africa. It is cruel, inhuman, wrong, and I appeal to the good sense of the American nation against it. Look at John Bull; he has bound us to catch all we can, and we send them back at an expense of twenty-five dollars per head. We send them back, but what does John Bull do when he gets them? He apprentices them out again, and makes slaves of them. That is the hypocritical treaty that you are bound by, and yet I hear no Southern voice, or Northern voice, raised against this aggression upon the law of nature and of nature's God, but I intend to raise my voice against it, humble as it is.

Now, this may be a secondary question before us tonight. The great point is harmony and union in the Democratic party. Let us whip the Black Republicans, let us win the fight, and *when we have settled these things,* let us act together and all will be right.

Chapter VI
What "Popular Sovereignty" Has Done

It will be admitted that Mr. Douglas is a good judge of what his dogma of "Popular Sovereignty" has accomplished during the past six years. Therefore, we let him tell the result in his own words, quoting from his speech in the Senate on the 16th of May, 1860, as printed in the *Congressional Globe:*

But, we are told that the necessary result of this doctrine of non-intervention, which gentlemen, by way of throwing ridicule upon, call squatter sovereignty, is to deprive the South of all participation in what they call the common Territories of the United States. That was the ground on which the Senator from Mississippi (Mr. Davis) predicated his opposition to the compromise measures of 1850. He regarded a refusal to repeal the Mexican law as equivalent to the Wilmot proviso; a refusal to recognize by an act of Congress the right to carry a slave there as equivalent to the Wilmot proviso; a refusal to deny to a Territorial Legislature the right to exclude slavery as equivalent to an exclusion. He believed at that time that this doctrine did amount to a denial of southern rights, and he told the people of Mississippi so; but they doubted it. Now, let us see how far his predictions and suppositions have been verified. I infer that he told the people so, for as he makes it a charge in his bill of indictment against me, that I am hostile to Southern rights, because I gave those votes.

Now, what has been the result? My views were incorporated into the compromise measures of 1850, and his were rejected. Has the South been excluded from all the territory acquired from Mexico? What says the bill from the House of Representatives now on your table, repealing the slave code in New Mexico, established by the people themselves? *It is part of the history of the country that under this doctrine of non-intervention, this doctrine that you delight to call squat-*

ter sovereignty, the people of New Mexico have introduced and protected slavery in the whole of that Territory. Under this doctrine they have converted a tract of free territory into slave territory more than five times the size of the State of New York. Under this doctrine slavery has been extended from the Rio Grande to the Gulf of California, and from the line of the Republic of Mexico, not only up to 36 deg. 30 min., but up to 38 deg.—GIVING YOU A DEGREE AND A HALF MORE SLAVE TERRITORY THAN YOU EVER CLAIMED. In 1848 and 1849 and 1850, you only asked to have the line of 36 deg. 30 min. The Nashville Convention fixed that as its ultimatum. I offered it in the Senate in August, 1848, and it was adopted here, but rejected in the House of Representatives. You asked only up to 36 deg. 30 min., *and non-intervention has given you slave territory up to 38 deg.*—A DE-GREE AND A HALF MORE THAN YOU ASKED; and yet you say that this is a sacrifice of Southern rights?

These are the fruits of this principle which the Senator from Mississippi regards as hostile to the rights of the South. Where did you ever get any other fruits that were more palatable to your taste or refreshing to your strength? What other inch of free territory has been converted into slave territory on the American continent, since the Revolution, except in New Mexico and Arizona, under the principle of non-intervention affirmed at Charleston. If it be true that this principle of non-intervention has conferred upon you all that immense territory; has protected slavery in that comparatively northern and cold region where you did not expect it to go, cannot you trust the same principle further South when you come to acquire additional territory from Mexico, which was surrounded on nearly every side by free territory? will not the same principle protect you in the northern States of Mexico when they are acquired, since they are now surrounded by slave territory; are several hundred miles further South; have many degrees of greater heat; and have a climate and soil adapted to southern products? Are you not satisfied with these practical results?

CHAPTER VII
SLAVERY IN NEW MEXICO—SERFDOM OF WHITE LABORERS

It is appropriate to inquire in this connection *what kind of slavery* Popular Sovereignty has been instrumental in introducing into New Mexico; "a Territory," as Mr. Douglas says, "more than five times the size of the state of New York." The reader will be surprised to learn that it includes the serfdom of white men as well as the slavery of the blacks, and that it allows any man who employs other men in the capacity of laborers to FLOG, BEAT, CUFF, AND OTHERWISE PUNISH THEM, to his heart's content, irrespective of color or sex, and denies to the party so flogged and beaten *any redress at law!* We copy the following sections from "an act amendatory of the law relative to contracts between masters and servants," passed by the Territorial Legislature of New Mexico, January 26, 1859:

> SEC. 1. When any servant shall run away from the service of his master, he shall be considered as a fugitive from justice, and in such case it shall be the duty of all officers of the Territory, judicial or ministerial, on being informed that such persons are within the limits of their jurisdiction, to ascertain whether such persons are runaway servants or not, and if they ascertain that they are, said officers shall immediately arrest them and put them to work at public labor, or hire them out to any person so that they may be employed, with security, until their master shall be informed thereof, in order that they may demand them, and to whom they shall immediately be delivered.
>
> SEC. 2. Every person of this Territory, either a contracted servant according to the law of contracts, or engaged on trips or as shepherds, shall be compelled to serve for the time stipulated for in the contract; and any servant so contracted who shall fail to serve by abandoning his master or property placed under his care, shall be held responsible for all costs and damages which through his neglect may result to the owner.
>
> SEC. 4. *No Court of this Territory shall have jurisdiction nor shall take cognisance of any cause for the correction that masters may give their servants* for neglect of their duties as servants, for they are considered as domestic servants to their masters, *and they should correct their neglect and faults;* for as soldiers are punished by their chiefs, without the intervention of the civil authority, by reason of the salary they enjoy, *an equal right should be granted those persons who pay their money to be served in the protection of their property: Provided,* That such correction shall not be inflicted in a cruel manner with clubs or stripes.

The concluding proviso is similar to that which prevails in all the slave codes of the Southern States—leaving it discretionary with the "master" as to *what constitutes* "correction inflicted in a cruel manner." The slave code of New Mexico, by the terms of Sections 12, 13, 14, and 15, allows *any person* to arrest any one whom he calls an absconding slave, *by force,* and without any legal process from any court or magistrate, and to deliver such person so arrested to the sheriff of the county in which the arrest may be made, which sheriff shall imprison such person for six months, (without a commitment,) and advertise for a master, and if no master come, shall imprison six months longer, and advertise for sale; and at the end of twelve months' imprisonment, the sheriff shall sell such person, at the door of the jail or courthouse, to the highest bidder, for cash, and his *bill of sale* "shall vest in the purchaser a good and indefensible title against all persons whatever."

On the 16th of February, 1860, the Hon. John A. Bingham, of Ohio, from the House Community on Territories, reported a bill declaring these infamous acts null and void. A vote was thereupon taken in the House of Representatives, on Mr. Bingham's bill, resulting as follows:

YEAS		NAY	
Republicans, ...	97	Democrats and South Americans . .	91
Democrats.	00	Republicans.	00
South Americans	00		

Among the nays were Messrs. John A. Logan, Isaac N. Morris and James C. Robinson, of Illinois, (Messrs. Fouke and McClernaud not voting,) Chas. H. Larrabee, of Wisconsin, Geo. B. Cooper, of Michigan, and all the other Democratic members from the Northwest, who thus sanctioned, in express terms, the serfdom or peonage of persons of their own color and kindred, in New Mexico. It was this bill of Mr. Bingham's which Mr. Douglas refers to in the extract from his speech of the 16th of May, quoted above.

Chapter VIII
Slavery in Nebraska—Ineffectual Efforts to Abolish It

It is not deemed necessary to revert to the workings of Popular Sovereignty in Kansas—the violence, rapine and bloodshed which followed the repeal of the Missouri Compromise. These things are too fresh in the recollections of the people. But it is well to call to mind the unavailing efforts of the Republicans in Nebraska, to abolish slavery in that Territory, and the successful exertions of the Democracy to thwart that beneficent purpose. Early in the session of the Nebraska Legislature, last winter, Mr. Dundy, a Republican member of the Council, and Mr. Collier, a Republican member of the House of Representatives, introduced bills in their respective bodies, for the abolition and prohibition of slavery in the Territory. The Omaha *Nebraskian* and the Nebraska City *News,* the Democratic organs of the Territory, immediately denounced the measure as a wanton agitation of the slavery question, designed to create "political capital." The Chicago *Times* cordially seconded its confederates in Nebraska by reprobating the proposed law, and pronouncing it "a most unnecessary piece of buncombe." The Republican journals and members of the Legislature replied that slavery did exist in the Territory, and urged the Democrats to assist in passing the law as the easiest way to *destroy* all the political capital which might be made out of it by the Republican side. The bills were referred to a select committee of whom a majority were Democrats.

First, an investigation was had into the fact whether slavery did or did not exist in the Territory. The Democratic majority reported that there were "four and a half persons" held in slavery in the Territory, and that it was unwise, unnecessary and inexpedient to pass any law prohibiting the institution. The Republican minority reported that the fact was notorious and indisputable that slaves were held at a number of places in the Territory, and that parties of slave hunters had frequently sallied across the river into Iowa, in pursuit of fugitives from service and labor held in Nebraska. They also recommended the passage of the law abolishing and prohibiting the institution. A vote was taken on the 20th of December, 1859, and the bill was defeated *by the Democrats.* Every Republican in the two houses voted for it, and all but two or three Democrats against it. Thus was "Popular Sovereignty" vindicated!

But this was not all. The bill was resuscitated on a motion to re-consider, and was forced to a second vote on the 3d of January, 1860. It was proposed by both parties to call a convention for the formation of a State Constitution, and some of the Democrats became frightened by the evidences that they would be utterly defeated if they allowed the slavery record to stand against them. Hence, when brought to the scratch a second time the bill passed both houses on the 3d of January, aforesaid, by the following vote:

In the House of Representatives.

Ayes—*Bain, Barker, Bowen, Burbank,* Campbell, *Collier,* Crowe, *Davis,* Fanscum, Lake, *Latta, Marquette, Maxwell,* Myers, *Rogers,* Reck, *Stephenson,* Stewart, *Taffe*—19.

Nays—Adams, Arnott, Barnard, Belden, Brodhead, Goshen, Hinsdale, Johnson, Kelling, Kennedy, Malcolm, Noel, Nuckolls of Otoe, Nuckolls of Rich, Reynolds, Shields, Tufft—17.

Absent—Bates, McCasland.

In the Council.

Ayes—Messrs. Boykin, *Cheever,* Doane, *Dundy,* Furnas, *Porter, Reenes*—7.
Noes—Messrs. Collier, Little and Scott—3.
[Democrats in Roman, Republicans in *Italics.*]

The bill was as follows:

Sec. 1. Be it enacted by the Council and House of Representatives of the Territory of Nebraska, that slavery or involuntary servitude except for the punishment of crime, be and the same is forever prohibited in this Territory.

Sec. 2. This act shall take effect and be in force from and after the first day of July, A. D. 1860.

On the occasion of its passage in the Council, Mr. Little, an ardent advocate of popular sovereignty, delivered his views as follows. We quote from the Omaha *Nebraskian,* of January 4th:

Mr. LITTLE—Mr. President:—I have heretofore been, as I am now, a zealous follower of Stephen A. Douglas, in so far as I have regarded him the leader of the principles of popular sovereignty in the Territories; believing, as I do, that the people have the right to legislate upon this subject, and if necessary, to prevent Southerners from bringing their slaves here among us. But, sir, I shall vote to-day as I have heretofore done, against this, or any similar bill, in whatever shape it may come up, from principles of policy. There is no need of this legislation now. If we could actually see a black cloud rising in the South, and should a horde of slaves be precipitated upon our fair soil to-day, no one would vote quicker than I to repel such an evil from the land. But where is the danger? Where is this dreaded African spectre that, like Hamlet's ghost, fits ever before the hallucinated vision of the supporters of this bill? Our soil is yet unstained with slavery; we are free, and surrounded with free soil; Iowa on the east is free. Kansas, on the south, is free, and is there danger on our northern and western borders? Sir, I too, like the gentleman from Burt, take issue with Mr. Buchanan. I believe that Congress has no power over the Territories upon this question. But I shall not vote for what is now uncalled for. This bill had its origin in Black Republican buncombe. As a Democrat, I shall not vote to honor their political caprices, and exercising common sense, I shall not vote to dispel a phantom. Sir, I vote "no" upon this bill.

So far, so good. The bill was passed, and nothing was lacking but the signature of the Governor to give it the authority of law. But hardly had the vote been recorded, when the Democratic organs began to hint that it was the duty of the Governor to apply his negative to the "unnecessary piece of buncombe." Four or five days later the Democratic Governor of Nebraska, *vetoed the bill.* Gov. Black's reasons for withholding his signature, were substantially these:

1st. The existence of Slavery in the Louisiana Territory, ceded to the United States, is recognized by the treaty of cession; hence, until the formation of a State out of the Territory so conveyed or any portion thereof, the abolition of Slavery is impossible without a violation of the treaty stipulations.

2d. The equality of the States demands that the people of the Slave, as well as the people of the Free States may take their "property" to the Territory belonging to all States in common; hence the abolition of slavery by a Territorial Legislature becomes impossible, because, by denying the citizens of the Slave States the right of migrating with their negroes, the equality of the States would be destroyed. In other words, *the Dred Scott decision which* Gov. Black *recognizes as in force forbids the Legislature to prohibit Slavery.*

So Slavery exists in Nebraska to-day in spite of the effort of the Legislature to abolish it! It is there, a fixed fact in the Territory, above and beyond the reach of Congress or of the people! As to the question whether slavery does or does not exist in the Territory, it is in evidence, as a matter of public record, that a citizen of Page county, Iowa, a few weeks since, recovered damages in the amount of $8,000 from a gang of scoundrels who broke into his house while hunting for two negro girls, *held in Slavery in Nebraska,* who had "escaped from service or labor," a year and a half ago.

It may be added in this connection, that the legislature of *Kansas,* also, passed a bill last winter, abolishing Slavery in that Territory, and that the Democratic Governor, (Mcdary,) vetoed it!

Chapter IX
All Votes Cast for Douglas Are Given Practically to Breckinridge or Joe Lane

When the Charleston Convention assembled, on the 23d of April, in the present year, it became apparent that Mr. Douglas had no strength in the Southern States. It was proclaimed with great volubility by his opponents, that while the delegates from the Republican States were all in favor of Douglas, the Democratic States were all against him. It is sufficient for our purpose that the Convention split on the Douglas issue, and that the delegates from South Carolina, Georgia, Florida, Alabama, Mississippi, Louisiana, Texas and a majority from Arkansas and Delaware seceded, and, after a brief session apart from the regular Convention, adjourned to meet at Richmond, on the 20th of June. The other Convention took fifty-seven ballots without making any nomination, and then adjourned to meet at Baltimore on the 18th of June, "to enable those States which were unrepresented to fill up their delegations." Well, the South Carolina Democratic State Committee called a new Convention, which met in the time at Columbia, and appointed a new set of delegates, instructing them *not to go to Baltimore at all,* but to meet at Richmond, pursuant to the Seceders' adjournment. The Georgia Democratic Executive Committee called a new Convention to meet at

Milledgeville. Primary meetings were held in all the counties, and when the Convention assembled the vote stood 298 in favor of the Seceders, and 41 against them. The 298 thereupon re-appointed the old delegates to Baltimore, and the 41 withdrew and appointed a new set. The Florida Democratic State Committee called a new Convention, which met at Tallahasee, and did exactly what the South Carolina Convention had done. The Alabama Democratic State Committee called a new Convention to meet at Montgomery on the 4th day of June. Very soon after the call was issued, a number of private citizens, headed by John Forsyth, of Mobile, issued a sort of prospectus for a Convention to be held at Selma on the same day, to which "the Democracy and all other persons who were willing to abide by the action of the Baltimore Convention and support its nominees," were invited to send delegates. Both Conventions met. The Democratic concern re-appointed the Seceders by a unanimous vote, and the Forsyth men elected a new delegation. The Mississippi Democratic State Committee called a new Convention which unanimously re-appointed the Seceders, and no other Convention was held. The Louisiana Democratic State Committee called a new Convention to meet at Baton Rouge, which unanimously re-appointed the Seceders. The Hon. Pierre Soule and a few others in New Orleans, however, called a mass meeting to assemble at Donaldsonville, which appointed a new set of delegates. The Texas Democracy re-appointed the Seceders without opposition. The Arkansas Democracy held a Convention and endorsed the Seceders, and the Delaware Democracy did the same. Thus the delegations were "filled up" in pursuance to the resolution adopted at Charleston. Seven weeks transpired between the adjournment at that place and the re-assembling at Baltimore. The delegates all visited their constituents; *they* all had opportunity to learn the wishes of those who gave them their commissions. Those who took part in the secession at Charleston had all been sent back by their regular organization of the party, except in those States which utterly refused to have anything more to do with "National Democracy," and dispatched their delegates to an antagonistic Convention at Richmond. Those who adhered to the remains of Democracy—those who "stuck to the ship," and talked of going down on the last timber—also had conferences, anxious and prolonged, no doubt, with their neighbors and constituents. They had abundant time to consider the question in all its phases. The question itself had been of such magnitude—had been so overmastering in its importance to the people, that no man who carried the vote of his district could fail to learn exactly what was desired of him and exactly what it would be safe or unsafe for him to do. The Convention met again at Baltimore on the 18th of June. Five days later it was rent in twain. Douglas was nominated by the delegates from Maine, New

Hampshire, Vermont, Rhode Island, Connecticut, a portion of New York, a portion of New Jersey, a portion of Pennsylvania, a portion of Maryland, Ohio, Indiana, Michigan, Illinois, Wisconsin, Iowa, a portion of Minnesota, and a portion of Missouri. John C. Breckinridge and Joseph Lane were nominated by the delegates from Delaware, Virginia, North Carolina, South Carolina, Georgia, Florida, Alabama, Mississippi, Louisiana, Texas, Arkansas, Kentucky, Tennessee, California, Oregon, Massachusetts, a portion of Maryland, a portion of Missouri, a portion of Pennsylvania, a portion of Minnesota, and a small portion of New York. The Breckinridge and Lane Convention was presided over by the Hon. Caleb Cushing, the Chairman of the Charleston Convention. The question which arises here, is this: Did the delegates from the Southern States faithfully represent their constituents at Baltimore? If so, were they in earnest in nominating Breckinridge and Lane, or were they in fun? Are the Southern States going for Breckinridge and Lane, or for Douglas and Johnson? A few days ago, Mr. Johnson himself was hooted down at a public meeting, held at Macon, in his own State, and afterwards burned in effigy. He was not allowed to make his speech at all, and it has since been published in the Atlanta *Confederacy* as the only means of reaching the public. (The *Confederacy,* by the way, is a Douglas paper, which goes strongly *for the re-opening of the African slave trade.*) In Delaware, there is to be no Douglas electoral ticket. In Virginia there are only six newspapers supporting Douglas, while there are over forty for Breckinridge and Lane. Mr. Roger A. Pryor, who adhered to Douglas up to the final split at Baltimore, has publicly announced himself for Breckinridge and Lane. In North Carolina it seems probable there will be no Douglas electoral ticket. In South Carolina, the electors are chosen by the Legislature, and nobody is for Douglas. In Florida, Alabama, Mississippi, Texas and Arkansas, there is next to nobody for him. The Democratic State Convention of Kentucky met a few days ago, and endorsed Breckinridge with hardly a dissenting vote. In Tennessee, the few Douglasites that live in and around Memphis, have sold out body and breeches to Bell and Everett. In short, there is no Douglas party, which can properly be called a party, in any Southern State, except Missouri.

Now, if Mr. Douglas secures any electoral votes in the North, what is to be the result? The Electoral College consists of 303 votes. One hundred and fifty-two are required to elect a President. Deprived of Southern support, Douglas must carry almost the entire North to secure an election. Who believes that New England, New York, Ohio, Michigan, Wisconsin, and Iowa, which went so overwhelmingly for Fremont, are now going for him? But if he succeeds in taking from Lincoln the votes of the Northern States which went for Buchanan, four years ago, he merely carries the election into the present

House of Representatives, where he has only *one* vote, and where Breckinridge has *thirteen.* The Constitution of the United States, Article XII, *Amendments* says:

> If no person have a majority of the whole number of Electors, then from the persons having the highest numbers, *not exceeding three,* on the list of those voted for as President, the House of Representatives shall choose immediately, by ballot, the President. But in choosing the President, the votes shall be taken by states, the representation from each state having *one vote;* a quorum for this purpose shall consist of a member or members from two-thirds of the states, and a majority of all the states shall be necessary to a choice. And if the House of Representatives shall not choose a President, whenever the right of choice shall devolve upon them, before the fourth day of March next following, then the Vice-President shall act as President, as in case of the death, or constitutional disability, of the President.
>
> The person having the greatest number of votes as Vice-President shall be the Vice-President, if such number be a majority of the whole number of Electors appointed; and if no person have a majority, then, from the *two highest* numbers on the list, the Senate shall choose the Vice-President; a quorum for the purpose shall consist of two thirds of the whole number of Senators; a majority of the whole number shall be necessary to a choice.

Thus it appears that only the three highest candidates can be balloted for in the House, who in all human probability will be Lincoln, Breckinridge and Bell. But if we suppose that Mr. Douglas is one of the three highest, how will the case stand? Each State having one vote, the House would be divided as follows:

FOR LINCOLN	FOR BRECKINRIDGE
Maine,	Delaware,
New Hampshire,	Virginia,
Vermont,	South Carolina,
Massachusetts,	Georgia,
Rhode Island,	Florida,
Connecticut,	Alabama,
New York,	Mississippi,
New Jersey,	Louisiana,
Pennsylvania,	Texas,
Ohio,	Arkansas,
Indiana,	Missouri,
Michigan,	California,

Wisconsin,   Oregon—13
Iowa,
Minnesota—15.

FOR DOUGLAS   FOR BELL
Illinois—1.   Tennessee—

EQUALLY DIVIDED
Maryland, North Carolina, Kentucky—3.

The Maryland delegation in the House, consists of three Americans and three Democrats. The North Carolina delegation consists of four Americans and four Democrats. The Kentucky delegation consists of five Americans and five Democrats. Seventeen States being required to elect a President, Breckinridge will have to secure Maryland, North Carolina, Kentucky, and either Tennessee or Illinois, in addition to the thirteen which he has already. The Breckinridge faction believe that they can, without difficulty, get the votes of Mr. Webster, of Maryland, Mr. Vance, of North Carolina, Mr. Bristow or Mr. Mallory, or both, of Kentucky, and Messrs. Maynard, Branson and Hatton, of Tennessee, when the pinch comes—which would give them all of these States, and elect their man. All of these South Americans are intensely pro-slavery, and it is calculated they would unhesitatingly vote for Breckinridge, if there was no chance for Bell. But if no election should be made by the House, prior to the 4th of March, 1861, the Breckinridge faction are *sure* of success in the Senate. The Constitution declares, that only the *two* highest candidates for Vice-President, shall be voted for there. These will inevitably be Lane and Hamlin. The Senate is divided as follows: Republicans 26; Breckinridge Democrats, 37; Americans, 1; Douglas, 1. (Mr. Pugh, of Ohio, leaves the Senate on the 4th of March, and Mr. Chase takes his seat; Mr. Crittenden, of Kentucky, leaves on the same day, and Mr. Breckinridge takes his seat; Mr. Lane, of Oregon, leaves on the same day, and his successor has not been elected.) Of course, Mr. Lane would be elected Vice-President on the first ballot, and he would then assume the functions of President of the United States, for four years. What sort of a figure then does Mr. Douglas cut in the three or four cornered fight? Simply that of a catspaw, to rake the chestnuts out of the fire for Breckinridge, or Joe Lane, his bitterest enemies! It was a special cruelty, almost a satanic ingenuity, on the part of those who nominated Breckinridge and Lane, to so order the battle that *all the electoral votes carried for Douglas, should, in reality, play the game into their hands and not into his.* Are the honest supporters of "Popular Sovereignty," to be cheated in this way? Will they allow the election to go into the House, and thus insure the success of Breckinridge or Lane, by throwing away their votes on Douglas?

The following sharp article from the Buffalo *Commercial Advertiser,* of July 12th, the old and influential Fillmore organ, of Western New York, still further elucidates this question:

We have the highest regard and respect for Gov. Hunt, and that gentleman will not misinterpret our motives or accuse us of undue personality, if we remind him of a business transaction with which he was once familiar. A gentleman, whom he knows very well, had built a boom across the Genesee river, at Mt. Morris, and profited by the spring freshet to float down several thousands of saw-logs. Other people relied upon the same boom; so many of them, in fact, that the boom went out and the logs of all parties were carried down the river, some of them fetching up in Lake Ontario. Mr. ———— was making his arrangements to chase up his vagabond logs, when one day he received a call from a person who was a loser by the boom. Person wanted to make an arrangement: he had trusted the boom, and its insecure construction had occasioned him serious loss; *ergo,* Mr. ———— should make him reparation. Whereupon, the following proposition was made: Mr. ———— owned a tract of land in Scio; 18,000 acres; great many deer on it. He would give a deer for every saw-log; Mr. ———— to take the logs where he could find them, the other party to do the same with the deer.

Now it seems to us that the result of the late Union Convention, at Utica, is pretty much after the fashion of this proposition. The Union men agree to deliver to the Douglas men some 60,000 American saw-logs, running down stream like mad in a Republican freshet. The Douglas men pass over to the Union party something still more tangible, and if ever the Union leaders see anything more than the tail of that Douglas venison, we shall be astonished. We are tolerably well posted on the American vote of New York. It is recalcitrant, individualized, independent, knows no leaders, and now that the boom is broken, it will float off on the swift rolling tide of the Lincoln flood, beyond the reach of bargain and sale. Said a distinguished American—not Union—leader, a few days since, "I always found it easy enough to sell out the American vote: the trouble was to deliver."

We take it for granted that Americans and old Whigs will shy off from this bargain, for the following very evident reasons: Douglas is as far from any resemblance to Americanism or Whigism as can well be conceived. Nothing can be gained for principle by electing him; and even the slavery issue will not be quieted. Douglas is the leading agitator of the question. He re-opened the quarrel after it had been satisfactorily closed by the compromise of 1850, and it would be queer policy now to look to the agitator as the source of quiet. Then again, they know perfectly well that even should the election go to the House, nothing can be done there as long as Bell has only one and Douglas one of thirty-three votes, seventeen of which are required to elect. *And the House failing to elect, what can they expect of the Senate? The choice then would be between Lane and Hamlin, and Lane would win.*

CHAPTER X
"THE EVERLASTING NIGGER QUESTION"

Senator Douglas has been marking out for himself a departure from the dignified course of all the Presidential candidates we have ever had, by making a stumping tour in behalf of Douglas and Johnson. In his Boston speech, as we find it reported in the newspapers of that city, he said:

For the last few years, the whole time of Congress has been employed in the discussion of the slavery question, to the exclusion of the important business affecting the whole country. (1.) Whenever you ask your representatives why they did not revise the revenue system, and order to defray the expenses of the government, without borrowing twenty millions of dollars a year, they will tell you they had not time. The whole time was occupied in the discussion of slavery, and there was no time to raise money to pay your honest debts. (2.) When you ask your representatives why it is that the Pacific Railroad has not been made, you were told that there was no time, because the Slavery question absorbed the entire session of Congress. (3.) When you ask your representatives why it is that the mail system has not been reformed and carried on with vigor throughout the country, you are told that the bill was lost for want of time. (4.) When you ask why it is that you have no overland mail route to the Pacific, and no steam lines, you are told that the slavery question occupied the whole session, and the bills were lost for want of time. (5.) Thus you find that all the great measures which affect the commercial interests, the shipping interests, the manufacturing interests, the industrial interests of the country, have been lost for want of time. (6.) My fellow-citizens, there never will be time to perform the duties for which the government was made, unless you banish forever the slavery question from the halls of Congress, and remand it to the people of each State and each Territory, according to the platform of the Democratic party.

Mr. Douglas makes haste to pronounce his own condemnation. His remarks constitute one of the best Republican arguments that has been put forth since the nomination of LINCOLN. We proceed to notice them in the order in which they are numbered above.

I. "Whenever you ask our representatives why they did not revise the revenue system in order to defray the expenses of the Government, without borrowing twenty millions of dollars a year, they tell you they had not time. The whole time was occupied in the discussion of slavery." At the last session of Congress the Republicans in the House of Representatives *did* revise the revenue system in order to defray the expenses of the Government without borrowing twenty millions of dollars a year, but *Senator Douglas* was too busy discussing the slavery question to give his influence or even his vote for the measure! The bill passed the House by a large majority, and was defeated by the Democrats in the Senate—by the opposition of some, and by the pre-occupation of others with the nigger question. Mr. Douglas was found in the latter category. He could "find no time" to attend to the revenue system.

II. "When you ask your representatives why it is that the Pacific Railroad has not been made, you were told that there was no time, because the slavery question had absorbed the entire session of Congress." The Republicans in the House of Representatives did essay, earnestly and manfully, to pass a Pacific Railroad bill at the last session of Congress. They were thwarted at every point by the Democracy, some of whom were Mr. Douglas' peculiar friends! Did Douglas himself display any zeal for the measure? No. He was too busy discussing Sedition Laws and the various phases of the slavery question.

III. "When you ask your representatives why it is that your mail system has not been reformed and carried on with vigor throughout the country, you are told that the bill was lost for want of time." "The bill" which Mr. Douglas talks of was prepared and carried through the House of Representatives by the Republicans, *in opposition to the votes of the five Douglas members from Illinois!* Mr. Douglas was too much occupied discussing the slavery question to give it any assistance, and all his friends voted squarely against it. It was finally defeated, by Democratic votes in the Senate—Douglas himself not voting for it at all! He was doubtless preparing a new speech or magazine article on the "everlasting nigger question."

IV. "When you ask why it is that you have no overland mall route to the Pacific, and no steam lines, you are told that the slavery question occupied the whole session, and that the bills were lost for want of time." Both measures were carried through the House by the Republicans, and were defeated by the Democracy in the Senate. Mr. Douglas was so busy discussing the slavery question.

V. "Thus you find that all the great measures which affect the commercial interests, the shipping interests, the manufacturing interests, the industrial interests of the country, have been lost for want of time." This is rather the coolest thing of all. A single debate on the slavery question, initiated by Mr Douglas on the 23d of February, and mainly carried on by himself, filled forty columns of the *Globe*. Another speech of his in May occupied two days in delivery. Another (on the Sedition Law) consumed the better part of two different days.

Another (his wanton and disreputable attack on Senator Seward filled six or eight columns of the *Globe.* In short, he occupied about three times as much of the public attention in discussing the slavery question during the last session of Congress as any other member!

VI. "My fellow citizens, there never will be time to perform the duties for which the government was made, unless you banish forever the slavery question from the halls of Congress, and remand it to the people of each State and each Territory according to the platform of the Democratic party." In 1852 the platform of the Democratic party declared that they would "resist all attempts at renewing, in Congress or out of it, the agitation of the slavery question, under whatever shape or color the attempt may be made." One year and a half after the adoption of the platform, this Douglas set about repealing the Missouri Compromise, and by that act laid the foundation of all the slavery agitation which has since followed. Was there ever impudence like this, which he now puts on before the good people of Boston? Where else is it to be found?

CHAPTER XI

LINCOLN AND HAMLIN'S LETTERS OF ACCEPTANCE

SPRINGFIELD, Ill., May 28, 1860

Hon. George Ashmun, President of the Republican National Convention

SIR: I accept the nomination tendered me by then Convention over which you presided, and of which I am formally apprised, in the letter of yourself and others acting as a Committee of the Convention for that purpose. The declaration of principles and sentiments, which accompanies your letter, meets my approval, and it shall be my care not to violate it or disregard it in any part, imploring the assistance of Divine Providence and with due regard to the views and feelings of all who were represented in the Convention; to the *rights* of all the States and Territories and the people of the nation; to the inviolability of the Constitution and the perpetual union, harmony and prosperity of all, I am most happy to co-operate for the practical success of the principles declared by the Convention.

Your obliged friend and fellow citizen,
ABRAHAM LINCOLN.

WASHINGTON, May 30, 1860.

GENTLEMEN:—Your official communication of the 18th inst., informing me that the Representatives of the Republican party of the United States, assembled at Chicago on that day, had, by unanimous vote, selected me as their candidate for the office of Vice-President of the United States, has been received, together with the resolutions adopted by the Convention as its declaration of principles. Those resolutions enunciate clearly and forcibly the principles which unite us, and the objects proposed to be accomplished. They address themselves to all, and there is neither necessity nor propriety in my entering upon a discussion of any of them. They have the approval of my judgment, and in any action of mine will be faithfully and cordially sustained. I am profoundly grateful to those with whom it is my pride and pleasure politically to cooperate, for the nomination so unexpectedly conferred, and I desire to tender through you to the members of the Convention my sincere thanks for the confidence thus reposed in me. Should the nomination which I now accept be ratified by the people, and the duties devolve upon me of presiding over the Senate of the United States, it will be my earnest endeavor faithfully to discharge them, with a just regard for the rights of all. It is to be observed, in connection with the doings of the Republican Convention, that a paramount object with us is to preserve the normal condition of our Territorial domain as homes for free men. The able advocate and defender of Republican principles whom you have nominated for the highest place that can gratify the ambition of man, comes from a State which has been made what it is by the special action in that respect of the wise and good men, who founded our institutions. The rights of free labor have there been vindicated and maintained. The thrift and enterprise which so distinguished Illinois as one of the most flourishing States of the glorious West, we would see secured to all the Territories of the Union and restore peace and harmony to the whole country by bringing back the Government to what it was under the wise and patriotic men who created it. If the Republicans shall succeed in that object, as they hope to, they will be held in grateful remembrance by the busy and teeming millions of future ages.

I am, very truly yours,
H. Hamlin.

To Hon. G. Ashmun, Pres't, &c.

The Culmination of the Battle for the Soul of America
1861–1876

✶ 14 ✶

An Address to the People of the United States, and Particularly to the People of the States Which Adhere to the Federal Government (Washington, 1864)

THE DEMOCRATS, politically marginalized first by their crushing defeat in 1860 and then by the war, came roaring back in the state and congressional elections of 1862, in the face of persistent Republican "oppressive government," "misgovernment," corruption, unacceptable racial experiments, and the "wild passions" their policies had unleashed, all of which severely threatened American stability. As they prepared this 1864 address to the party faithful, Democratic congressmen declared that their worst fears had come true. As predicted, the long assault by consolidationists (Federalists, Whigs, Republicans) on the people's liberties, firmly advanced by the Lincoln administration, had become a reality. The presidential election of 1864 was an opportunity for the American people to save themselves. "The sound elements of society must be brought to the surface, the body politic be purged of its unhealthy elements, and in places of public trust, just and broad-minded, pure and tolerant men be substituted for radicals and corruptionists."

As members of the Thirty-Eighth Congress, politically opposed to the present Federal Administration and representing the Opposition Union sentiment of the country, we address ourselves to the people of the United States: and our object will be to show (as far as may be done within the limits of an address) that there is good reason for changing the Administration and Policy of this General Government through the instrumentality of suffrage in the elections of the present year.

It is our settled conviction that men now in public station, who control the policy of the Government, cannot or will not perform those duties which are necessary to save the country and perpetuate its liberties. Many of them are engrossed by political and personal objects which do not comport with the public welfare, and will not subserve it; others have false or perverted views of our system of free government, or are inspired by passions which continually mislead them; and the Opposition in Congress are powerless to check the majority, and are unable even to secure such investigation of the Executive Departments and of the conduct of Government officials, as will prevent abuse and secure honesty, economy, and efficiency in the public service.

Profoundly, painfully impressed by passing events, we turn from the President of the United States and from the majority in Congress, upon whom all remonstrance against misgovernment would be wasted, to address ourselves to our fellow countrymen at large; and we appeal to them to interpose in public affairs, and by a proper exertion of their sovereign electoral power, to decree that these United States shall be justly governed, re-united, tranquilized and saved!

Engrossment of Power

What we propose to notice in the first place, as introductory to our examination of public affairs, is, the consolidation of all power in the Government of the United States into the hands of a single political interest. The party of the Administration has not been subjected to any efficient check upon its action from an opposing interest or party, since its attainment of power in 1861. Carrying all the Northern, Western, and Pacific States, with a single exception, at the Presidential election of 1860, and being relieved from all southern opposition in Congress by the withdrawal of the States of that section, it was able to do its will and pleasure without check or hindrance in the Government of the United States. All public patronage was subsidized to its uses; all Government outlays (and they were enormous in amount) were disbursed by its officials; all public power was wielded by its arm; and this condition of things has continued to the present time. It has revelled in power, and of inevitable necessity, from its very nature and from the opportunities presented it, it has abused its powers; it has forgotten or despised and trampled under foot the duties imposed upon it by the people, and the objects announced by it in the outset have been supplanted by others, which now inspire its action and occupy its hopes.

No truth is more certain, none better established by history, than this, that political power is aggressive; that it will always seek to enlarge itself and to increase its domination, and that no free government is possible where by the very constitution of the Government itself, power is not made a check to power. Freedom is secured by the action and reaction upon each other of

political forces, so organized and so limited that no one can absolutely dominate over or control the rest. And hence, the necessity of constitutions which
shall so divide and arrange the powers of government, that no single interest,
class, or individual, shall become supreme and engross the whole mass of
political power. Now the capital mischief (or rather source of mischief and
evil) in the Government of the United States during the past three years and
at this moment, is, that a single political interest or party, of evil constitution,
has obtained and exercised the whole mass of Government powers, free from
all check or limitation whatsoever. The fatal results are obvious. It has been
false to its promises made as a condition upon which it attained power; it has
broken the Constitution shamefully and often; it has wasted the public treasure; it has suspended the ancient writ of liberty, the *"habeas corpus,"* rendering
it impossible for the citizen to obtain redress against the grossest outrage; it
has changed the war into a humanitarian crusade outside of any constitutional or lawful object; it has grossly mismanaged the war in the conduct of
military operations; it has degraded the currency of the country by profuse
issues of paper money, and confiscated private property by a legal tender enactment; and, to retain its power, that it may riot in plunder and be subjected
to no check and to no restraint from public opinion, it has undertaken to
control State elections by direct military force or by fraudulent selection of
voters from the army. These are some of the results already achieved, and "the
end is not yet." No impartial observer can contemplate the future without
apprehension of still greater evils, or can doubt that some real division of
public power or its lodgment in new hands, is necessary not merely to the
success but to the very existence of free government in the United States.

The Democratic Party

The evil of uncontrolled party domination in government will be greater or
less according to the character and objects of the party in power. The Democratic party, which ordinarily has administered the Government of the United
States, even in the utmost plentitude of its power, did not fall into gross abuse
or threaten the liberties of the country. Although it required to be checked
upon occasion, and that its policy and conduct should be subjected to rigid
scrutiny by an active opposition, there was great security against its abuse of
its powers in the principles and doctrines to which it held; for its creed was
established for it by men of the most sterling virtue and profound wisdom,
who justly comprehended the nature of free governments and the dangers to
which they are exposed. Strict construction of the Constitution, a sparing use

of the powers of Government, moderate expenditures and equal laws, became the articles of a political creed which preserved the Government from abuse and degeneracy, kept the States in harmony, and secured the growth and development of a material prosperity unexampled in the history of nations. Its great merit was that it was a constitutional party, (in the true sense of that term,) subjecting itself cheerfully, thoroughly and constantly, to all the rules and limitations of the fundamental law. Its principles themselves, checked it and kept it within bounds. As its contests for power were upon the very ground that there should be no over-action of government but only a due exertion of its authorized powers, there was the less necessity to confront it with a powerful opposition. Yet such opposition always existed, and was no doubt necessary to the safe and successful action of the Government under its management.

The Party of the Administration

But with the party now in power the case is widely different. Its main strength lies in States which voted against Mr. Jefferson in 1800, against Mr. Madison in 1812, against Andrew Jackson in 1828, and against Mr. Polk in 1844; and it embraces that school of opinion in this country which has always held to extreme action by the General Government, favoritism to particular interests, usurpation of State powers, large public expenditures, and, generally, to constructions of the Constitution which favor Federal authority and extend its pretensions. Besides, it is essentially sectional and aggressive—the very embodiment of that disunion partyism foreseen and denounced by Washington and Jackson in those Farewell Addresses which they left on record for the instruction of their countrymen, and by Henry Clay in a memorable address to the Legislature of Kentucky. That it could not safely be intrusted with the powers of the Federal Government is a conclusion which inevitably results from this statement of its composition and character. But the question is no longer one of mere opinion or conjecture. Having been tried by the actual possession of Government powers and been permitted to exhibit fully its true nature, it has completely justified the theory which condemns it; as will plainly appear from considering particular measures of policy pursued by it. From among these we shall select several for particular examination, in order that our general statement of Republican unfitness for the possession of Government powers may be illustrated, established, and made good against any possible contradiction.

Military Interference with Elections

This has taken place in two ways:

First. By the selection of soldiers of the army to be sent home temporarily to participate in State elections.

This practice, in connection with sending home on such occasions large numbers of Government officers and employees in the civil service, has changed the result of many State elections and given to the party in power an unjust advantage. With the large powers possessed by the Administration for the purposes of the war; with the large increase of appointments to civil office and the employment of vast numbers of persons in all parts of the country in the business of Government, the Administration and its party have been enabled to influence elections to an alarming extent. The powers conferred by the whole people upon the Government, and the revenues derived by taxation from the whole people or derived from loans which become charged upon the whole mass of individual property, have been used in an infinite number of ways for party purposes and to secure to the Republican interest, in the Federal and State Governments, the continued possession of power. The injustice and corruptive tendency of this system cannot be denied, and alone should be held sufficient to condemn the party of the Administration. It is notorious that time after time, on the eve of doubtful elections, thousands of voters have been sent home from the army to turn the scale between parties and to secure an Administration triumph. And this has been done, not upon the principle of sending home citizen soldiers indiscriminately and without reference to their political opinions and attachments, (which would have been just,) but upon the principle of selecting republican soldiers, or of granting furloughs upon the condition of a promise from the persons favored that they would support Administration candidates. We mention elections in New Hampshire, Connecticut, and Pennsylvania, as instances of such most base and unjust proceeding, by which unscrupulous power has defeated the true expression of popular opinion, and obtained political advantages which were shameful to it and deeply injurious to the country. Will a free people consent to have their system of elections thus perverted and corrupted, and expect to enjoy, in spite thereof, the peaceable fruits of good government and honest rule?

Second. A still more grave offense against the purity and independence of elections has been committed by the Administration in the States of Missouri, Kentucky, Maryland and Delaware. The particular circumstances of

Government interference were somewhat different in each of they States, but the substantial facts in all, were these:

1. That the military power of the General Government was directly applied to control the elections, and that officers and soldiers of the army of the United States were openly used for the purpose.

2. That the States in question were at the time in a state of profound peace and quiet, and that with the exception of a single congressional district in Kentucky, no Rebel raid or invasion into them was then in progress or expected.

3. That in each of them there existed an adhering State government, exercising complete and unquestioned jurisdiction under Government and other State officials whose devotion and fidelity to the Government of the United States were unquestionable.

4. That there was no official call upon the Federal Government by the Executive or Legislature of any one of those States for protection against domestic violence, (under the particular provision of the Constitution of the United States, authorizing such call,) but that the interference, in most cases, was against the desire, and notably in the case of Maryland against the protest of the State authorities.

5. That thousands of qualified persons were prevented from voting at those elections, and in most of those States the result of the election was changed from what it would have been without military interference. The aged and timid were deterred from attending the elections; many who attended were kept from approaching the polls; and, in many cases, actual outrage prevented the legal voter from exercising his right. The full proof of all this appears in a number of contested-election cases in Congress, in official papers from the Governors of several of the States in question, in reports of committees of the State Legislatures, and from other reliable sources; and we recommend the whole subject, as one of fearful importance, to the examination and judgment of our countrymen.

Creation of Bogus States

The steps taken towards establishing a system of false and unjust representation in the Government of the United States, should also be carefully considered.

In the first place, let us consider what has taken place in regard to the State of Virginia. In 1860, Virginia had a population, (including slaves,) of 1,596,318; Pennsylvania a population of 2,906,215; New York a population of

3,880,735. While the two States last named adhered faithfully to the Government of the United States, and have since borne on its behalf, their proper share of the burdens of the war, Virginia revolted, and two thirds of her population was thrown into the scale of the enemy. What result followed as to the representation of that State in the Congress of the Union? The comparatively small part of the State which adhered to the Union was recognized as constituting, for political purposes, the State of Virginia; an improvised Legislature of this adhering fragment of the State, elected two Senators, who were admitted into the Senate of the United States, and Representatives from the same territory were admitted into the Federal House of Representatives. The liberal principles of construction upon which this was done, may stand justified by the peculiar circumstances of the case. But there was a further proceeding for which no warrant of power or pretence of necessity can be shown. a part of the adhering Virginia territory was permitted to form itself into a new State, was admitted into the Union under the name of West Virginia, (although the Constitution of the United States declares that no State shall be divided for the formation of a new one without the express assent of the Legislature thereof,) and Senators therefrom were admitted into the United States Senate. A very small part of the old State, not included within the boundaries of the new one, remained within our military lines, to be, as well as the new State, represented by two members in the Senate. Thus, under Republican manipulation, one third of the ancient State of Virginia has four votes in the Senate of the United States, and may neutralize the votes of both New York and Pennsylvania in that body. The "Ancient Dominion," with a population a little exceeding one half that of Pennsylvania, is represented by four Senators in the Congress of the United States, and by two in the Confederate Congress at Richmond! Pennsylvania, with her three millions of people, remains true to the Union, and retains her former vote in the Senate; Virginia turns traitor, sends two thirds of her population under the Confederate flag, and forthwith has her representation doubled in the Senate of the United States, and that, too, in defiance of a constitutional provision forbidding it, and avoided only upon a strained construction or implication totally at variance with the plain fact Against the plain truth of the case, and without necessity, it was assumed that the Legislature of a fragment of the State represented the whole for the purpose of assenting to its division and the erection therefrom of a new member of the Federal Union.

We pass from this case to speak of matter more recent. A State government has been set up in Louisiana, under the supervision of a major general of the United States Army, which, although it holds the allegiance of but part of the population, we suppose is to have the former representation of that State in

Congress; and in Tennessee and Arkansas there have been proceedings of a similar description. The indications are clear and full, that in these cases and in others of similar character which may follow them, the President of the United States, through his officers of the army in command in the States to be represented, dictates and will dictate and control the whole proceeding for renewed representation, and upon principles most unequal, unjust and odious.

A recent attempt to set up one of these bogus States in Florida, under a presidential agent, must be fresh in the recollection of the country, as must also be the military disaster by which that attempt was rendered abortive.

But why refer to particular cases? Why reason upon events that have happened, or upon probabilities which present themselves before us? The President of the United States has, himself, in his message at the opening of the present session of Congress, and in his proclamation appended thereto, announced his programme for the reconstruction and consequent representation of the States which may be rescued in whole or in part from the Confederates during the existing war.

The Proclamation extends a pardon to all persons in the rebellious States, (except certain Confederate officers, &c.,) upon condition that they shall take, subscribe, and keep a prescribed oath, one provision of which is, that they will abide by and faithfully support all proclamations of the President made during the existing rebellion having reference to slaves, so long and so far as not modified or declared void by decision of the Supreme Court. And it further proclaims, that whenever in any one of the Confederate States, "a number of persons not less than one tenth in number of the votes cast in such State at the Presidential election of 1860, having taken and kept the aforesaid oath, &c., shall re-establish a State Government which shall be republican, and in nowise contravening said oath, such State shall be recognized as the true government of the State."

This presidential paper must be regarded as the most remarkable one ever issued by an American Executive. The one tenth part of a population are to exercise the powers of the whole, and, if Congress concur, are to be represented in the Government of the United States and in our electoral colleges for the choice of President, as if they were the whole! And this one tenth is to be made up of men who will solemnly swear that they will obey and keep all the President's proclamations upon a particular subject, issues during the present war; not proclamations which he may have issued already, but future ones also. A more abject oath was never framed in the history of the whole earth. Was a religious obligation ever before required of citizen or subject, in any age or country, to obey and keep the future and unknown edicts of the

Executive will? And if usurped authority can accomplish its object, a handful of men in a State, degraded by such an oath, are to wield representative votes in the Government of the United States, and enter electoral colleges to extend the power of the master to whom their fealty is sworn.

The lawless and dangerous character of the Administration must most evidently appear from the foregoing review of its policy and conduct regarding popular elections and the organization of States.

But its incapacity (if not profligacy) will as clearly appear from an examination of its measures in the prosecution of the war, and to some of those measures we will now direct attention.

RAISING OF TROOPS

In April, 1861, at the outbreak of hostilities, the army of the United States was small and wholly inadequate to meet the exigency of war which had arisen. The President called for seventy-five thousand troops from the States to serve for a period of three months, and subsequently made other calls. Finally, in the latter part of 1862, drafts were ordered in several States to fill up their quotas, and the proceeding for that purpose was under the State authorities, pursuant to State laws and some general regulations of the War Department framed for the occasion. Thus the case stood as to the raising of troops at the commencement of 1863, and the troops in service at that date consisted of the Regular Army of the United States as it stood at the outbreak of hostilities, with subsequent enlistments added, and of volunteers and drafted militia of the States, organized and officered as companies and regiments by State authority. Volunteering had at one time been checked by the Administration, upon a statement by it that all the troops needed were already in service. Soon, however, the demand for men was renewed, and at the beginning of 1863 the number called for and raised had become enormous. But for the after purposes of the Administration it was perfectly feasible for it to call for additional troops in the manner theretofore practiced, which involved State assistance and co-operation and secured to the troops raised their regular organization as State militia under the laws of their respective States. The army bore, mainly, the character of a public force contributed by the States under the fifteenth and sixteenth clauses of the eighth section of the first article of the Constitution, which authorize Congress "To provide for calling forth the militia to execute the laws of the Union, suppress insurrections, and repel invasions," and "to provide for organizing, arming and disciplining the militia, and for governing such part of them as may be employed in the service of the United States, reserving to the States respectively the appointment of the officers," &c.

The power of the Federal Government to call for troops, and the power of the States to supply them, organizing them into companies and regiments and appointing their officers, were unquestionable, as was also the power of the States to select those troops which they were to contribute, by draft or lot.

CONSCRIPTION

But early in 1863 a new system for the raising of troops was established by act of Congress. This was a system of conscription, (the word and the idea being borrowed from the French,) and was without example in the history of the United States. Passing by the State authorities and by the clauses of the Constitution above mentioned, it put the General Government in direct communication with the whole arms-bearing population of the country, and assumed for the General Government exclusive and absolute control over the whole proceeding of raising troops. The validity of this enactment has been questioned, and it is one of the debatable points which belong to the history of the war. For it has been argued with much of force and reason that the power of Congress to raise armies although a general power is not unlimited, and that laws of conscription by it are not "necessary and proper" when the forces required can be raised with perfect certainty and convenience from the militia of the states under the provisions of the Constitution above cited. But, passing this point, the inquiry arises, why was the former system involving State co-operation abandoned, and a new and questionable one substituted? No clear and adequate reason for the measure appears in the debates of the Congress which passed it, unless the suggestion made by one of its leading supporters in the House of Representatives that it was in hostility to "the accursed doctrine of State rights" be accepted as such reason. We must, therefore, conclude that it was the policy of the authors of the law to deprive the States of the appointment of the officers of the troops raised, and to absorb that power into the hands of the Federal Administration; that the act was the measure of a party to increase its influence and power, and to prevent the possibility of any participation therein by the Governments of the States.

We believe it to be certain that this measure has entailed great expense upon the Treasury of the United States; that it has created unnecessarily a large number of Federal officers, distributed throughout the country; and that, while it has been no more efficient than the system which required State co-operation, it has been much less satisfactory.

If a necessity for raising troops by conscription be asserted, then it would follow that the revolutionary policy of the Administration has alarmed and disgusted the people, and chilled that enthusiasm which in the earliest days of the contest filled our patriot army with brave and willing volunteers.

BOUNTIES

What is further to be mentioned in this connection is the payment of bounties by the United States, by the State governments, and by cities, counties, and other municipalities. In their payment there has been great want of uniformity and system. The policy of the General Government has not been the same at all times, and in the States there has been infinite diversity. Upon the whole, the system of bounties has been costly and unequal; the amount of indebtedness created by it is enormous, and unequal sums have been paid to soldiers of the same grade of merit. Under any system of local bounties to avoid conscription, the wealthy parts of the country enjoy an advantage over others, and especially where manufacturing and other interests find it to their profit in providing the supplies of the war to retain their laborers at home, substituting payments of money in their stead, unless each State shall be firmly required to furnish the substitutes to fill up its quota from its own citizens. But the General Government has permitted the agents of such interests in a State to go into other States and into the southern country and obtain enlistments for bounties, both of white and black troops, to be credited upon the quota of the State of the agent. If it shall happen hereafter that local payments of bounties, whether by States or by municipalities within them, be assumed by the Government of the United States, the inequalities of the system and its extravagance in many cases will become a matter of concern to the whole people. And it is just matter of complaint against those who have held authority in the Federal Government, that by their policy and want of policy on this subject the burden of the war has been vastly increased, and been distributed irregularly and unfairly.

The pecuniary outlay and indebtedness caused by payment of local bounties, being mostly incurred by powerful and influential communities, it is quite possible that they may be recognized hereafter by Congress as a legitimate object of national assumption; and if this happen, those communities that have retained their laborers at home, and thereby secured their prosperity during the war, will cast a part of the burden of their exemption upon other sections.

Obviously what has been wanting has been wisdom and foresight in those who have controlled the public measures of the war, and who have resorted to one expedient after another without a fixed policy; who have acted where they ought not, and have failed to act where action and regulation were demanded.

Negro Troops

But a subject which requires particular notice is, the employment of negro troops in the war. An act of Congress, passed the 17th day of July, 1862, authorized the President "to receive into the service of the United States for the purpose of constructing intrenchments, or performing camp service, or any other labor, or any military or naval service for which they might be found competent, persons of African descent; and such persons should be enrolled and organized under such regulations, not inconsistent with the Constitution and laws, as the President might prescribe;" and further, that they "should receive ten dollars per month and one ration, three dollars of which monthly pay might be in clothing."

Without any other law on the subject prior in date to the present session of Congress, (except an imperfect provision in an act of 1862,) the President in his message of December 8, 1863, announced, that "of those who were slaves at the beginning of the rebellion, fully one hundred thousand are now in the United States military service, about one half of which number actually bear arms in the ranks."

At the present session, on the 24th of February, an act amendatory of the conscription law of 1863 was approved, the twenty-fourth section of which provides for the enrollment of colored persons between twenty and forty-five years of age; that slaves of loyal masters enrolled, drawn and mustered into the public service, shall be free, and one hundred dollars for each shall be paid to the master; and that in the slave States represented in Congress, the loyal master of a slave who volunteers into the public service shall be paid a sum not exceeding three hundred dollars, out of the military commutation fund.

By the army appropriation bill, approved June 16, 1864, it was further provided, "that all persons of color who have been or may be mustered into military service of the United States shall receive the same uniform, clothing, arms, equipments, camp equipage, rations, medical and hospital attendance, pay and emoluments, other than bounty, as other soldiers of the regular or volunteer forces of the United States of like arm of the service, from and after the first day of January, 1864; and that every person of color who shall hereafter be mustered into the service, shall receive such sums in bounty as the President shall order in the different States and parts of the United States, not exceeding one hundred dollars [each]."

This enactment is similar in terms to a bill which passed the Senate in March last, upon the consideration of which it was announced, that at least two hundred thousand colored troops would be raised. Adding to this number the number stated by the President to be in service in December last, would make one quarter of a million troops of this description.

The measures above mentioned would establish the following points in the policy of the Government. *First.* The employment of black troops generally, both slave and free. *Second.* The equality of black troops with white as to compensation and supplies; and *Third,* The payment to the loyal master of a slave of a bounty of one hundred dollars when the slave is drafted into the service, or of a bounty not exceeding three hundred dollars, when he volunteers.

The practical results of this policy are, to obtain an inferior quality of troops at the highest rate of expense; to impose upon the Treasury the support of an enormous number of undisciplined and ignorant negroes; to recognize the principle of buying negroes from their masters, whether the public interests require it or not, and to incur the risk of breaking down in the war because of the inefficiency of the forces employed in its prosecution. Besides, it is notorious that in pursuing this policy, the negro women and children must, to a great extent, be thrown upon the Government for support or be left to perish.

There has never been extensive objection to the employment of negroes under the act of 1862, in those war employments for which they are fitted as laborers and teamsters, and for camp service. In the warm parts of the country, especially, they could be thus usefully employed, and a reasonable number doubtless might also be employed for some sorts of service in the navy. But to employ an unwieldy number of them at such prodigious expense, is most evident folly and wrong, and it will be well if signal disaster does not result from it. We know no reason for this extravagant, costly, and dangerous policy, except a desire of the majority in Congress to establish (if indeed their enactments could accomplish such object) the equality of the black and white races with each other. But doubtless, the employment of blacks in the war is to be made the pretext for extending to them the right of suffrage and also social position, and to be followed, probably, by the organization of a considerable body of them into a standing army.

Increase of Soldiers' Pay

The immediate result of this policy of negroism in the war had been to postpone, and at last to limit the increase of compensation to our citizen soldiers. Bills providing such increase were permitted to lie unacted upon in Congress for more than five months of the present session, and the bill finally adopted for that purpose was inadequate and made to take effect only from the first day of May, 1864. It increased the pay of privates from thirteen to sixteen dollars per month, (without distinction of color,) and the pay of officers in somewhat similar proportion. But the smallness of this increase, as well as the delay in enacting it, was occasioned by the extravagant measures above mentioned. The Treasury, strained by the payment of enormous sums to negroes by reason of their employment in increased numbers and at increased rates of expense, could illy respond to the just demands made upon it in behalf of our citizen soldiers.

Besides it is instructive to observe that in this legislation by Congress, while increased pay to white troops begins on the first of May, an increase to colored troops dates from the first of January. And a provision contained in the act of 15th of June authorizes the Attorney General of the United States to inquire whether increased pay under former laws cannot be allowed to negroes employed in the public service before the beginning of the present year, who were free on the 19th of April, 1861, and if he determine in favor of such allowance his decision shall be carried into effect by orders of the War Department. The majority in Congress, in pursuing the phantom of negro equality, are as improvident as they are impassioned. The decision of the War Department (in accordance with the opinion of its solicitor) as to the compensation of negroes under former laws, is to be opened and subjected to review by the Attorney General, in the hope that some additional meaning may be wrung out of the old statutes justifying additional expenditure upon a favorite object.

It ought to be manifest to every reasonable man that negroes in service should be paid less than white troops, and that the increase of their pay from ten to sixteen dollars per month was unnecessary and profligate. The market value of their labor is known to be less than that of citizens, and it is equally clear that their services are much less valuable in the army.

We have but to add under this head that additional pay to our citizen soldiers in service is but just and reasonable, and ought long since to have been provided. The great depreciation in the value of the currency in which they are paid, and the increased rates of price in the country affecting all their purchases and outlays, have demanded the notice and consideration of the Government. It is upon their exertions that reliance must be placed for success in the war, and even for the preservation of the Treasury from embarrassment and the country from pecuniary convulsion; and whatever differences of opinion may exist as to measures of Government policy, their merits and sacrifices demand recognition and gratitude from the whole mass of their countrymen.

This gigantic scheme for the employment of negro troops at full rates of expense is, therefore, unwise as regards the prosecution of the war, and operates unjustly as to our citizen soldiery in service. In other words, it is dangerous, profligate, and unjust.

But limited space requires us to forego further examination of particular points of Administration policy, (however instructive and useful such examination might be,) and to confine ourselves to some general considerations which may be more briefly presented. And these will relate to the dangers which will threaten us (as results of Administration policy) during the war and afterwards.

Dangers in Connection with the War

Under this head may be mentioned the state of our

Finances and Currency

The unnecessary waste of the public resources in the war; the enormous sums expended upon foolish and fruitless military expeditions, (sometimes badly planned and sometimes badly executed and supported,) and the other enormous sums corruptly or unwisely expended in obtaining supplies and materials of war, would, of themselves, have been sufficient to deeply injure the public credit, and to create fears of our future ability to bear the pecuniary burdens created by the war. And what ought to sting the minds of reflecting men, is the consideration that the general political policy of the Administration has been such that it has prolonged the war by depriving us of allies and sympathy in the enemy's country, and frittered away the public energy upon other objects beside military success.

In addition to which stands forth the fact, that this occasion of war has been seized upon to establish a system of Government paper money, which has caused the public expenditures and the public debt to be one half greater than they would otherwise have been, and introduced numerous and most serious evils and dangers into all the channels of commercial and business life. The crash of this system, and the failure of all the delusive hopes and arrangements based upon it, is not merely a possible but a probable event in the future. The ruin and suffering which such an event would entail cannot be overstated, and to avert it, or to mitigate its force, is one of the main objects which should be had in view in settling our future policy. Upon questions of currency and finance, we must revert to the ideas of former times in which alone can safety be found.

In speaking of financial prospects and future pecuniary conditions, we do not overlook the fact that opinions very different from ours are expressed by the friends of power. But the appearances of prosperity to which they refer us, are delusive.

Production in the country is now decreased, for great numbers of laborers are employed in the war, and abstracted from industrial pursuits.

Increased rates of value press hardly upon persons of fixed incomes, and upon all who are disabled or engaged in unprofitable employments.

The war does not create wealth but consumes it, and consumes also the laborers by which it is produced. It devours the products of past and present industry, and checks the growth of population upon which future prosperity depends.

And the inevitable evils of a state of war—the injury and destruction of material interests, the waste, spoilation and improvidence that characterize it—are aggravated by profuse issues of Government paper money which incite to reckless expenditure, public and private, and disguise for the time the fearful consumption of wealth and the sure approach of a day of suffering and retribution.

This expenditure and the accumulation of debts, public and private, cannot go on indefinitely or for any considerable time. The day of payment, which will be also the day of trouble, will surely come. Great suffering will fall upon the people. Those who suppose themselves independent of the frowns of fortune, will realize the retribution which always follows upon excess, and even those wholly innocent of any complicity with financial mismanagement or other evil feature of public policy, will be smitten equally with the guilty.

The vast debt, created in great part by profligacy and mismanagement, is a source of profound anxiety to the people, who must pay it, and to the capitalists who hold it. Its obligation rests upon the security of the national ability and honor. But to prevent its growth beyond the point where bankruptcy threatens it with destruction, the folly and corruption which now waste and devour the wealth of the people must meet with speedy and condign overthrow.

Foreign Intervention

Another danger to be apprehended under our present rulers; one which has been speculated upon often since the war began, and which is possible hereafter, is the intervention of some foreign nation in the pending struggle. There is an example of such intervention in our history, which deserves contemplation by those who would justly judge our present situation, and make provision against future dangers. Our fathers revolted and were sorely chastised therefor by their monarch. The sword smote them in all their coasts; their wealth was dried up, their cities occupied by their foes, their land ravaged. They were pushed to the extremity of endurance; they became spent and exhausted by the conflict. But in their hour of extremest peril, France, at the instance of a Pennsylvania diplomatist, extended them her powerful assistance, and they emerged from the struggle triumphant and independent. Is this war to be mismanaged and perverted and protracted, until a foreign power may be induced to assist our antagonist, as France assisted the revolted colonies of the third George? Unquestionably the feeble, changeful, arbitrary and unwise policy of the Administration, begets this danger of intervention, and will produce it if it ever take place. Nor has its diplomacy abroad been calculated to avert the evil consequences of its action at home. That diplomacy has not been wise, judicious and manly, but feeble, pretentious, and offensive. It should therefore be one of the leading objects in selecting an Administration for the next four years, to avoid this danger of intervention by the selection of rulers who will not provoke it, and whose policy will command respect at home and abroad.

Dangers beyond the War

But other dangers menace us under Republican rule, even if success in the war be secured. And as these, in a still greater degree than those already mentioned, deserve careful and earnest attention, we proceed to state them distinctly.

Oppressive Government

If already we have experienced the arbitrary disposition and unlawful practices of our rulers, what may we not experience after some time has elapsed, and when military success has rendered them still more insolent? If their assaults upon law and upon right be so numerous and flagrant while they are subjected to opposition and struggling to maintain their position against an open foe, what may we not expect when all constraint upon them is removed? In considering what they have already done in opposition to liberty and lawful rule, we may exclaim, "If these things be done in the green tree, what shall be done in the dry?" Let no one be deceived by the assertion, that the arbitrary and evil acts of the Administration indicate but a temporary policy and are founded upon necessities which cannot long exist. Not only is the excuse that this policy of the Administration is necessary in view of the public interests, false in point of fact, it is equally untrue that if unopposed, if not put down, it will be of short duration and expire with the war. If it be necessary now to do unlawful things and trample upon individual rights in adhering communities, the same pretended necessity will exist hereafter. Will it not be as necessary to uphold arbitrary government in order to prevent renewed revolt, as it is to support arbitrary government in order to subdue existing rebellion? When did a ruler who had deprived his country of its liberties ever voluntarily restore them? That people who will accept excuses for tyranny, will always be abundantly supplied with them by their rulers, and especially will they be furnished with this argument of necessity which will expand itself to the utmost requirement of the despotic power under all circumstances.

Our ancestors who settled this country and established the Government of the United States, fortunately did not admit this doctrine of necessity, but proceeded, under the guidance of a most wise and just policy, to tie up the hands of official power by constitutional limitations, by checks and balances established in the very framework of Government, and by inculcating among the mass of the people, in whom was to be lodged the ultimate or sovereign power, a profound respect for all private rights and for the laws by which they are secured and vindicated; and we will do well to act upon their policy and follow in their footsteps. They trod the road of safety and made it plain before all succeeding generations, and we will be recreant to duty and false to our lineage, if we surrender the principles to which they held, or permit ourselves to be deluded by those arguments of power which they despised and rejected.

Success itself in the odious policy now urged by the Administration, of the subjugation of one-third or more of the States of the Union, were it possible, could be so only at the price of liberty of the whole country; for our system would not admit of military rule over them. Necessarily populations within them must conduct local governments, and exercise the proper portion of power pertaining to them in the Federal Government. In short, they could not be held as conquered Territories unless we should change our whole constitutional system and abandon altogether our experiment of freedom; and therefore the imperative necessity of changing the issue between the sections from one of conquest to one of restoration. Men must be chosen for public station who will know how to save a bleeding country what is left, and restore what is lost, by securing peace on constitutional and just terms.

CORRUPT GOVERNMENT

Another danger to be considered is, corrupt government, the necessary consequence of arbitrary principles practically applied in the affairs of the nation, or rather an accompanying principle. The vast increase of officers in all branches of the public service; the administration of a great public debt, including the management of a revenue system of gigantic proportions, will create numerous avenues of corruption, and when the Government is administered upon principles of coercion, it must necessarily subsidize large numbers of persons in order to maintain its authority. It is ever thus that strong governments, as they are called, must be corrupt ones, and the interests of the great mass of the people be sacrificed to the interests of classes or individuals. A truly free government, where the authority of the rulers is supported by the free and uncoerced action of the people; where the laws are kept in perfect good faith and individual rights perfectly respected, is the only one which can be pure.

INSECURITY

But, it is equally true, that a free government, not one free in form merely but in fact, is the most secure, both as regards danger from external force and from internal convulsion. If it be established for a people not base minded but civilized and honorable, it will impart to them enormous force for resisting foreign aggression, while it preserves them from internal revolt. Unquestionably, under ordinary conditions, that government is most secure which is most free. But in the hands of a sectional party, the future of this country is not secure. Not only is the danger of renewed revolt a possibility of the future, but the dangers of a foreign war are immensely increased. A disaffected population weakens the Government in resisting invasion, and if such disaffection be sectional, then the country has a weak part through which a foreign foe may strike its effectual and fearful blows.

Corruption of Race

A still more important consideration remains to be stated. We mean the social question—the question of the relations of race—with which our rulers are so little fitted to deal, and upon which such extreme, offensive and dangerous ownership are held by their prominent supporters. Whatever may be determined as to the negro race amongst us, it is manifest it is unfitted to participate in the exercise of political power, and that its incorporation, socially, and upon a principle of equality with the mass of our countrymen, constitutes a danger compared to which all other dangers are insignificant. We suppose the men who established suffrage in this country, and from time to time have subjected it to new regulation, proceeded upon the principle of vesting it in those who were fitted for its exercise. Political powers being in their nature conventional, it is proper that they be established upon a basis of utility and convenience, and in such manner that they will not be subjected to abuse. Pursuing the same line of action pursued by our fathers, suffrage is to be withheld from those members of the social body who are manifestly unfit to exercise it, and whose participation therein must necessarily lead to abuse. Manifestly, a race of mankind who cannot support free institutions, regular government, productive industry, and a high degree of civilization, of themselves, acting in an independent capacity, are unfit for performing the functions of freemen in conducting the business of government amongst us. The argument of equality of rights for all men fails in their case, because of the absence of the conditions upon which it is founded. In the organization of a State, it is perfectly manifest that the social body cannot be identical with the political; that vast numbers comprised within the former are not to be included in the latter. We do not, in this country, include females, minors, unnaturalized foreigners, particular criminals, nor the insane, among those who exercise the right of suffrage. Incapacity or unfitness exists, to a greater or less extent, with all these extensive divisions of human beings, and the same ground of exclusion precisely exists in the case of the negro or other inferior race, who may be casually or permanently placed amongst us. Chinese, Malays, and the uncivilized Indians, fall within the same principle of exclusion. There is no reason why any general incapacity or insufficient capacity for electoral action, should be ignored in the case of one of these classes and not in another. Our governments were established by white men and for white men and their posterity forever, and it is for the common advantage of all states and conditions of human beings, that the exclusion of the inferior races from suffrage should be permanently continued. Thus only can this great experiment of freedom begun by our ancestors and continued by us, be carried forward successfully, and be made to accomplish the great and beneficent results of which it is capable.

But the social aspect of this subject of the "relations of race," is equally important with the political, and intimately associated with it. It is of the highest policy, it is of the greatest necessity, that the races should be kept distant, socially; that they should not blend together to their mutual corruption and destruction. If an example were needed to admonish us upon this high point of policy, it would be furnished by the Spanish American Republics, who have run their troubled and inglorious career under our observation, and whose present condition may well awaken the pity or contempt of mankind. The Spaniard in the New World had not self-respect enough to keep himself uncontaminated from the Negro and the Indian, and he inflicted upon his colonies all the curses and horrors of hybridism, until their social state has become degraded and poisoned beyond apparent redemption. Throughout all those extensive countries brought under control by the arms or policy of the Spanish crown, and which within the present century and in imitation of our example, have assumed republican forms of government, this disregard of natural law, this ignoring of the differences of race, has been the prolific cause of the social and political evils which scourge and afflict those unhappy countries. Social vices prevail to a fearful extent; society is enfeebled and eaten out by them; there is no steady productive labor, no increase of population, no uniform and just administration of law, but constant revolutions and insecurity of all those rights which governments are established to protect and defend.

OPPOSITION TO BE ORGANIZED

In view of the foregoing considerations, and of many others which might be mentioned, an appeal for popular action against the evils of the time and the dangers which threaten us, must be thought timely and proper. The sure restoration of the Union and of a true administration of our system of constitutional government, await the success of a great opposition party actuated by just aims and inspired by an earnest, patriotic determination to save the country and perpetuate its liberties.

The idea of ignoring party in the accomplishment of great public objects, cannot be accounted one of wisdom. Great masses of men in a free country can act usefully and steadily only through some organism which combines their power and gives it direction. Without organization, their strength (all powerful when concentrated,) is dissipated and wasted, and the adventurous few seize upon the powers of government and pervert them to their own sinister designs.

No truth is more certain than this, that the destructive elements of society, (for instance fanaticism and rapacity by both of which we are now afflicted,) can be held in permanent check in a republic, only by uniting patriotic and just men against them in some enduring association, which shall act steadily and powerfully upon government and preserve it in its due course.

The problem for us now to solve is this: Are the people of the United States competent to organize themselves in defense of their system of free government and voluntary union, or must they resort to a dictator, armed with large powers, who will crush faction and restore peace and union at the sacrifice of liberty? Evil in the State will not die out, if left to itself. Some instrument adequate to its extirpation must be sought and found, in the direction of either dictatorial or popular power.

Instead of looking to a dictator, to the despotic principle, to a strong executive government of large and concentrated powers, those who have faith in our American principles will look to the people, and will seek to rouse and organize them and direct their united strength against the evils of the time. Thus we believe the nation may be saved, and saved by itself, and be prepared to resume its career of prosperity rudely interrupted by the war.

A great opposition party, made strong enough to carry the elections of 1864, is now the appropriate instrument for national redemption, and its success will be the triumph of free government and will extricate us from the jaws of destruction.

That the party of the Administration is both vicious and incapable, has been most abundantly proved and ought no longer to be denied. It has failed to restore the Union after three years of trial, though possessed of all the powers of Government and of all the resources of the country. And meantime it has struck heavy blows at liberty, and is carrying us away from all the old landmarks of policy and administration. We are literally drifting toward destruction, with the knowledge that those who have charge of our vessel of State are unfit to direct its course.

But there is yet time to avert much of calamity. The future at least may be made secure. To all who really desire the Union restored, and along with it honest, constitutional government, the appeal may now be made to assist in elevating a party to power which will be faithful to the Constitution, which will unite together the union elements of the whole country, will chastise corruption and fanaticism from the public Administration, and will secure the future from convulsion and despotism.

Let the fact sink deeply into the hearts of our countrymen, that the great obstacle to peace, to re-union, to integrity in public affairs, and to the renewal of prosperity, is the presence at the capital of the nation of the chiefs of a sectional party, who have been instrumental in plunging the nation into "a sea of troubles," and who are both incapable and unwilling to save it.

POLICY OF THE OPPOSITION

Having already spoken with just freedom of the Administration and of its policy and conduct, we proceed to indicate the position and views of the Opposition, who contend with the Administration for the possession of popular favor.

We hold that all laws duly established and existing shall be kept, and kept as well by persons in official station as by the mass of the people. Disregard of law and of rights established and guaranteed by it, is one of the great evils of which just complaint must now be made. A change of Administration and of party power, will secure throughout the whole country subject to our jurisdiction, a just, faithful, and uniform administration of the laws by the courts and by the President and his subordinates, and it will secure in the Congress of the United States, faithful obedience to the Constitution and an honest construction of the powers conferred by it upon the legislative authority. The interruption of justice caused by an unnecessary suspension of the *habeas corpus* in the unrevolted States will, forthwith terminate; arbitrary arrests of persons in civil life will become unknown, and a pretended necessity overriding justice and right, and made the pretext for various forms of oppression and injustice, will disappear before a returning sense of obligation and duty in our rulers.

In the policy of the Federal Government there will be no recognition of doctrines which tend to the social debasement and pollution of the people. The profligate and pernicious theories which, under the garb of philanthropy and a regard for human rights, would overthrow the natural barriers between different races and ignore wholly organic laws of difference between them, will not be promoted or favored in the policy of the Government of the United States.

There will be an earnest and proper effort made to retrace the steps already taken in debasing the currency of the United States by large and unnecessary issued of paper money; a system at once unauthorized and injurious, which impoverishes the country and distributes the earnings of labor to hands that have not earned it, will invite immediate revision and ultimate removal from the statute book of the United States.

The troops raised for the public service, whenever a necessity for raising them shall exist, will be rightfully obtained through the agency of the State Governments and be officered by State authority; thus securing, in the raising of armies for extraordinary occasions, the true intent and meaning of the Constitution, and preserving the armies of the United States from the undue political control of the Federal Executive.

The action of the Government in its financial disbursements and other features of its administration, will be thrown open to full investigation, and an earnest effort be made to purge it in all its branches of corruption.

Economy of outlay, so much spoken of by those who now hold power previous to their election and so little regarded by them since, will be reinstated in the practice of the Government as one of the essential rules of its action.

The doctrine that the States shall possess and exercise all ungranted powers, and shall be free within their jurisdiction from the encroachments of Federal authority, shall be rigidly maintained.

The system of public revenue shall be adjusted so as to bear equally upon all sections and interests, and the unnecessary increase of officers in collecting it, as well as in other departments of public service, shall be avoided.

The exertion of public force in the war to be exclusively for the object for which the war was begun, to wit: the restoration of the Union and the jurisdiction of our laws over the revolted country; and being confined to that object, and relieved from the incumbrance of other objects, to be brought to a speedy and honorable conclusion. But further, it may be confidently asserted, that an opposition triumph in our elections will call into existence moral forces more powerful even than physical force for securing peace upon the basis of re-union. And it may be the only means for securing that great object, hitherto unrealized, and postponed and prevented by the policy and incapacity of our rulers.

Beside the revision of our domestic policy and the restoration of constitutional principles therein, the great objects to which we look, are, the conclusion of the war and the just determination of the questions connected therewith. The burden of this contest has become intolerable. Patience has been exhibited by the people of the United States to the utmost extent of forbearance. They were told the war would last but sixty days; they were told the South was not united; they have been deluded throughout the contest, now more than three years in duration, by promises of speedy success; they have been told to trust and applaud military chieftains who were afterwards retired from service, and denounced and calumniated by those who had inculcated their praise; they have seen a variety of enterprises, both by land and water, miscarry outright, or fail in securing the objects for which they were undertaken; they have seen the prices of all the necessaries and comforts of life go up to enormous rates, beyond the ability of all who are not rich, or favored by Government patronage; they have undergone domestic bereavement and bitter sorrow in all their homes, from losses incurred in the war; they have been constantly supplied with false information about current events, and have still offered them promises of speedy and complete success quite unwarranted by the past achievements of their rulers, and which ignore all the real, indubitable difficulties, original and created, which attend the struggle. But one thing they have not been told—one great and important fact has not been disseminated under Government censorship, nor appeared anywhere in official documents—to wit, that success in the war and the speedy return of peace, have been all this time prevented, and will be hindered if not prevented hereafter, by the evil and odious policy and the incapacity of the Administration itself! These, have united the South; these, have nerved the arms of Southern soldiers in the field and inspirited them to united, earnest, determined resistance to our arms; these, in the darkest moments of the contest, have rendered their submission impossible. They, and the populations they represent, have seen before them the alternative of complete independence on the one hand, as the possible result to be achieved by valor, skill, and endurance, and on the other, as the result of submission, confiscation, emancipation, disgrace, and the iron rule of the conqueror; and viewing their position as presenting only a choice between these results, they have girded themselves up to herculean and desperate efforts and still stand defiant and unbroken.

It is not for us to, foretell the future, but it is possible to conceive its dangers and to make reasonable provision against them. Certainly, it is possible for the people of the United States, by selecting new rulers, to put their public affairs, including this business of the war, upon a new footing—to remove the main obstacle to peace and reunion, which has impeded their great efforts hitherto, and rendered their sufferings and sacrifices unavailing for the object for which they were incurred. That is the great and necessary work to be done by them in regaining the road of safety, and to its performance they are earnestly invited.

When the members of the present Administration are removed from power, and patriotic and just men are made to fill their places, the people of the adhering sections of the country will have done their part in removing the cause of war and the obstacle to peace, and will be represented by men competent alike to conduct war and to secure peace, who will call into existence, for the redemption and reunion of the country, moral influences more potent than physical force, and who will achieve their mission before exhaustion and intolerable suffering have been incurred.

RECONSTRUCTION

The propositions which should obtain in the reconstruction of the Union are not difficult of statement, and when contrasted with the policy of the Administration will appear to peculiar advantage.

The first is, that the States shall stand as before the war, except as to changes which may be agreed upon between or among them. The Constitution of the United States is the rightful and only bond of union for the States composing the Confederacy, and it is to stand as it is, in its full integrity, until the parties who are bound by it shall change its terms or add to it new provisions. Any other doctrine is revolutionary and destructive and to be utterly rejected, whether founded upon Presidential proclamations or statutes enacted by Congress. The powers of the Federal Government in all its branches are confined within the provisions of the Constitution and cannot transcend them. Therefore the Constitution as it is, including its power of regular amendment, is the leading doctrine of the great party which proposes to save the nation in this the day of its sore trial. Let the false and guilty doctrine that the President of the United States by proclamation, or the Congress thereof by statute, can prescribe, alter, add to or diminish the conditions of union between the States be discarded at once and forever, and most of the difficulties which appear to attend the question of reconstruction will wholly disappear. Those departments of the Government are confined to particular legislative and executive duties, and cannot touch or determine the relation of the States with each other. That field of power is sacred to the great organized communities by whom the Union was formed and by whom alone it can be subjected to modification or change. We have fought to restore the Union, not to change it, much less to subvert its fundamental principles, and the accomplishment of its restoration is the compensation we propose to ourselves for all the cost and sacrifices of the struggle.

But what is impossible to the President or to Congress it is competent for the States, in their sovereign capacity, by free mutual consent, at the proper time, to perform.

The American States required a compact of union to go through the war of the Revolution, and it was made. Subsequently they required an amended compact, creating a more intimate union, to secure to them the fruits of independence. From their deliberations on the latter occasion there resulted that most admirable instrument, the Constitution of the United States, under which the Republic has existed and prospered for more than seventy years. And now, under our experience of revolt and war and misgovernment, we may conclude that additional securities for liberty and Union should be established in the fundamental law. But these securities must consist of limitations rather than of extensions of Federal authority, and must not invade those fields of power which were left sacred to State jurisdiction in the original scheme of Union.

The Constitution should provide against the uncontrolled domination of sectional parties, South or North, in the Government of the United States, as the most indispensable and vital regulation possible for our safety and continued existence as a Republic. We refer upon this point to our remarks at the beginning of the present address, as exhibiting the grounds upon which this most important proposition may stand, and as illustrating its utility and necessity beyond all cavil or question. An adequate, real, and efficient check in Government, securing a balance of power between political interests, is unquestionably the highest and most important point in constitutional science; and it is most evident that because our system has been found defective in this particular, we are now involved in war and scourged by misgovernment in its most intolerable, odious and lawless forms. The checks already provided in our Constitution and which have been so salutary in their action and influence upon the Government, must be supplemented by some proper provision which shall more perfectly perform the office and function for which they were designed. For it is now proved amid the blood and tears of this nation, that all balance in our Government may be lost and all its checks be found insufficient to curb the insolence and guilt of faction and secure obedience to those fundamental principles of liberty, law, and right, which were established by our fathers. We are at war, and blood flows, and wealth is wasted, and fanaticism runs riot, and the Constitution is broken, and we are bowed down by bitter grief and sorrow in all our homes, because a sectional faction rules the Government of the United States, free from restraint, or curb, or limitation of its powers. And it should be made impossible that this condition of things can again exist, after we have once extricated ourselves from the grasp of calamity.

There should also be a judicious limitation upon the distribution of Federal patronage. The prodigious growth and present extent of that patronage in official appointments, constitutes a fertile source of corruption and danger. Nearly the whole mass of Federal appointments are poised every four years upon a presidential election, intensifying and debasing the struggle for power, and sowing the seeds of corruption broadcast throughout the land. Purity, economy and justice in government become almost impossible under this system, and their restoration and maintenance demand its amendment. A change by which the great body of public officers would hold for fixed terms, and be removable only for lawful cause, would be one of great men and wisdom, and is among the most desirable objects to be sought in our public policy.

AMNESTY

Another proposition pertaining to reconstruction is, that as to individuals there shall be amnesty except for particular offences. All the excesses of a state of war cannot be visited with judicial punishment. Both necessity and policy require that, at the conclusion of such a struggle, the mantle of oblivion shall cover the past. A nation torn by civil war demands repose at its conclusion, that society may be reorganized and that the passions and demoralization produced by war may disappear before the renewed action of moral forces. Laws of confiscation and treason may be politic and necessary to prevent insurrection or to check it in the outset, but they become inapplicable when revolt has ripened into public war, and one entire people are organized against another. Penal enactments when directed against a whole population are odious and useless, and their tendency is to prolong and intensify war, and to embarrass or prevent its just conclusion. Their office is to chastise individual offenders within Government jurisdiction, and not entire communities contending for independence or other public object. The laws of war necessarily and properly obtain between the parties to a war pending the contest, and displace or supersede those of municipal enactment. Amnesty therefore, within the limit of public safety, follows of course the termination of such a contest as that in which we are now engaged.

It may be added that clear justice requires that Unionists who have fled from the revolted country should be restored to their estates, and that the particular wrongs inflicted upon them should as far as possible be redressed.

A CONTRAST

We have thus taken notice of several questions connected with the subject of Reconstruction and indicated our views upon them. How much opposed those views are to the policy of the Administration will appear upon the most cursory examination. They point to the determination and settlement of disputes upon a just and reasonable basis, and to the security of the country against the recurrence of war hereafter; while the policy of the Administration points to a simple alternative between the subjugation and independence of the South. If we succeed in the war, we have a conquered country to hold and govern as we best may; and if we fail in the war, a rival and hostile power will be established beside us. The Administration has no instrument for national redemption except physical force, (which it has shown itself hitherto incompetent to wield,) and whether it succeed or fail, the future is encompassed with dangers. Representing radical and violent elements of population among us, its party interests require of it an uncompromising and hostile attitude not only towards the confederate government but to the whole Southern people. In fact, the President virtually announces to us in his bogus State proclamation, that he can trust no men in the South except under most stringent oaths of approval of his policy and within the direct military influence of the army. Under the present administration, therefore, each party to the war strives for a clean victory or an utter defeat, and no agreement between them except one of disunion is proposed or is possible. We submit to our countrymen that this statement of fact pronounces the utter condemnation of the Administration and establishes solidly the argument for its removal from power, and this, too, independent of the other considerations which we have presented. Impotent in war, incapable of securing a just and speedy peace, competent only to waste the blood and resources of the people, it stands as fully condemned in its policy against the enemy as it does in its measures of internal administration. And we are justified in concluding upon the whole case, that if the Union is to be restored, liberty preserved, and prosperity renewed in this country, those results must follow the defeat and rejection of the Administration by the American people.

THE DEFEAT OF MR. LINCOLN REMOVES THE MAIN OBSTACLE TO REUNION AND RESTORES AT ONCE THE JUST RULE OF THE CONSTITUTION OVER THE ADHERING STATES.

CONCLUSION

There are but two classes of men in this country who may rejoice in existing conditions: *First.* Those who make money out of the war, and *second,* those who desire to achieve emancipation by it. As to the former, their thirst for sudden wealth is gratified and it is not in their nature to regret deeply those calamities which fall upon their fellow-countrymen but from which they are exempted. And as to the radical abolitionist, his cup of enjoyment is almost full. He believes that emancipation will take place or the Union remain broken forever. Either result satisfies him profoundly and wholly, and no possible event during his existence can compete with either of these in merit and excellence.

But has not the country borne all it can reasonably bear, in fact much more than it can reasonably bear, for the gratification of these two classes of men, and shall not the Administration of the Government under favor of which they nestle in power and gratify their unholy greed and their detestable passions, be thrown out of power, thus relieving the country from this nightmare of corruption and fanaticism which is pressing out its very existence?

Short-sighted and passionate men rush on to accomplish an immediate object, unable to perceive the consequences which lie beyond the present moment, and unwilling to believe that new obstacles in their path of passion and vengeance will succeed to the existing ones. They vainly think that if slavery be struck down by force, regardless of law or civil obligation, and negro equality be established in its stead, no subject of difficulty, no cause of national peril, no "stone of stumbling" will remain in the path of our national progress. Vain delusion! Such expectations are proved to be false by a thousand examples in history. The source of danger is in these wild passions let loose in the land which will not regard civil obligations, and which in their headlong fury tread under foot both public law and individual right. We do not decry theory, but we assert that statesmanship is concerned mainly in the domain of the practical, and that in the present imperfect condition of human affairs it is obliged to modify general ideas and adapt them to existing conditions, which are infinitely diverse in different countries and at different times. And as all political powers are conventional, that is, established by express or implied consent, the validity of any political act must rest upon the ground that it is authorized. Some distinct authority for it must be shown, or we must determine against its existence. And to the existence of a free government, and to the harmony and prosperity of a country wherein it is established, there must be a profound and constant respect by rulers and by people for all those things which have been agreed upon or instituted in affairs of government, and there must be a careful repression of all the destructive forces by which the bands of society are loosened and license or abuse introduced into public or social action. Of destructive forces constituting capital causes of danger, corruption and fanaticism (before mentioned) must be ranked as chief; and are they not now both in existence, and conspicuous beyond any former example in these United States? Are they not predominant characteristics of the party which achieved success in 1860, and has since held and now holds possession of political power? And can there be hope of the future so long as these destructive principles run their course unrebuked and uncurbed? The sound elements of society must be brought to the surface, the body politic be purged of its unhealthy elements, and in places of public trust, just and broad-minded, pure and tolerant men be substituted for radicals and corruptionists. Then will the laws be kept; then will free individual action be permitted and permissible; crime only will be punished, and harmony and peaceful relations and widely-diffused prosperity succeed to violence, intolerance, waste, bloodshed, and debauchment of the national life!

C. R. BUCKALEW,
SAMUEL J. RANDALL,
JOHN D. STILES,
S. E. ANCONA,
MYER STROUSE,
PHILIP JOHNSON,
CHARLES DENISON,
WM. H. MILLER,
A. H. COFFROTH,
   Pennsylvania.

GEORGE H. PENDLETON,
J. F. McKINNEY,
F. C. LEBLOND,
CHILTON A. WHITE,
S. S. COX,
WILLIAM JOHNSTON,
WARREN P. NOBLE,
W. A. HUTCHINS,
WILLIAM E. FINCK,
JOHN O'NEILL,
GEORGE BLISS,
JAMES R. MORRIS,
J. W. WHITE,
   Ohio.

THOMAS A. HENDRICKS,
JOHN LAW,
JAMES A. CRAVENS,
JOSEPH K. EDGERTON,
JAMESF.McDOWELL,
   Indiana.

W. A. RICHARDSON,
C. M. HARRIS,
JOHN R. EDEN,
LEWIS W. ROSS,
A. L. KNAPP,
J. C. ROBINSON,
W. R. MORRISON,
WILLIAM J. ALLEN,
   Illinois.

CHARLES A. ELDRIDGE,
   Wisconsin.

L. W. POWELL,
GARRETT DAVIS,
   Kentucky.

JOHN S. CARLISLE,
   Virginia.

W. SAULSBURY,
GEORGE READ RIDDLE,
   Delaware.

A. J. ROGERS,
   New Jersey.

DANIEL MARCY,
   New Hampshire.

Washington, July 2, 1864.

[After the preparation of the foregoing Address, at the very conclusion of the session of Congress, two extraordinary measures relating to subjects treated in the Address, were enacted into laws. They were both approved by the President, on the 4th day of July, and fitly concluded the labors of the Congressional majority. Those measures were: 1*st*, a further supplement to the conscription law; and 2*nd*, a joint resolution imposing a special and *second* income-tax for the year 1863. The former was entitled "An act further to regulate and provide for the enrolling and calling out of the national forces, and for other purposes," and authorized the President, at his discretion, to call out troops for one, two, or three years; provided for bounties of one, two, or three hundred dollars to each recruit, according to the time of service, payable in three equal instalments; and authorized drafts for unfilled quotas after fifty days from the date of the call; but in case of any such draft no payment of money should be accepted or received by the Government as commutation to release any enrolled or drafted man from personal obligation to perform military service.

The third section reads as follows:

"Sec. 3. That it shall be lawful for the Executives of any of the States to send recruiting agents into any of the States declared to be in rebellion, except the States of Arkansas, Tennessee, and Louisiana, to recruit volunteers under any call under the provisions of this act, who shall be credited to the State, and to the respective subdivisions thereof, which may procure their enlistment."

The sixth section provides, that in drafts one hundred *per centum* of names more than the quota shall be drawn.

The eighth section reads as follows:

"Sec. 8. That all persons in the naval service of the United States who have entered said service during the present rebellion, who have not been credited to the quota of any town, district, ward, or State, by reason of their being in said service and not enrolled prior to February twenty-fourth, eighteen hundred and sixty-four, shall be enrolled and credited to the quota of the town, ward, district, or State in which they respectively reside, upon satisfactory proof of their residence made to the Secretary of War."

Such is the law which abolishes commutation, and provides a plan by which certain States may escape the pressure of a draft. They are to be authorized through their agents to obtain negroes in the southern country to fill up their quotas, (the bounties for this purpose being paid by the United States,) and in the commercial States all the sailors and marines who have entered the service since the outbreak of the rebellion, are to be enumerated and credited to the States of their residence, whether citizens or not. The States which are most enterprizing in the race for negro recruits, and have most facilities for obtaining them, will reap the main advantages of this arrangement. But the public interests will suffer, and States remote from the seaboard will be subjected to an unjust discrimination.

The vote in the Senate, July 2, upon adopting the report of the Committee of Conference, which gave this act its final form, was as follows:

"YEAS—Messrs. *Anthony,* Chandler, *Clark,* Conness, *Fessenden, Foot, Foster, Hale,* Lane of Kansas, Morgan, *Morrill,* Pomeroy, Ramsey, *Sumner,* Van Winkle, Wade, Wilkinson, and *Wilson*—18.

"NAYS—Messrs. Buckalew, Carlile, Davis, Doolittle, Harlan, Harris, Henderson, Hendricks, Howe, Lane of Indiana, McDougall, Powell, Riddle, Saulsbury, Sherman, Trumbill, and Willey—17."

It will be observed that one half the whole affirmative vote was from the States east of the Hudson.

But, to meet the expenditure for bounties under this law, the joint resolution before mentioned, imposing a special income tax, was passed. It provides that, upon the first day of October next, a tax of five *per centum* upon incomes of 1863 (in excess of $600) shall be assessed and paid. These incomes having been already subjected to a tax, this tax is a second imposition upon the same object for the same time, and swells the tax in most cases from three to eight per cent. The pressure of this measure upon persons of fixed incomes is severe, and it sets aside the doctrine that the same article or object shall be taxed but once by Government for a given period, its form and use remaining unchanged. Upon this ground, a tax upon liquors on hand (which had already been taxed) was voted down at the late session after prolonged debate.]

❧ 15 ❧

"Union" on Dis-Union Principles!
The Chicago Platform, McClellan's
Letter of Acceptance, and Pendleton's
Haskin Letter, Reviewed and Exposed.
A Speech Delivered by Abram Wakeman,
of New York, at Greenfield Hill,
Conn., Nov. 3, 1864 (New York, 1864)

ABRAM WAKEMAN (1824–1889), a former Whig legislator, then briefly a congressman in the 1850s and New York City postmaster during the Civil War, was one of thousands of minor Republican politicians who spoke at party rallies throughout the presidential election of 1864. His, and their, message, widely distributed in pamphlet form, was clear and direct: "Every other election has been trivial, compared with this," because the Democrats, since 1861, had either flirted with treason or fully engaged in it in their subversive antiwar activities, which were intended to destroy the Union. Whatever their deceptions (including the nomination of a general as their presidential candidate), the Democratic party's basic position had been set since the outset of the war. Its leaders called for compromise, negotiation and peace, but always in ways that favored the South and insured the permanent separation of the Union.

Mr. Wakeman was received with applause, and said:

LADIES AND GENTLEMEN: I thank you most heartily for your kind reception, and I think I can repay it best by proceeding at once to the subject I propose to take in hand. That will be to find out the real meaning of the

Chicago Platform, McClellan's Letter of Acceptance, and Pendleton's Haskin Letter.

The necessity of doing this appears from the

Importance of Political Parties.

We are told that in our country the people rule, but the more practical and important truth is that they rule only by political Parties. The *party* that has the majority at a Presidential Election governs for the next four years, and cannot be changed. In England the Executive is dependent upon the House of Commons, and must resign as soon as it looses its majority there. Our President is fixed in his term of office, and is independent of Congress—nay, unless it have a majority of two-thirds against him, he can control it by his veto. But there is one thing that he cannot control—one thing that dictates his measures, his appointments, and makes him all that he is—that is, his *political party.* Upon that he must rely or have no support at all.

The Nominee that kicks the Platform of his *Party* from under him must fall from want of support as soon as he reaches the realities of government; he cannot hold himself up by his own waist-band in politics any more than he could in the circus.

John Tyler, you remember, made the attempt, and it nearly convulsed the country in times of profound peace. Instead of being the powerful and respected "Tyler too" that he was when elected, his position became so ridiculous and impotent that it is certain he will never have an imitator.

We cannot but see, then, that the personal claims or merits of candidates, and our preferences for, or prejudices against them, are of little moment. Our country's fate depends upon the policy, principles and instincts of the *party* that will control it for the next four years. *It is our country's future and not men that we are electing!*

The Principles and Policy of the so-called Democratic Party were in grand National Convention, August 30, 1864, unanimously embodied in the Chicago Platform. Mr. Vallandigham was the active man of the Committee that framed it, and he it was who moved that Gen. McClellan be unanimously placed upon it as their and its candidate—to execute it if elected.

It is our duty, then, to scan this Platform closely. It was built by astute lawyers and politicians, who weighed and measured every word. It is the indictment of the Convention against President Lincoln's Administration. But above all, if adopted, it will be the future history of our country. It is the chart by which their party proposes to steer our noble old ship of State through the storms and breakers of civil war.

Let us, then, turn up each of its six planks and see if its timber will stand the fearful test.

The First Plank Is This:

Resolved, That in the future, as in the past, we will adhere with unswerving fidelity to *the Union under the Constitution,* . . . as the only solid foundation of our strength, security, and happiness as a people, and as a *framework of government* equally conducive to the welfare and prosperity *of all the States, both Northern and Southern.*

If they have the same understanding of words that the loyal people and democracy have, there would seem to be nothing objectionable in this plank. But notice, they only say, "*we will adhere.*" The Southern half of the so-called Democratic prty refused to "adhere." Does the portion of the party now in the loyal States propose to compel them to submit to the constitution as it is?

The history of the plank throws light on this question. It was offered in their full Convention by Ex-Gov. Washington Hunt, of this State, an old line whig, who it seems was there playing the part of the goose among cranes, and very soon was he stripped of his patriotic feathers. As he offered the resolution it read, "Union *and* Constitution *and insist on maintaining the national unity,*" &c. The resolution with these invaluable words in it was referred to the Committee on the Platform. Neither grammar nor style required these words to be changed, but the word "*and*" was changed to "*under,*" and the whole clause "*insisting upon maintaining the national unity,*" was stricken out and *THEN* it was adopted by the Convention and is their first plank.

Why was this patriotic clause stricken out? The "*national unity*" is the very point at issue between us and Rebels in arms. These Rebels are principally Southern Democrats, who refused to "adhere" to the Constitution, and are now making desperate efforts to destroy it by arms. Why is it that their old political associates refuse to insist upon maintaining the national unity?

Do not these people propose to sit still and "adhere with unswerving fidelity" to the ship that floats them, while rebel pirates scuttle and send her adrift?

Why, then, do the Convention use the word "adhere," why change "Union *and* the Constitution" to "Union *under* the Constitution"—why speak of

"the welfare and prosperity of all *the States,* both Northern and Southern?"—
why *strike out* the clause to "maintain the national unity?

It is because they have adopted the rebel theory of the constitution! What that is
will appear from a moment's glance at

The True Theory of Our Government.

The old and true doctrine was and is, that the Constitution of the United
States is the CHARTER by which THE PEOPLE formed and ordained a
National Government, to which, every man, woman and child owes allegiance. That the laws and treaties made in pursuance thereof are paramount
to, and above, all state constitutions and laws. This national Constitution
binds together indissolubly the people individually, and also the states, *both
having joined to form it and give it life.* No individual, nor state, nor number
of individuals, acting as a state legislature or convention can break the governmental bond thus entered into, or absolve the allegiance of any person or
state from this national government—called the "United States of America."
The States exercise all the functions of government not provided for in the
Constitution, particularly functions relating to local or domestic affairs.

The President is required by his oath of office to protect and defend the
Constitution of the United States. He has under him for this purpose an
army and navy, and is expressly empowered to put down insurrections and
rebellions.

This national government is Republican in form, and by the Constitution
is made to guarantee a Republican form of government to each state; and in
time of peace, to protect every individual in his life, liberty and property,
except when arrested for crime.

This is the most perfect government the human race has ever yet achieved.
It rests on three firm pillars.

1. DEMOCRACY, securing individual liberty and equality before the
   law.
2. REPUBLICANISM, by which the citizens frame and administer their
   own government and laws in state and nation.
3. A National Government *of unity and strength,* protecting the liberty and democracy of the people and guaranteeing the Republicanism
   of the states, against foreign nations and rebels and traitors at home.

History shows us governments, in all ages, resting upon one or the other of these pillars, but never before were they made to stand *together* as the supports of one *Grand Republic* securing individual liberty—a government by the people, and a *Union* of national power superior to the mightiest monarchy. But this is not all. It is capable of unlimited extension. Its states controlling local affairs, and the national government binding them and their people into *one nation*—the more it includes, the stronger it is. Unlike the Roman empire, it may be safely extended—by annexation of states, without breaking, until it includes all the people of this continent, and perhaps, in future ages, all the people of the whole world!

Time reserved the founding of this magnificent structure for a new hemisphere, and a people selected from all nations.

God grant that the crime of letting it fall to pieces may not rest upon us!

The Rebel or Chicago Theory of Our Government

is told in a few words.

The southern colonies, unlike the northern, were settled by aristocrats, adventurers and convicts. Neither of these classes would work if they could help it. Those that could, therefore, procured slaves. As the country grew, slavery grew, and those who held slaves became the aristocrats. The first result was that all true democracy, all free labor, all equality among the people vanished. The states then changed from republics to oligarchies, controlled by slave-owners. The non-slaveholders being the dependents of, and voters for, the oligarchs.

Thus democracy and republicanism were destroyed. The next attack was upon the "*national unity.*" They controlled the slave states. States rights were, therefore, the only political power they could make the basis of their movement. Calhoun was their leader. Seizing upon some loose expressions in the Virginia and Kentucky resolutions of 1798, and wresting them from the meaning affixed to them by Madison, their author, Calhoun asserted *that the States* still remained *sovereign* and *independent.* That the constitution was only a compact or treaty between them, by which they delegated certain duties to a general government, which was the creature and agent of the states, and from which they might secede at will.

The States thus *formed* a "Union *under* the Constitution." They denied that *the people* by *the Constitution* formed "the Union" as a national government; binding alike on the people and the states.

The slavery-based aristocracy made their first attack under this theory in South Carolina, in 1833, under Calhoun, for the purpose of nullifying the tariff.

President Jackson expressed his determination to hang Calhoun upon the first overt act. Would that he had! Who can estimate the blood, the suffering, and treasure it would have saved us?

Henry Clay, unfortunately, stepped in with a compromise, and the glorious opportunity of crushing the monster *Secession* in its infancy was lost. Both Jackson and Webster regretted that the power of the government was not then brought to a test and vindicated. The conspirator Calhoun was baffled, not defeated. He and the Southern aristocracy commenced to educate the Southern youth and the Democratic party of the whole Union. He was successful at the South and partially so at the North. The changes were rung first on the RESOLUTION OF '98, then on STATE RIGHTS, then on STATE SOVEREIGNTY, then on the RIGHT OF SECESSION, until the pillar of NATIONAL UNITY was undermined and ready to fall. His political descendants at the Charleston Convention purposely broke up the Democratic party, in order that a pretext might be had in the election of President Lincoln, and then the rebellion threw off disguise and took up arms.

Now, when you see men decline to pledge themselves "to maintain the National unity," and hear them talk of "adhering" to a "Union *under* the Constitution," and when they say nothing about our national glory and prosperity, but are careful and jealous of the "welfare of the States Northern and Southern." You may judge at once by these stray feathers what bird they follow. You may be sure it is not our National American Eagle, but that low nauseous Southern turkey buzzard Secession. Not insist upon the national unity! Ah, my friends, this first plank won't do. It is fatally defective—dry-rotted to the very centre!

Put this plank beside the first plank of the Baltimore Platform on which Abraham Lincoln stands firm and square, and mark the contrast!

Resolved, That it is the highest duty of every American citizen to maintain, against all their enemies, the integrity of the Union, and the paramount authority of the Constitution and laws of the United States; and that laying aside all differences of political opinion, *we pledge ourselves as Union men, animated by a common sentiment, and aiming at a common object, to do everything in our power to aid the Government in quelling,* BY FORCE OF ARMS, *the rebellion now raging against its authority,* and in bringing to the punishment due to their crimes the rebels and traitors arrayed against it.

This is like a breath of pure air; it needs no praise. Every patriot feels at the first touch of his knuckle that this plank is sound. He knows that the future of our Government built with such timber will stand the test of war and time.

THE SECOND PLANK OF THE CHICAGO STRUCTURE IS THIS:

Resolved, That this Convention *does explicitly declare,* as the sense of the American people, that, *after four years of failure to restore the Union by the experiment of war,* during which, under the pretense of a military necessity or war power higher than the Constitution, the Constitution itself has been disregarded in every part, and public liberty and private right alike trodden down, and the material prosperity of the country essentially impaired, *justice, humanity, liberty, and the public welfare, demand that* IMMEDIATE EFFORTS BE MADE FOR A CESSATION OF HOSTILITIES, with a view to an ULTIMATE Convention of all the States, or other *peaceable* means, to the end that at the EARLIEST PRACTICABLE MOMENT PEACE MAY BE RESTORED ON THE BASIS OF THE FEDERAL UNION OF THE STATES.

This resolution was written by the hand of Vallandigham himself, and in style and substance it is singularly worthy of its author.

Every patriot feels uneasy about it.

1. Notice, that this *whole* resolution is declared "*explicitly*" to be "*the sense of the American People.*" You may say the three tailors of Tooley street did no harm, and this is innocent enough. Not so. If the American people adopt this platform "as their sense" by electing the candidates placed upon it, it then becomes their will, and must and will control the next Administration. That is the *catch* in these words. Adopt them, and the copperhead sends his fangs into the vitals of the Nation, and it never can recover from his poison.

2. But look further, it says—"*after four years of failure.*" False to begin with! The war has not yet lasted but three years and six months. The rebels began the war by firing on Fort Sumter, April 13, 1861, and President Lincoln called for 75,000 men a few days after. What reason had that Convention to say—as the sense of the American people, that there will be a failure for four years, viz., until April 13, 1865?

The American people believe nothing of the kind. It is their "sense," hope and will, that the war will by that time have ended the Confederacy. The American people will never understandingly resolve, that their armies have failed for four years—certainly not until the four years are up!

3. But has the war failed? Its object was to compel the rebels to submit to the Constitution and laws, and to recover the territory possessed by them.

It was a gigantic undertaking. Our enemies in Europe said at once the task was beyond our strength, and exulted in the fall of the great Republic. But the American people rose to the height of the mighty argument. If they succeed in four years, as I believe they will, it will be the most glorious and successful war history has yet recorded.

Why, when the rebels began the war they held everything south of the Ohio River and the Pennsylvania line, except the City of Washington,—and that city their Secretary of War declared they would take within three months. They held the State of Missouri, running up far north of the Ohio line, and the whole of the vast territory south of the line of Kansas. *Where are they now?* They have lost the States of Maryland, Kentucky, Tennessee, Missouri, Arkansas, Louisiana, Mississippi, more than half of Alabama and Georgia, all the Territories, and the last ghost of a chance of ever taking Washington!

When the rebels began the war they had seized and captured, by treachery, every fort and military post along their Atlantic seaboard, except Fortress Monroe; every one on the Gulf of Mexico, and all on the Mississippi River. Our army and navy have taken from them every one of these forts except those that protect Charleston harbor, and every seaport except that and Wilmington. *Does that look like* "FAILURE!"

When they began the war they had 1,063,850 square miles of our territory in their possession; now they have only 345,666. Then they numbered 12,121,314 of inhabitants; now they number only 4,553,241. Then they counted four millions of slaves within their dominions. Our armies have set free, or withdrawn from their control, at least half this number, and have shaken the accursed institution to its very foundation. *Does this look like* "FAILURE?"

They began the war with a million of fighting men—slaves tilling their fields, and allowing all their able-bodied whites to rally around the rebel standard. They had splendid officers, educated at our expense, troops thoroughly drilled in preparation for this rebellion, arms and munitions of war stolen from our arsenals, navy yards treacherously seized from us in which to fit out pirate craft to prey upon our commerce, the aid and comfort of foreign nations, and everything needed to enable and encourage them to wage a long, costly and bloody war. We have destroyed nearly every one of their armies, used up the whole of their available fighting material, exhausted their supplies of arms and of food, captured their guns, destroyed their privateers, seized their fortifications, driven them back upon the Gulf, and brought them at last to the very verge of military annihilation. *Does this look like* "FAILURE?"

4. The convention next try to make the American people declare the war an "EXPERIMENT." Not so at all. The rebels were in arms, and arms were the only means God and Nature had left us wherewith to save our country and government from total destruction, and the constitution prescribed their use. The only other "experiment" was, to have permitted Jefferson Davis to have taken Washington and installed himself there. In other words, to have allowed our constitutionally elected President to be ejected by a Usurper, and to have submitted to an armed despotism for the sake of peace.

5. The convention next say, the "experiment of war" as "to *restore* the Union." Not so. The UNION, meaning the Government of the United States, has never been destroyed; and it is the "sense of the American people" that it never shall be.

But if the Union is a mere compact or league of States, by the secession of one State, its destruction is an accomplished fact—the Union is dead and gone. That is the reason they say "restore." That is the reason copperheads say "war is disunion." You can't coax States back by war, AND THEREFORE IT MUST ALWAYS BE A FAILURE AS A MEANS OF "RESTORING" THE UNION, AND SHOULD BE STOPPED AT ONCE. There is under this Calhoun-theory no power to coerce a State. The Union is at the mercy of their choice to return.

No defeat of the national arms could so thoroughly destroy the national Union as the adoption of this sentiment by our people. Fair words are deceivingly used to obtain this fatal result.

With the same meaning they next arraign the Administration as having "*disregarded the Constitution in every part*" by exercise of the war power. This is a kind of stump speech injected into the belly of this Resolution, and I shall refer to it under the 4th Resolution, where it belongs. Benton says, President Jackson vetoed more than one bill for "*amphibology.*" It is evident enough the so-called Democracy that adopted this Resolution did not take their lesson from old Hickory either in style or patriotism.

6. They next declare as the sense of the American people "that *justice, humanity, liberty and the public welfare demand that immediate efforts be made for a cessation of hostilities,*" *with a view to an ultimate convention of all the States,* or *other* PEACEABLE *means,* to the end that at the earliest practicable moment, peace may be restored *on the basis* of the *Federal* union of the *States.*"

Mark well, this is the *only* thing in their whole platform that the Convention order their party and candidates TO DO. The rest of their Resolutions contain only sentiment, doctrine, complaints and advice—cheap material and of no practical importance.

If the American people adopt this as their sense by electing the candidates of this convention, they are on the 4th of March next, or soon thereafter, to ask Jefferson Davis for a "cessation of hostilities," which, of course, must be by armistice, or a total abandonment of the war at once.

Mr. Davis may find it convenient to run the blockade by that time, but if he can be found this side of the Rio Grande, he will grant the request at once. Like every wrong-doer he says, he only wants "to be let alone"—a cessation of hostilities is just what he wants. They evidently inconvenience him beyond all measure. Let us follow out the programme.

Time must be taken then to suspend hostilities, to convene Congress, to "*ultimately*" call a Constitutional Convention, to get it ratified by the people of two-thirds of the States, to get delegates elected, to coax Mr. Davis and his friends to attend, which they never will do, unless the doctrine of State sovereignty is conceded to them. And *then,* suppose they should be outvoted! They certainly would be. Would they submit? Not at all. That is what they took up arms about in the first instance, and, by conceding State sovereignty, we relinquish the right to subdue them. But if we did not, they would then be in fighting trim again on the same question. His confederacy would be recognized by foreign powers and our blockade gone. His cotton would be converted into British gold and ammunition. His recruited army would crush out all unionism in the South. A new crop would be on his hands. His defiance, stimulated by our cowardice, would know no bounds. He would strike out clauses about "national unity" quicker than the Chicago convention. "The best he could do for us" would be, to resolve our national government into a confederacy *under* the State sovereignty, Montgomery version of the Constitution!

You have the traitor now by the throat, and at the last gasp. If you loosen your hand and let him get his wind again, you are conquered!

The whole scheme of coaxing the rebels into a Constitutional Convention, in order to *whip them,* is impracticable. They will never come except to win—failing in that, they have us at their mercy.

7. But if the rebels refuse to come into this Constitutional Convention, or bolt from it, what are we to do? The Convention leaves us in no doubt—we must submit, *surrender!* The cessation of hostilities is to be continued with a view to "other PEACEABLE means." The word "*peaceable*" was used to preclude the idea of *warlike* means being resorted to in any case.

The restriction was purposely made; the *Daily News* of this city shows this, by some revelations of the labors of the committee room in Chicago. It says:

We especially italicise the word *"peaceable,"* because it is the key to the whole purport and purpose of the resolution, and because it excludes all possible honest belief that the convention meant to countenance further resort to any means, of any sort, which should not be peaceable. Nay more—we assert, as part of the history of the platform, that the resolution, as originally presented, did not contain the word "peaceable," which was introduced in committee, upon the special motion of ex-Governor Pratt of Maryland—an uncompromising peace man—and upon the explicit ground, as stated by that gentleman when he proposed it, that in its absence war might possibly be considered as among the "other means" intended to be suggested. The word "peaceable" was introduced then to exclude a conclusion in favor of war, in any contingency, and the signification of the whole phrase, as modified and adopted, is so plain to that effect, that no intelligent man in the convention could have understood it in any other sense.

You say can this be true? That they mean by this, to obtain a peace by surrender at discretion to the rebels? The words do mean that and nothing else. The best expounder of the Resolution should be its author, and what does Mr. Vallandigham say of it. Commenting on this second resolution, in a speech at Dayton, shortly after the adjournment of the Chicago Convention, he said:

It declared as its grand purpose, not to be surrendered, the reconstruction of the Union—the *federal* Union of the States—pointing out the stopping of the war and a convention of the States as the constitutional, lawful, necessary and proper means of accomplishing the work, and it went not beyond. What should be necessary hereafter; what our duty shall be in one, two or three years, Time will be our grand instructor, and he teaches wisely and well. They who are in public life then, filling the high places of responsibility and trust, will discharge their duty, and you will demand of them that which they shall do— always having in view never to surrender that one great object, the reconstruction of the *federal* Union—*not territorial unity,* a unit of despotism—but the *old* federal Union, a union founded on the principles of *federation and compact between sovereign and independent States,* delegating certain powers to their common agent, and withholding from it those not delegated. * * * * * But that *great doctrine of State rights is implied in the living words inserted in the last clause of the resolutions relating to peace on the basis of the* FEDERAL *Union, as distinguished from* ANY OTHER *union or any community.*

These last enlightening remarks of Mr. Vallandigham prove what is meant by the last clause of the resolution—*"that peace may be restored on the basis of the* FEDERAL *Union of the States."* It is plain, these people have no idea of preserving the National *Government* of the United States. Their "Union" is to be a mere confederation like the one that existed before our present Constitution was adopted. They are, State right, sovereign State, secession men of the Calhoun Jefferson Davis doctrine, that a State can vote itself out of the Union, and the General Government being a mere creature of the States, has no right to coerce it or its people. It can only coax it and them back again. The result of this doctrine is, that the war is unconstitutional and wrong—a wicked usurpation! That was not the doctrine of Washington, Jackson and Webster, and if the American people adopt it "as their sense" the Nation is gone! This resolution is so worded that the people are made, if they adopt it, to vote the law of the case to be just as Jeff. Davis claims it to be. It fully justifies him and all the rebellion. President Lincoln is a usurper and Gens. Grant and Sherman are trespassers and murderers, if that is the law. Yet this is their chart for the future of our country—all they propose *to do.* It is ignominious surrender, pure and simple. It is *National suicide!*

8. But why should there be a

Cessation of Hostilities?

What reasons do they assign for this wonderfully strange course? What requires or *compels* us to abandon our national unity—and break up the Union and Government of our fathers?

1. *Justice,* they say, demands it. Why? Is it *justice* to our fathers, who gave their lives or endured all the horrors of war to gain this goodly heritage for us, that we should basely abandon it to rebels.

Is it *just* to our noble brothers, who have fallen and suffered in this war, that we tell them, "You have bled and suffered for nothing—we commenced the war wrongfully, in a freak of passion; but on reflection we don't think our country worth preserving. 'It is the sense of the American people,' *now,* that they ought to use only "peaceable means," and let the rebels grant us such a country as they choose."

Is it *just* to those now living, that we should let the only great republic of the world fall to pieces? It has fostered and secured our prosperity—it is the protector of us and ours—the land of promise and hope to the poor and oppressed in every part of the world.

Is it *just* to those who will come after us? We live for our children. Through the dim future they call to us not to let their patrimony be lost by our cowardice, not to leave them the legacy of a broken government—a mass of petty, discordant, and belligerent states. No! whether we look to the past, present, or future, *justice forbids* us to abandon this war and claims it as her own.

2. Ah! but say they "*humanity and liberty*" demand it. Is it not evident by

immigration, if nothing else, that the people or every land look to our *government* as the home and guardian of humanity and liberty? Every fibre of strength that is taken from our national government weakens the cause of humanity and liberty the world over.

We know well enough that the trouble with these people is, that liberty and humanity are being specially vindicated in this war. As slavery had formerly rooted out true democracy and republicanism at the south, so it stood out as the *Soul* and *Strength* of the rebellion.

SLAVERY.

If fifty years ago the Constitutional right of a free press and free speech had been allowed the Abolitionists and Emancipationists in the Southern States, they would have organized a free society there, and by moral influences have removed the cause of the rebellion and saved us this desolating war. The Constitution framed to perpetuate *liberty* was shamefully disregarded in order to protect *slavery* from the moral influences of the age. The Abolitionists and Emancipationists were banished to the north, and there sat in "constitutional bonds," uttering Cassandra prophecies from year to year until our fate overtook us. Many of our people had so long worshipped the "black serpent" that they scarcely knew any other God. But the triumph of "liberty, justice and humanity" was nigh. We had refused them when they plead with us from year to year as angels of peace; they came to conquer at last in the terrors of civil war. The army; the people, saw that it was necessary this monster should die, that the nation might live. The President saw that the military necessity of emancipation made it his Constitutional duty—and the deed was done. Since that emancipation proclamation, and by aid of it, our victories have been won.

Now think that these Chicago people mean.

By this war some two millions of poor slaves have struggled into liberty and the hope of enlightenment; and some 200,000 of them are helping to fight our battles in our places. What a beautiful offering to *justice, humanity and liberty* it will be to hand them back to the "tender mercies" of their traitor masters and the "blessings" of slavery? Never fear, the human soul is not mean enough for that!

3. But they insist the "public welfare" demands it; and they say, "the material prosperity of the country is essentially impaired."

This is an appeal to our interest. We are asked to give up our country because it will cost us too much to insist upon its unity.

The answer to this is, we cannot pay more than it is worth as long as we have anything to pay with.

THE STRENGTH AND WEALTH

Of our nation consists of its people and property. Let us see if they are exhausted.

Of course I can only give results here which I, and others, have tested and found to be correct. I confess I had little idea of the immense strength and wealth of our country, until I began to calculate it.

In July, 1864, our public debt was $1,750,000,000 The population of the loyal states 24,900,000. This gives but $72.92 debt to each person, and the interest on the whole of this debt would be at 5½ per cent. $96,000,000, which would give the interest each person has to pay of $3.90. This is too high, for there are $500,000,000 of the public debt on which no interest is paid, it being in the shape of stamps and currency.

This, then, is our debt.

Now what have we to pay with? The value of the real and personal property of the loyal states, July 1, 1861, is correctly estimated at $15,300,000,000, divide this by our population, 24,500,000, and it gives $614.95 to each person; on which the interest at 6 per cent is $36.86.

It is clear enough we are in a solvent condition yet.

But it is urged the increase of the debt and interest on it, if the war goes on, will overwhelm us.

Let us see which grows the fastest, our debt or our resources.

From carefully prepared statistics it appears that while the population of the whole United States from 1850 to 1860 increased from 23,191,876 to 31,500,000, or 35.5 per cent. Our property increased from $7,135,780,000 to $16,159,000,000 or 126.45 per cent.

This is the most extraordinary growth ever made by any nation in the world. It is almost startling! Why Great Britain in those ten years increased her population only 1 per cent, and her property only 33 per cent.

Let us assume the war will end by defeat of the rebels in 1865, leaving a debt of $3000,000,000, we will then have the whole country under our government. But we will suppose that the check by the war, or other causes, to the increase of population and property, will reduce the ratio to 30 per cent, on the population, and 100 per cent, on the property for each ten years in the future, though this is too large a reduction by half. Commencing then with

1865 at those rates, we see by the following table how our debt would disappear during this century by the INCREASE of our wealth alone.

COMPARATIVE INCREASE OF WEALTH AND DEBT.

Years.	Population.	National Wealth.	Average Property to each Person.	Average [Debt assumed at $3000,000,000] for each Person.	Annual Interest for each person	Percentage of Debt to Property.
1860	31,500,000	$16,159,000,000	$510.00			
1865	34,000,000	21,574,000,000	634.52	$82.35	$5.35	
1870	40,950,000	32,318,000,000	789.00	73.26	4.38	9.28
1880	53,235,000	64,236,000,000	1214.00	56.35	3.38	4.64
1890	69,205,500	129,272,000,000	1878.00	43.43	2.60—	2.32
1900	89,964,150	258,514,000,000	2873.00	33.34	2.00	1.16

The burden of a national debt decreases just in proposition to the increase of national wealth. We have only to look after the interest, and our children can pay the principal without feeling it. The percentage of debt to property tells the story. This is seen in the last column.

This is the reason that Great Britain has so easily carried her national debt. In her case in 1816, after crushing Napoleon, her debt was 37½ per cent. on her property, but in 1858 her debt was only 13.4 per cent. on her property. Of course she was solvent and flourishing. With us the strength to bear grows faster than the burden, even in time of war—immensely faster will it grow, when peace comes with a vindicated government!

This seems like a fairy tale; can it be true?

Think a moment of the natural increase of our population every year, of the immense immigration, which will this year equal to 300,000. Think of the sources of increase of wealth; of agriculture carried over a whole continent by *free labor;* of mining of the precious and useful metals; of coal and petroleum; of labor-saving machinery, of which that of Massachusetts alone equals 100,000,000 of men; of the public lands; of commerce, shipping and fisheries, and the almost innumerable branches of industry and profit connected with each of these—think of these, stimulated by an immensely augmented population of free men, and improved upon by the progress of science and art, and who will say that our figures will not be true? They do not lie. This is no dream, but a firmly based and ever-growing reality of strength and grandeur that leaves all past achievements of our race behind as trivial and insignificant. But if we fail now—the national unity—the one condition necessary to the realization of this glorious future will be gone! The discordant States must pursue the arts of war instead of peace. The spring of the national intellect and enterprise will be limited by State lines and restrictions, and dwarfed by defeat. Foreign immigration must fall off when we can no longer protect the asylum it seeks, and when national enterprise ceases to reward industry. Despots will then point to America as to Greece, and say "Her patriotism failed to sustain her NATIONAL UNITY, and in the New World as in the Old, the cradle of liberty became its grave!"

No! Even if we owed all this debt to foreign nations, the "public welfare" requires us to pay it thrice over rather than abandon our national unity or surrender it to armed rebellion. But

To Whom Do We Owe This Debt?

NOT ABROAD, BUT TO OURSELVES! That debt is no burden, because the country is rich enough to pay it, and we get the interest as long as we hold it—*the debt is really individual property.* Throughout the country we have paid off our individual debts and taken the debt of the government to us. We have very generally ceased to be debtors and have become creditors of our government. If the government is sustained and vindicated, this credit is wealth. But if the government is abandoned, it is repudiation and dead loss! Does public welfare require us to make this sacrifice in order to lose our country?

Again Mr. Davis will certainly submit to no "*peaceable* means" of restoring peace that does not pay the rebel home and foreign debt, in case ours is paid. There is no mistake about this. Even his friends at the north, when they speak of compromise always include the payment or consolidation of the debt of both parties. We are to lose our cause,—our country, and pay the costs of both parties, in order to "secure the public welfare." Would it not be infinitely cheaper then, to continue the war till our debt was doubled before surrender?

Yes. Our country is still rich in men and means, and is growing richer almost beyond calculation. Courage, confidence, and unity of sentiment in using the immense resources we have, is all we need. Some people talk as though we had our last man in the field,—our last dollar in the treasury. Not so. We have not yet put forth half our strength. And what we are to purchase by this outlay is beyond any calculable price. Take the loans of your government then, freely. She will pay. When final victory touches her banners—

every one of her notes will command a premium over gold. Patriotism is a safe bank. Next to your God you may trust your Country with all you have.

Thank God and take courage! We can never purchase "public welfare" nor' 'material prosperity" by selling our country.

Now—look at the counterparts of this second Resolution as they stand in the Baltimore Platform.

> *Resolved,* That we approve the determination of the Government of the United States, *not to compromise with rebels,* nor to offer any terms of peace except such as may be based upon an unconditional surrender of their hostility, and a return to their just allegiance to the Constitution and laws of the United States, and that we call upon the Government to maintain this position and to *prosecute the war with the utmost possible vigor* to the complete suppression of the rebellion. in full reliance upon the self-sacrifice, the patriotism, the heroic valor, and the undying devotion of the American people to their country and its free institutions.
>
> *Resolved,* that the national faith, pledged for the redemption of the public debt, must be keep inviolate; and that for this purpose we recommend economy and rigid responsibility in the public expenditures, and a vigorous and just system of taxation, and that it is the duty of every loyal State to sustain the credit and promote the use of the national currency.

These ARE the "sense of the American people;" they mean peace and the Union by victory, not peace and *some* Union by surrender.

THE THIRD CHICAGO PLANK IS THIS:

> *Resolved,* That the direct interference of the military authorities of the United States in the recent elections held in Kentucky, Maryland, Missouri and Delaware was a shameful violation of the Constitution, and the repetition of such acts in the approaching election will be held as revolutionary, and *resisted with all means and power under our control.*

The interference complained of was guarding the polls, so that they could not be broken up by armed rebels, and in administering the oath of allegiance, so that rebels might not outvote loyal men.

This was all that was done. If it has not been done Jeff Davis would have carried every one of those states by marching his soldiers up to the ballot boxes. *That would have been far more easy and effective for him than fighting!*

The purity of the ballot box, the very first *democratic* principle, required that armed rebels should be kept away by "direct military interference," and traitors by the oath of allegiance. What Jackson Democrat would object to that, or would fail to charge it as the highest crime on the Administration, if it neglected this duty? But these Calhoun men—democrats so-called—think it a plain violation of state rights and the constitution. Of course if the constitution is, as they believe it, merely a compact of confederation, the exercise of military power to maintain the "national unity" is a criminal usurpation. But the most singular part of this resolution is the last clause. Such interference, they say, "*will be resisted with all means and power in our control.*" In the proceedings of this convention we find the following:

Mr. Wickliff, of Kentucky, then rose and said that the delegates from the West were of the opinion that circumstances may occur between now and the 4th of March next of the Democracy of the country to meet in convention again. He therefore moved the following resolution, which was *unanimously* adopted.

> *Resolved,* That this Convention shall not be *dissolved by adjournment at the close of its business, but shall remain organized* subject to be called at *any time* and *place that the Executive National Committee shall designate.*

This was unusual. No political convention had ever taken a like step before in our country. It meant *something*. But what? Honest democrats in this part of the country were at a loss to know—too, what *means and power* the Convention had in their control to resist the General Government.

We know *now* what the copperheads of the West were driving at. They meant to open the polls to the rebels by force, and to organize a conspiracy that would plunge the West and North into a revolution.

The Sons of Liberty, of which Dodd was one of the leaders, then numbered its tens of thousands. Dodd was arrested. His trial at Indianapolis proved him guilty, and proved the fearful nature and extent of this conspiracy. Dodd pretended boldness and innocence at first, but when he saw that his guilt was proved, he escaped from jail, was hurried into Canada by his confederates. But the loyal Democracy, the Jackson Democracy of Indiana, saw their danger, and at their State Election on the 11th of October, crushed the conspirators beneath a union majority perfectly overwhelming.

Think of this third plank and Wickliff's resolution being adopted *unanimously,* and be *forewarned!* It is much easier to defeat these conspirators *by ballot than it will be by bullets.* They must be taught by such majorities as were given against them in Ohio and Indiana, how little they understand the "sense of the American People," and the Jackson Democracy of the North!

I earnestly request every man to read the able and beautiful Report of Judge Joseph Holt, dated October 8, 1864, on the evidence obtained at the trials of these conspirators. This secret conspiracy under the name of Sons of Liberty, Knights of the Circle, &c., had its thousands of armed men aiding the rebels in Missouri, Kentucky, Indiana, Illinois, Ohio, and in a modified form under the name of "McClellan Minute Men," in New York. The *Rituals of these secret orders are based upon the very same Calhoun phrases that occur in the Chicago Platform, and were apparently written by the same hand—certainly with the same meaning.* They had actually commenced the inauguration of Civil War. *"Direct military interference" is all that saved the West from its horrors.*

Let no Jackson Democrat suppose that because he is honest and patriotic that the present leaders of the so-called democratic party are so too. The *children of Jackson and Calhoun are not of the same family!*

The Fourth Chicago Plank Is This:

Resolved, That the aim and object of the Democratic party is to preserve *the Federal Union* and *the rights of the States* unimpaired; and they hereby declare that they consider the Administrative *usurpation of extraordinary and dangerous powers not granted by the Constitution,* the subversion of the civil by military law in States not in insurrection, the arbitrary military arrest, imprisonment, trial and sentence of American citizens in States where civil law exists in full force, the suppression of freedom of speech and of the press, the denial of the right of asylum, THE OPEN AND AVOWED DISREGARD OF STATE RIGHTS, the employment of unusual test-oaths, AND THE INTERFERENCE WITH AND DENIAL OF THE RIGHTS OF THE PEOPLE TO BEAR ARMS, AS CALCULATED TO PREVENT A RESTORATION OF THE UNION, AND A PERPETUATION OF A GOVERNMENT DERIVING ITS JUST POWERS FROM THE CONSENT OF THE GOVERNED.

This Fourth Resolution opens with the "*Federal* Union" and the "Rights of the States." The idea that there is any such power as a National Government is entirely omitted from every part of their platform—they always qualify the word "Union" so that it shall not be taken for a National Government, but simply a union of States. The further we go, the clearer it is, that the SPIRIT of Calhoun wrote this Platform by the HAND of Vallandigham.

Charges against the Administration.

I cannot tax your patience to answer all the charges against the Administration set forth in this Resolution. They all rest on the same false basis. They are instances of the exercise of war powers. If by the Constitution the President is vested with such powers in order to defend and protect the Constitution and the National Government embodied in that charter, THEN THEY ARE NOT USURPATIONS, NOR UNCONSTITUTIONAL, NOR ILLEGAL, BUT THE CONTRARY. The Democracy of Jackson said, and still say, THE NATION MUST LIVE! The Calhoun Democracy said, and say by this platform, "THE FEDERAL UNION" *may* live, as long as the States can be coaxed to agree to support it, but the President cannot "coerce" a State, nor individuals acting under State authority. THAT IS THE ISSUE OF LIFE OR DEATH TO THE NATION. The decision of the people on this question settles its fate just as certainly as defeat or victory in the field.

I wish I had time to expose the injustice, exaggeration and falsehood of each of these charges, but I can only refer to

Military Arrests.

This is the greatest rebellion since the angels were thrust from Heaven, yet the President HAS NOT HUNG ONE TRAITOR. All the military arrests made in his name don't exceed 500, and most of these have been set free on taking the oath of allegiance, and in hard cases, giving security not to take up arms with, or aid the rebels. The writ of *habeus corpus* has been long ago legally suspended, yet we hardly know it. Such leniency we would hardly expect even in an ordinary insurrection or street fight in any other country. All the acts charged ARE ACTS OF WAR. In war, arrests are not made for the purpose of punishing the offender for a crime—not for trial under civil laws—but for the purpose of preventing the man from harming the government by aiding the enemy. It is like an injunction or preliminary arrest—a civil suit to prevent injury from being done, not to punish it. In that noble and beautiful letter of the President to Erastus Corning, of Albany, on the Arrest of Vallandigham, the whole matter is clearly and truly stated. I earnestly beseech all who have doubts on this subject to read that letter. The case of Vallandigham come up before Judge Leavett, a democratic Judge appointed by President Jackson. In deciding that case he thus stated the law.

In time of war the President is not above the Constitution, but derives his power expressly from the provision of that Instrument, declaring that he shall be Commander-in-Chief of the Army and Navy. The Constitution does not specify the powers he may rightfully exercise in this character. No one denies, however, that the President, in this character, is invested with very high powers." . . .

And in deciding what he may rightfully do under this power, where there is no express legislative declaration, the President is guided solely by his own judgment and discretion, and is only amenable for an abuse of his authority by impeachment prosecuted according to the requirements of the Constitution.

The power does exist to defend the Constitution from traitors and conspirators. When necessity calls, the duty must be exercised. The President has used this power rarely, and with remarkable clemency. It will be the fault of such conspirators as Dodd, and Vallandigham, and Wickliffe, acting under the inspiration of the Chicago Platform, if it is ever exercised again. The President is mild but firm. He has undertaken to maintain the National Unity, and as long as he is President he will do it—the Chicago Convention the Calhoun Democracy, and the Sons of Liberty to the contrary, notwithstanding! He relies upon the true "sense," the common sense of the American people for support.

The last clause complains that all these acts of war are "calculated to prevent a RESTORATION of the Union, and the PERPETUATION OF GOVERNMENT DERIVING ITS JUST POWERS FROM THE CONSENT OF THE GOVERNED.

Here we have the same story, the Union to be *restored;* thus admitting it is dissolved—"perpetuation of government," but not *the* government of the United States, but *some* government or other "deriving its just powers," not from the constitution as it now stands, but from the consent of the "governed."

But who are the "governed," whose consent is necessary?

In the Declaration of Independence, the sentence of which this is meant to be the echo, refers to a majority of the people. Here it means the Rebel States "whose consent is necessary to restore the "FEDERAL UNION," and whose "consent," must be obtained by coaxing and surrender, not by exercise of war powers. The same words occur in the Ritual of the Sons of Liberty, with this meaning. No one can fully understand the Chicago Platform without reading that Ritual and seeing how these very phrases are there made the basis for conspiracy, revolution and murder.

The Fifth and Sixth Chicago Planks

are too light timber to stand any examination. We place them before the corresponding Baltimore planks to show their hollowness and mockery.

CHICAGO.

Resolved, That the shameful disregard *of the Administration* to its duty in respect to our fellow-citizens who now and long have been *prisoners of war* in a suffering condition, deserves the severest reprobation, on the score alike of public interest and common humanity.

Resolved, That the *sympathy* of the Democratic party is heartily and earnestly extended to the soldiery of our army, who are and have been in the field under the flag of our country; and, *in the event of our obtaining power,* they will receive all the *care and protection, regard and kindness,* that the brave soldiers of the Republic have so nobly earned.

BALTIMORE.

Resolved, That the Government owes to all men employed in its armies, without regard to distinction of color, the full protection of the laws of war, and that any violation of the laws or of the usages of civilized nations in the time of war by the rebels now in arms, should be made the subject of full and prompt redress.

Resolved, That the *thanks* of the American people are due to the soldiers and sailors of the army and navy, who have periled their lives in defense of their country, and in vindication of the honor of its flag; that the nation owes to them *some permanent recognition of their patriotism and valor, and ample and permanent provision* for those of their survivors who have received disabling and honorable wounds in the service of the country; and that the memories of those who have fallen in its defense shall be held in grateful and everlasting remembrance.

Let us sift the meaning out of

McClellan's Letter of Acceptance.

It is well for the Committee of the Convention that the Candidate to whom they presented this Chicago Platform was not General Jackson, or a General upon whom his mantle had fallen. How sublime would have been the storm of indignation with which he would have hurled it back upon them? Alas! it was presented to a General in every respect the exact opposite to the Hero of New Orleans. For nine days he was silent. In those days Atlanta fell, and Grant moved upon the Weldon Road. It became evident that this platform would not stand even the storm of an election, unless it was touched up with war paint. It might do pure and simple for the western Conspirators and Butternuts, but not for the more honest Democrats of the Atlantic slope. There was a hurrying to and fro of Committee men. The letter of acceptance must accept the peace platform, and it must make it palatable to war democracy. How was that possible? They tell me that in hard times in Mexican mountains when the mules refuse to eat their provender of dry leaves, it is found sufficient to but a pair of green goggles over their eyes, whereupon the innocent animals, thinking the greenness is in their fodder, instead of themselves, devour it readily. This letter is a mere blind. If possible, it is even more dangerous than the avowed surrender it is to make palatable.

It is evident that neither McClellan nor any ONE man wrote it as it now stands. It has been terribly doctored by peace and war men alternately, until its dislocated, non-committal paragraphs got so weak that neither party could tell who would be cheated by them, and then it was sent to the public.

1. He says "the nomination comes unsought."

Unless he, together with his personal friends have been seeking this nomination ever since he was at the head of the army, his and their conduct belongs to the unaccountable singularities of human conduct.

2. He next is "happy that the convention kept in view the record of his public life."

His record is so short that the convention had little difficulty in so doing. He never held a civil office in his life.

3. He next says, that service in the army in war and peace had made the love and reverence for the union, constitution, laws and flag of our country impressed upon him in early youth "indelible."

His education in early youth, and in the army in peace and war, was of the pro-slavery, state right, aristocratic kind, prevalent at West Point and under the Pierce and Jeff Davis Administration. No! love and reverence won't do, NOW! We want acts, facts, and principles that can't be misunderstood. When Jeff Davis visited Portland in 1860, he exceeded all I ever heard in expressions of "love and reverence," &c., for the Union.

4. He says these feelings have guided the course of his life, and must continue to do so to its end.

Do these feelings *now* guide him to *preserve* the *National* Union by continuing the war and subduing the rebels by arms, or to *restore* the *Federal* Union "by cessation of hostilities?" We shall see in a moment.

5. His next idea, is that "the existence of more than one government over the region which once owned our flag is incompatible with the peace, the power, and the happiness of the people."

Must that "*one* government" be our present government vindicated by arms, or a new one "deriving its just powers" from the consent of the Rebel States? We shall learn soon from this letter.

6 and 7. The next *two* paragraphs (for I must hurry on) are luminous with theory of the war. It was "commenced," he says, "with the sole avowed object to preserve the Union. It should have been conducted for that object, [just as though it had *not* been] and in accordance with the principles which he took occasion to declare while in active service." That is, in his letter to the President from Harrison-Landing, where his defeated army lay under the protection of our gunboats.

"Thus conducted," he says, "THE WORK OF RECONCILIATION WOULD HAVE BEEN EASY, and we might have reaped the benefits of our many victories on land and sea."

If the phrase "*thus conducted*" refers to carrying on the war to preserve the Union, it has been so done. But if it had been carried on according to the notions in the Harrison Landing letter, we never should have had any victories to reap the benefit of. This we know, for, it was by rejecting those notions and their author, and by using all the means we could, that we gained those victories. But the luminous idea and singular confession is, that if we had BEATEN THEM ONLY A LITTLE, AS HE DID, they might have been reconciled. Thus it appears that he was all the while a political General, using his arms for the purpose of making a "reconciliation easy," instead of subduing the rebel armies by decisive victory, and vindicating the laws. This confession should never be forgotten.

8. He next says, that because the Union was formed by conciliation and compromise it must be restored by the same means.

Not so. We may compromise to make a bargain or a government, but after it is made all parties must be held to it. It is the end of all popular government, if it must be the subject of a new compromise every time the defeated minority choose to rebel. No doctrine more dangerous than this was ever announced to the American people. In ten years it would render our government no better than that of New Mexico and the South American republics.

9. The next paragraph looks at first as though the war people were getting

the upper hand, but the contrary is the fact. "The *re-establishment* of the Union in all its integrity is, and must continue to be, the indispensable condition in any *settlement*."

We are then to have a *settlement* or compromise with the rebels for the purpose of *re-establishing* the Union, which must in that case be a "federal Union." For he goes on to say, that as soon as "our present adversaries are ready for peace on the basis of the Union, we should exhaust all the resources of statesmanship practised by civilized nations, and taught by the traditions of the American people, consistent with honor and interests of the country *to secure such peace, re-establish the Union and guarantee for the future the constitutional rights of every State.*"

Mark, he says "as soon as the rebels are ready for peace" we should go on and make all these frantic exertions by compromise to secure it. If they are "*ready*," it seems to me we could except their submission to the laws without any such "exhaustion of statesmanship and traditions," &c. This language seems mere twaddle, but it is not. It is meant to prepare and suborn our patriotism to accept the conclusion "guarantee for the future the constitutional rights of every State," that is, accept a "federal Union" and a confederate peace. For what does a man, educated under Jefferson Davis and the disciples of Calhoun, mean by such phrases as "guaranteeing the rights of every State." Alas! we know too well! He concludes, "The Union is the one condition of peace—we ask no more." If it is a confederate Union, to be made by the rebel States, upon the ruins of the national government—we do ask more.

10. That I am giving no forced construction to this language, the next paragraph shows clearly.

He says: "Let me add, what I doubt not was, although unexpressed, the sentiment of the convention, as it is of the people they represent, that when *any one State* is willing to return to the Union, it should be *received at once, with a full guarantee of all its constitutional rights.*"

That is, the States are to return to the Union *as States* with full guarantee to each State of "its constitutional rights." The people are wholly left out of the account. The government is not to be preserved as a national government of the people. But the Union is to be a reconstructed federal league of States. And the resources of STATESMANSHIP, &c., not WAR—are to be "*exhausted*" (think of that terrible word) to make the best bargain we can with them, on claiming admission to this new confederacy.

This is the exact view of Alexander H. Stephens, the rebel vice-president. Let those, who would understand this letter, read *his* letter of September 22, 1864. He goes into poetic ecstasies over the State sovereignty doctrine of the Chicago platform.

The next paragraph says:

11. "If a frank, earnest and *persistent* effort to obtain *those objects* should fail, the responsibility for *"ulterior consequences"* will fall upon those who remain in arms against the Union."

Such "effort" would not fail, unless Mr. Davis should be too blind to know when his enemies surrender to him, in that case the responsibility, and blunder would be certainly with him and his friends.

You see this letter adopts and proceeds upon the programme of the Chicago Platform—first, we are to stop hostilities and exhaust "statesmanship and the traditions of the country" in making compromises, and if then the rebels won't accept the "federal Union," or, in other words, won't admit us into their confederacy, he talks of "ulterior consequences." He says the "ulterior consequences will fall upon those who remain in arms against the Union." What consequences? Why the consequences of having a divided country, which he thinks "incompatible with the interests of the people." For, as I have shown, if we let up the rebels, as he here proposes, for the purpose of first compromising with them in convention, if we there fail to get low enough to suit them—they, "who remain in arms against the Union," will have their confederacy acknowledged and invincibly established and us at their mercy.

It is in this connection, and after compromising, that he says, "But the *Union* must be preserved at all *hazards*." What Union—what *hazards* should we have the choice of *then?* There can be but one answer. Such a Union as Mr. Davis and the rebel States might choose to preserve after throwing away our national government, and *that* we must take at the hazard of seeing that our "exhausted statesmanship" had established a separate southern confederacy! When President Jackson, in fighting Calhoun and these same State-right doctrines, said, the "Union must, and shall be preserved!" we knew he meant the national government, of which he was the head, and that he was not going to leave it stripped of its power, at the mercy of armed rebels, for some two years, to see if he could not then rescue it from their grasp by exhausting the resources of "statesmanship and traditions." The candidate cannot now be trusted who is bound by his party and binds himself to preserve the Union by exchanging the hazards of successful war for the hazards of such a compromise with rebels.

12. His respects are next paid to his comrades of the army and navy. He says he "could not look in their face and tell them their sacrifices had been in vain." He need not do it; for, has he not just told us that he and his comrades conducted the war not to hurt the enemy, but to make "reconciliation easy"

for them. He need not tell them that "THAT UNION," for which WE have so often perilled our lives, is abandoned." Certainly not, until the resources of his statesmanship are exhausted without effect.

13. He next concludes that he and a vast majority of our people in the army and navy or at home would hail, with unbounded joy, the permanent restoration of peace, on the basis of the "UNION UNDER THE CONSTITUTION." We know what school this phrase belongs to. It is the Calhoun dialect, and means a Union as a confederacy of States—a "federal Union" as distinguished from the National Union and Government, of which Jackson was and Lincoln is President. That I do not mistake his meaning, the next line shows: "But no peace can be permanent without UNION." What kind of Union? The Chicago convention could not say THE government. Why this shying at the definite article THE? Because he expects to take SUCH a Union as the rebels will grant peace upon when his statesmanship is exhausted.

14. The next clause might be innocent enough, if we did not know that some of the party phrases seemingly fair describe limitations of the war power in favor of the rebels. He promises "to seek in the Constitution" for "limitations of executive power," not for power to put down the rebellion; he is to "restore economy" and re-establish the law." The "cessation of hostilities" would doubtless stop the expenses of the war for a time, and do away with the suspension of the HABEAS CORPUS. He next promises "THE OPERATION of a more vigorous nationality." How this vigorous nationality is to "OPERATE" we are not told, but by it, we are to resume our COMMANDING POSITION among the nations of the earth. This, if it means anything but twaddle, seems to indicate that after we compromise with Mr. Davis, we are to unite with him in a foreign war. May it not be a basis of this projected compromise that we should conquer enough of Mexico or Cuba and Central America, to enable the number of slave States to equal the free States. This equality was the pet theory of Calhoun and his aristocracy. In fact, they did not rebel as long as they were able to keep up that equality.

15. The next clause is, "The condition of our finances, the depreciation of our paper money, and the burdens thereby imposed on labor and capital, show the necessity of a return to a sound financial system."

This means that our present financial system is unsound, and that we must return to the one we had, before our paper money depreciated. If this means anything, it means REPUDIATION! If not, why does he not intimate some system to which he proposes to return. He conjures up "burdens" (which I have shown to be imaginary) "imposed on labor and capital" by our present system, thus aiding the rebels by breaking it down, and promises them, that if he is elected, he will return to the one before the war. He cannot do so without giving up the war. No country ever carried on a war without making its credit money. To try to "return" to what was or might have been a sound system before the war made the issue of paper currency necessary, is not only "cessation of hostilities"—it is, REPUDIATION and RUIN.

But he goes on to say, "While the rights of citizens and the rights of states, and the binding authority of law over President, army and people, are subjects of not less vital importance in war than peace."

I have shown before that, by the constitution, the civil law is silent in time of war, to the extent that the President is obliged to use war powers to put down the resistance to the Constitution, the laws and the government thereof. If by "law" he means military law, the laws of war he asserts a stale flat truism; but if he means by "law" that the "civil law" is "binding" "authority over President, army and people" in war, he says what is ridiculous. According to that Grant has no right to execute a rebel spy until he has been indicted by a grand jury, tried by a United States judge, and sentenced. But that he does so mean is evident, because he describes the "law" he refers to as "just as vitally important in war as in PEACE." As military law is not binding on the people in time of peace, it must therefore be the civil law he is talking about. Thus the PRESIDENT, ARMY AND PEOPLE are bound by the civil law in time of civil war! And he says the "rights of citizens and rights of states" are just as important, that is, are to be respected the same "in war as in peace." A war according to civil law, respecting the rights of rebel citizens and rebel states just as though we were at peace with them, is an utter impossibility. In every way this paragraph is viewed, it is absurd and ridiculous.

16. He next says: "BELIEVING THAT THE VIEWS HERE EXPRESSED ARE THOSE OF THE CONVENTION AND THE PEOPLE YOU REPRESENT, I ACCEPT THE NOMINATION."

When he wrote this, he had the Chicago platform lying before him, for he refers to it in the 14th paragraph—it expressed the UNANIMOUS views of the convention, and he knew it. He says that he believes the views he has expressed in this letter are the same, and I fully agree with him. He confirms all I have said—he hereby puts substantially the same construction on his phrases that I do—he says, they "are those of the convention" the same identical ones in meaning. Such a "Christian gentleman" would never have accepted the nomination of this convention if his views had differed them theirs.

Why then was it necessary to send to the world such a mass of dubious incoherent platitudes? Why raise such a fog if there was nothing to hide? The reason is, that after the fall of Atlanta green goggles were necessary to make northern democrats take copperheadism, Calhoun semi-treason, and base surrender in the place of Jackson democracy. Many were thus a little blinded at first, but if they chew the cud a little, they will soon find out the mistake.

17. He says, "I realize the weight of the responsibility to be borne should the people ratify their choice."

If the weak man who would put, or permit his name to be put, to such a letter as this, although backed by Wood and Vallandigham and Pendleton, ever undertakes to "exhaust resources of statesmanship" with Jefferson Davis, in whose hands poor Pierce was like clay in the hands of a potter, the sharp incisive intellect, the clear stern will, the reckless daring of the American Cataline will soon leave him no choice but surrender. In such a defeat, he would not have even a gunboat for a refuge. He says he is "conscious of his own weak ness." Then we had better not let him loosen the rebel giant to see if HE can't throw him on the field of compromise.

18. He next talks of fervently seeking the guidance of the Ruler of the Universe and relying on His all powerful aid." I have observed that the Almighty aids those men and nations who call upon Him not by words alone but by acts. Who in time of war instead of longing for a surrender, keep their courage up and their powder dry; but that a nation like a woman, who hesitates when her honor is in question is lost.

He is, however, moderate in his demands upon the Divine Power. He is to do his best to "RESTORE UNION [not the Union] and peace to a SUFFERING people [including those great sufferers, the rebels,] and to establish and guard THEIR rights and liberties.

The rights and liberties of the loyal people of the United States are not yet lost, nor likely to be. The Rebels at the South and their fellow Conspirators at the north, if they get their "rights" will be deprived of their "liberty" to destroy our National Government, and continue so to be, until they submit to its Constitution and laws like the rest of us.

This is the end of the letter.

The Peace Copperheads, the Woods, Vallandighams, Voorhies, Longs, and McMasters, pretended to be put out by it, but on consultation, saw it was all right for them, and turned right in and supported McClellan heartily. The DAILY NEWS says it was a blind, that the Chicago Platform had been substantially presented to McClellan before the Convention met and been approved by him—and its statement has never been denied. Wood knew, as McClellan says, that it was, when examined, the same thing as the Chicago Platform; but what if it is not? Says he in a speech in New York, "If elected I am satisfied he will entertain the views and execute the principles of the great party he will represent WITHOUT REGARD TO THOSE HE MAY HIMSELF POSSESS. HE WILL THEN BE OUR AGENT, THE CREATURE OF OUR VOICE."

And he is right. Pendleton, who must be voted for by the same electors as McClellan, was on the floor of the Convention and gave his hearty consent to the Chicago Platform, and afterwards glorified it in a short speech from the steps of Vallandigham House, at Dayton, Ohio, as those "BENEFICIENT PRINCIPLES RECENTLY SOLEMNLY ANNOUNCED IN NATIONAL CONVENTION." On the same occasion Vallandigham made a few remarks—referred to Pendleton "as his own familiar friend," and said:

> The Chicago Platform enunciated its [the Democratic party's] policy and principles by authority, and was binding upon every democrat, and by them the democratic administration MUST and SHOULD BE GOVERNED.

These speeches were published in the Dayton EMPIRE just after the publication of McClellan's letter.

There is no mistaking the voice of this platform as expounded by its candidates, authors and principal supporters. If adopted, it is the end of our country as a Nation.

I have chosen to consider Gen. McClellan, like Pendleton, to be honest, and also intelligent enough to know the meaning of his platform and letter. Some of his friends, however, seem to intimate that he does not understand them thoroughly, or does not intend to be bound by them.

If he does not understand his own chart, certainly he ought not to be put at the helm. If he intends to deceive and mislead a large part of his employers and crew as to his course, the ship of state, will certainly be subjected to new divisions, mutinies and disasters in his hands.

Abraham Lincoln is sound, honest and experienced. He has brought us within sight of the peace we hope to gain. Certainly it is not safe to charge him for a green and uncertain hand until this voyage is over.

Now for

PENDLETON'S HASKIN LETTER.

What Atlanta did for McClellan, the Union majority of 75,000 in Ohio did for Pendleton. It made the dumb speak! When the Copperheads begin to cry Union, they know their end is near. As the last hope, Pendleton writes a private letter to John B. Haskin, dated October 17, 1864. He complains in a line or so about "falsehoods," &c., and then says:

> I MAKE NO PROFESSIONS OF A NEW FAITH—ONLY REPEAT MY REITERATED PROGRESSIONS OF AN OLD ONE, when I say that there is no one who cherishes a greater regard for the Union—who has a higher sense of its inestimable benefits—WHO WOULD MORE EARNESTLY LABOR FOR ITS RESTO-

RATION BY ALL MEANS WHICH WILL EFFECT THAT END, than myself. The Union is the guaranty of peace, the power, the prosperity of this people; and no man would deprecate more heartily, or oppose more persistently the establishment of another government over any portion of the territory ever within its limits.

All talk about "cherishing regard for the Union"—"sense of its benefits"—its being the "guaranty of peace" &c., "deprecating" or "opposing the establishment of another government," &c., &c., amounts to just the same thing as the "adhering" and "unswerving fidelity" of the first plank of the Chicago platform and no more.

The people are sick of empty professions. They want to know what their candidates will DO. They must have WORKS, or at least the honest PROMISE of them. He says he professes his old faith. His record shows what that is—and that he is an EXTREME CALHOUNITE opposed to the war in word, act and vote.

Thus, in Congress, January 18, 1861, he said: "To-day, sir, four States of the Union have, as far as their power extends, seceded from it. Four States, as far as they are able, HAVE ANULLED THE GRANTS OF POWER MADE TO THE FEDERAL GOVERNMENT; THEY HAVE RESUMED THE POWERS DELEGATED BY THE CONSTITUTION; they have cancelled, as far as they could, EVERY LIMITATION UPON THE FULL EXERCISE OF ALL THEIR SOVEREIGN RIGHTS, they do not claim our protection; they seek none of the advantages of the CONFEDERATION. On the other hand, they renounce their allegiance; they repudiate our authority over them, and they assert that they have assumed, SOME OF THEM THAT THEY HAVE RESUMED THEIR POSITION AMONG THE FAMILY OF SOVEREIGNTIES AMONG THE NATIONS.

"Sir, I deal in no harsh epithets; I will denounce no State, no body of men. I will not pause to enquire whether they have done all this legally or wisely or upon sufficient cause. THEY HAVE DONE IT, AND I RECOGNIZE THE FACT." In conclusion, he says: "SIR, THE WHOLE SCHEME OF COERCION IS IMPRACTICABLE. IT IS CONTRARY TO THE GENIUS AND SPIRIT OF THE CONSTITUTION.

Mr. Pendleton says further, "My voice to-day is for conciliation; my voice is for compromise. I beg you, gentlemen, to hear that voice. If you will not, if you find conciliation impossible, if your differences are so great that you cannot or will not reconcile them, THEN, GENTLEMEN, LET THE SECEDING STATES DEPART IN PEACE, LET THEM ESTABLISH THEIR GOVERNMENT AND AND WORK OUT THEIR DESTINY ACCORDING TO THE WISDOM GOD HAS GIVEN THEM."

As late as January, 1863, he advocated, in Congress, Vallandigham's resolutions to amend the Constitution, by breaking up the Union into four sections. A most infamous proposal. I have no space to give his record. He voted against all war measures or dodged them. Not a man nor dollar has he voted to put down the rebellion. His record has been published, showing his hostility to the National Government. He has been brought to New York to cry "Union," and in so doing he says that his published record is a forgery, and his only proof is, that one of his votes is put down for July 7, 1864, And Congress, he says, adjourned on the 4th of July, 1864. It should be January 7, 1864. This misprint of July for January is all he can find to object to. What difference does it make whether he voted against the Union in January or July? He does not deny the fact! Read that record and be sure the more such a man cries "Union," the more anxious he is to surrender the Union to rebels. He is for a UNION on DISUNION principles.

In the Haskin Letter he promises "to labor for the restoration of the Union BY ALL MEANS THAT WILL EFFECT THAT END!!

Here is the cloven foot in plain sight. He means by this COMPROMISE, SUBMISSION, not WAR! He tells us "the whole scheme of COERCION is IMPRACTICABLE." It is "CONTRARY TO THE GENIUS AND SPIRIT OF THE Constitution." And his constant voting in the house against raising money, men and means for the war shows that he is honest in his belief that the war is "impracticable" and against the Constitution.

"War is disunion," according to his Calhoun theory, pure and simple.

He is then to labor for "the restoration of the Union," according to his old faith, he has no new one he is careful to tell us.

What does that mean? Simply that he is to join McClellan in "EXHAUSTING THE RESOURCES OF STATESMANSHIP," INSTEAD OF GOING ON WITH THE WAR.

Instead of saying, that if elected, he will go on with the war, or favor that course—as he could do in one line—he refers to his damning record, and uses the deceitful phrase that he and all his Calhoun friends use to describe the "cessation of hostilities," and submission in a national convention, with a Southern Confederacy as the only alternative from our necessity if not choice.

That he might THERE, "persistently oppose a Southern Confederacy—MAY BE But after your head is in the lion's mouth, the more "persistently" you oppose his taking it off, the more certainly he will do it.

The last clause of his letter makes this meaning clearer. He says:

I am in favor OF EXACTING NO CONDITIONS, INSISTING UPON NO TERMS NOT PRESCRIBED IN THE CONSTITUTION; and I am opposed to any course of policy which will defeat the RE-ESTABLISHMENT OF THE GOVERNMENT upon its OLD FOUNDATIONS, and in its territorial integrity. I am, very truly, yours, &c.

He "is in favor of exacting no conditions, insisting upon no terms not prescribed in the constitution!!"

Here he is plainly talking about the terms of the compromise which must be as the Chicago Platform prescribes in National Convention.

The CONSTITUTION can PRESCRIBE no terms nor conditions to a CONSTITUTIONAL CONVENTION. Such conventions are called for the very purpose of ALTERING the Constitution and doing away with it. The rebels would only come into it for that purpose, and for the purpose of abrogating or changing the National Government. Again, according to his Calhoun theory, if the Constitution can't keep states from SECEDING, and we recognize that fact, by asking them into a convention—how can it limit sovereign states with "terms" or "conditions?" The idea is ridiculous. The phrase "NOT PRESCRIBED IN THE CONSTITUTION" means just nothing, except as a BLIND. When he says he "is in favor of exacting no conditions, insisting upon no terms," he MEANS UNCONDITIONAL SURRENDER TO THE REBELS, through the forms of a convention. That is all of it. The rebels will enter a convention for the very purpose of doing away with our present constitution and government. THEIR ARMS not OUR CONSTITUTION WILL DICTATE what TERMS WE SHALL give THEM—or rather THEY US!

He is "opposed to any course of policy which will defeat the RE-ESTABLISHMENT OF THE GOVERNMENT ON ITS OLD FOUNDATIONS, and its territorial integrity."

What does he mean by RE-ESTABLISHING THE GOVERNMENT ON OLD FOUNDATIONS?

You see the government is to be established AGAIN! I supposed it was already ESTABLISHED, and that the only question was whether it SHOULD STAND OR NOT.

His "own familiar friend," Vallandigham, would mean by "old foundations," the old Articles of Confederation, and it is not clear but that he does, too. If not that, he certainly means that he is opposed to everything that will prevent a "RESTORATION of the Union" upon the Sovereign State construction of the Constitution, with the Southern Aristocrats in full control of what National Government they choose to leave us. It is by such concessions that he promises us the mockery of "TERRITORIAL INTEGRITY." If he spoke truly he would rather say the Extension of the Southern Confederacy over the North! That is what it amounts to!

Thus ends his letter. It is just as expressive as his silence, but not as honest.

If he differs in meaning from the Chicago Platform why does he not say so? He was present when it was made—he approved it before the people—and he does the same by this letter.

There are

But Two Courses before the Country:

Either to go on and subdue the rebels by war, leaving it to the loyal people of the Southern States to send members to Congress and reorganize their States:

Or, to give up beat—ask the Rebel States into a convention to reorganize the National Government, and to pray them to grant us "territorial integrity" and some sort of a Union on "old foundations,"—with no help for it if they won't!

McClellan and Pendleton by their party platform and equally by their letters and record are pledged to the latter course.

I complain that they deceive the people about it. one plain honest sentence could make it known if they were for the war. That word WAR upon which the fate of our country hangs is carefully avoided in all their platforms and letters. The only war they propose is against their own government in the third and fourth Resolutions of their platform.

Our Saviour said:

"Let your communication be yea, yea; nay, nay; for whatsoever is more than these cometh of evil." By this rule nothing could be more surely "of evil" than the "communications" of these candidates.

Their art of letter writing is worthy of Macbeth's witches. They palaver about "Union"—"Constitution" and "Government"—and at last even "Territorial Integrity!" But we find they mean by those words things that the loyal people of the nation would not accept for a moment if they understood them.

> Be these juggling fiends no more believed!
> That palter with us in a double sense;
> That keep the word of promise to our ear,
> But break it to our hope!

This, the corrupt ambition of Macbeth said too late. May the pure Spirit of American Liberty say it in time, and thus escape not only the violence of war—but the GREATER DANGER OF DECEPTION AND TREACHERY AT HOME.

I do not ask you to vote for men or party, as such. This is not a party contest—or, rather, the Union party is now the ONLY support of the great pillars of the Union. Every other election has been trivial, compared with this. The choice is to be made by each one of us, whether we wish that the Nation—the Great Republic—shall live or die.

> Choose well! Your choice
> Is BRIEF, yet ENDLESS!

You choose in a day, the fate of your country for ever!

✵ 16 ✵

Modern Philanthropy Illustrated.
How They Tried to Make a White
Man of a Negro Twenty Five
Hundred Years Ago. Will Better
Success Attend the Experiment Now?
(n.p., 1868)

THE DEMOCRATS found in the wartime (and later) behavior of their opponents issues that they believed were both familiar and helpful vote winners. Whatever their advocacy and activities had been during and since the war, the Democrats felt their behavior had been justified because they were opposing a determination on the part of the Republicans (as the Federalists and Whigs before them) to use the power of the national government illegitimately to overpower the people and their liberties. Going further than their predecessors, Republicans also sought to impose a social revolution on the American people under the guise of wartime necessity, a claim that hid their deeper motives. Making an issue of the Republicans' desire to bring African-Americans to equality and, in Democratic eyes, to political power by granting them the right to vote had paid off handsomely for the Democrats as a campaign issue in the state and local elections in 1867. With the first postwar presidential election looming, they increased their emphasis on the issue, the extremism of their presentation, and their lurid racism. They had high hopes that the Democrats' return to power was imminent.

The history of the African in this age and country was—curious to note— told more than two thousand years ago, by a celebrated and remarkably pointed Greek writer; when, as he relates, certain persons—doubtless "philanthropists"—then, as now, not content with having the colored man about them as a "blackamoor," deliberately determined upon making him *white!* The story—as Æsop tells it—was both comical and sad. They put him in a tub, began upon him with scrubbing-brushes and brooms, and, not succeeding in the endeavor to make him white, they *did* succeed in giving him a cold and sickness which caused his death.

And although the world at large, and our own people in particular, cannot but be conversant with this most remarkable case; although it has the indubitable and invaluable stamp of antiquity to recommend it; and although its wonderful fidelity *to the tenor of events at the present time* cannot be questioned, there are those to-day just as deeply engaged in scrubbing the African, with a view to making him white, as were those who experimented so long ago in vain.

And what makes the matter more marked, too, in the nature of a warning to the present manipulators of the poor African, it has come to this—that whilst they kill "him with kindness," the experiment is just now proving *quite as fatal to themselves.*

If anybody doubts this, they have only to note the fate of that leading manipulator and philanthropist, the Chief-Justice of the United States, out of his abounding benevolence of heart one of the busiest and most earnest scrubbers known; his fate imminently threatening any one unwise enough to follow his example. As a case in point, the fact is notorious, that General Grant has already given strong evidence of having *caught a bad cold,* whilst hardly yet more than a looker-on where the African sits in his tub.

The colored man himself, too, is, it seems, so disgusted with his skin, that, under certain conditions and circumstances, he also is content, if not eager, to change it, even at the cost of life itself! An English authority in Australia tells us that, on one occasion, a native black was to be hanged for the commission of some crime. On the way to the fatal tree, he was observed to cut sundry fantastic capers; dancing, in fact—something that so surprised the good priest at his side, that the holy man was fain to inquire what could induce him to dance under such circumstances, adding, "Do you not fear death?" "No," was the instant and exultant reply, "I shall turn up a *white* man with plenty of money," proving thereby, very plainly, that, worse than the Greek African—who, it seems, was passive under the treatment he received—he would have stood the scrubbing with the *certainty* of its killing him, in order to become a "white man."

Now, then, if by both high antiquity and modern authority, it has been shown that Sambo himself is not open to any argument whatever, which prevents his trying every experiment possible, even to that of *death itself,* in order to become a white man, let no one suppose that he is going to stop short of the last possible endeavor in that direction at the present time, no matter how great the disaster it threatens, which promises even an approximation to the condition he so desperately covets.

Besides, when we know that for twenty years past, more or less, certain manipulators, *scrubbers* of Sambo, have, when not engaged with the broom and brush in the manner described, spent their luxurious lives on cushioned chairs, and on the carpeted floors of Congressional halls, merely on the credit of being anxious to perfect *the experiment,* mankind should not expect too much of these unselfish philanthropists, in presuming upon their readiness to give up their vocation, their only chance of comfort, and of accumulating available political capital.

To be sure, another class of men, whose cardinal belief it was that Sambo's skin is the very best skin he could possibly have, because in it he could stand a tropical sun in "cotton-picking," have unwittingly played into the hands of the *scrubbing* fraternity, Sumner and Co., by giving great provocations to *experiments;* and yet, whatever experiments are or have been tried, and whoever is benefited, Sambo is *not;* so that, this very moment, his chances of becoming a white man are further off than ever, since, betwixt those who would help him too much, on the one hand, and, on the other, those who are too disgusted and indignant to help him at all, neglect, filth, disease, and kindred troubles are likely to end at last all speculation, leaving the world nothing whatever to quarrel over finally—Æsop's case illustrated anew, exactly.

To be white, in this period of the world's history, and on this continent, means so much, so very much; the accumulated knowledge, the *audacity* (a terrible quality sometimes) and the property of eight or ten generations, running back in American annals at least three centuries; the property comprising so nearly all the land, especially, that the portion in the hands of Sambo is hardly worth consideration. And therefore, when men, carried away by false hopes, reckon that a race lacking all these elements of strength, these guaranties and solid pledges of *power,* are, suddenly, or short of centuries, or indeed *at all,* to mount to the same level, not to say to the *control* of those thus indubitably their superiors by so many tokens of mastery, who, with any discernment whatever, hopes or expects to make these beings white in hardly *any* sense? Who does not feel and know that the position of the negro is undeniably and hopelessly *under;* and that it must remain so, just so long as intellect, wealth, and numbers mean, in governing, more than ignorance, poverty, and numerical inferiority?

Again—for the matter is getting serious as we progress—let the tremendous and ominous fact be noted, that *the majority of no race can be made conspirators against themselves in favor of another and especially of an inferior race.* And, therefore, those politicians, who, like the Chief-Justice and his backers, expect to profit by so unheard of a phenomenon in human affairs, are blind, and deaf, and dumb to human probabilities, and must be disappointed accordingly.

Strange things occur, to be sure, at times, when a purpose is to be served. But, remembering that the time is drawing rapidly near, when the white race, *as a race,* as the dominating millions upon millions, will be heartily tired of being heavily taxed to make up the deficiencies in industry, in calculation, in food and raiment, of the black; and who can then expect miraculous forbearance and patience in dealing with him as an inferior, and more, as a most costly charge, let alone conceding to him any controlling influence over the destinies of the white race, now and always above him?

It is true there are those in the world who appear vastly unhappy because of their palpable inability to improve upon the work of the Creator; the same kind of people as those described by the old Greek writer, who appear unhappy and utterly dissatisfied because the negro was made *as he is.* And so, in some cases, when satisfied that, in dealing with the badge of inferiority itself—recognized as such since the days of Ham and of Æsop, and his contemporaries—they cannot change it or improve upon it, they, in a captious and monstrous sort of way, become enamored of it or affect to be so, insist that the mass of white civilization is in error, and end by hugging Sambo to their hearts.

But would it not be just as rational to arraign the Creator of all for fashioning any other creature of his—for allowing him, or fitting him, to move in an inferior sphere, and yet deny to him every noble attribute? And until these puzzled and indignant philanthropists can reconcile these difficulties, give good reasons why these concessions were not made *in the outset* to the confessedly inferior, by Him who rules and fashions all, men, rational men, will not be in too great haste to adopt their foolish creeds, espouse their quarrels, or condemn their opponents.

We have dwelt at some length on the "killing kindness" of the times, to question its wisdom and condemn it. Let us see what it has done, or is doing—what, at least, are its palpable results.

Not long since, a very remarkable sermon was preached on behalf of the negro, by the present able and kind-hearted Episcopal Bishop of North Carolina; the more remarkable, because it was an appeal to the wealth, and, we may add, the intelligence of New York, from the pulpit of old "St. Paul's;" it was a cry for "help." Under his teachings or expositions, in this instance, we say, were gathered the old and "solid" men of the great commercial metropolis; those whose superior enterprise had, through their shipping, visited every mart of civilization and trade, every recess of barbarism almost upon earth. And mark the good bishop's announcement to them, as he asked them for aid to help to stave off a fearful catastrophe. He said: "*The negro appeared doomed to extinction in this country*"—in other words, white philanthropy, in hastening to make a white man of him, was, in the act of destroying him, a repetition of the sad lesson conveyed by the ancient Greek fabulist precisely.

The bishop stated that in one city alone in North Carolina, where the negroes had flocked in the number of some ten thousand—that the Freedman's Bureau (the tub in which poor Sambo is seated for the whitening or scrubbing process) had furnished in a single year "twenty-five hundred coffins" for the dead of these ten thousand; they having perished in a single year—we repeat—from cold, and scant or bad food, neglect and disease. Think of this, ye Don Quixotes of the philanthropic school, and tell the world, if you can, where this thing is to stop.

The negro—the bishop reminded his audience—was emphatically a social being, particularly fond of gatherings with others of his race; that a comparatively solitary life on the farm, where he had few resources for pleasure, was his dislike; and that, acting upon this feeling and incentive, he, under the new order of things, naturally seeks the towns and cities, where he is not wanted, where there is nothing profitable for large bodies of them to do; and that, unemployed, or partially so, the very natural results followed—poverty, starvation, sickness, *death!*

Now, then, insisting upon the very obvious condition, that of poverty—which must be chronic for generations, because the negro is absolutely cut off from possession of the land in any great quantity, a land where the white race is fixed as monopolists, where nothing short of an impossible revolution, based upon the absurdity of expecting four millions of an inferior race to get on top of thirty millions of the superior—we say that such poverty means, to the end of the chapter, *ignorance;* and who is eloquent enough, plausible enough, conjurer sufficient, to persuade the white race to abdicate in favor of it?

And if *not;* if negro suffrage, legislation, government, can never have the sanction of the masses of the whites, what becomes of the "negro suffrage *party,*" with the designs of its leaders fully comprehended? Let it be noted, that the white race, hitherto careless in its strength, and conscious of its ultimate security, has looked on at the manipulations of the negro with something akin to utter indifference as to what was going on. But when negro suffrage, and, by consequence or possibility, negro *rule,* as started by Wendell Phillips, is afterwards supplemented in its efforts by the two great guns of the

Radical camp, Chase, Grant, or whoever is to be victimized by their proffered alliance and attempted support, the people, the thirty millions of white people are just as sure to extinguish their pretensions in regard to the *whole* country, as they have of late in certain of the Northern States where the case has been put to the test.

In view, then, of the almost inevitable fate of the colored man in the hands of his ostensible "friends," demonstrated, as we have seen, by facts and imminent probabilities; knowing, as all must know, that he cannot make progress, or even hold his own in the race marked out for him by them, provoking at every turn prejudices and antipathies which will aggravate the troubles and pile higher the burdens which keep him under, is it not time for the devotees to the theory of making him white to pause? Forcing him, or encouraging him, to accept this terrible and hopeless competition, appears cruel in the extreme; and yet, if ambition and heartlessness will still insist on making use of the colored man in this way, let them not wonder if the consequences are in the end as blighting to their success as to his own. Because the negro happens to be here; because of his inferiority, degraded unduly on one side, and championed unduly on the other, the white race has already paid so heavily, and still suffers so grievously, that no power on earth can LONG make even philanthropy popular, when overstrained in his behalf. The white people, we say, *both* sides, have suffered terribly on his account; and let those who are now expecting great things of him as an ally in political conflicts, once be thoroughly beaten and disappointed—as beaten and disappointed they *must* be—and who, after this, can expect the costly blunder to be repeated. Who?

THE INEVITABLE

Let us reduce this question of Negro Suffrage, and by consequence, Negro Government, Negro "Balance of Power," to its simplest conditions—to the INEVITABLE.

Let any one desirous of applying the test, take his position on any street corner, or go into any white assemblage of one of our great cities; and remembering that the proportion of whites to blacks in the nation, is "thirty millions" to "four millions."

Let the investigator of this subject, stop the first thirty white men who may pass and, placing them in a row, confront them with any four negroes whatever; beginning, for *intelligence,* with Fred. Douglas, and ending with the colored "Boston Lawyer" Bradley—would these thirty whites consent to be governed or controlled, *in any way,* by the four blacks?

Go to the farms or workshops of the land: would any thirty farmers or mechanics so consent?

And if not thirty, would *twenty?*

If not twenty, would *ten?*

If not ten, would *five?*

And if no *five* white men in this country, or indeed *on earth,* would consent to have *four* negroes govern or control them, what becomes, *inevitably,* we repeat—of the Negro Suffrage *party?* Is not its *ultimate* doom written as by the finger of Fate; is it anything whatever but a question of time?

The Three Secession Movements in the United States. Samuel J. Tilden, the Democratic Candidate for the Presidency; the Adviser, Aider, and Abettor of the Great Secession Movement of 1860; and One of the Authors of the Infamous Resolution of 1864. His Claims as a Statesman and Reformer Considered (Boston, 1876)

THE THEME, and the intensely bitter tone, of this pamphlet was familiar; they had been appearing in similar Republican efforts since 1864. In 1876 party leaders returned full force to the theme of Democratic treason, that party's loyalty to secession rather than to the Union, and its determination to turn back the clock to the troubled situation (which had benefited only the South) that had existed before 1860. The staying power of the wartime issues was, in Republican eyes, the dominant electoral reality of the day. What gave the pamphlet a (not entirely unexpected) twist was the weaving of Samuel Tilden into the web of treason and pro-Southernism. Tilden had been politically active for many years, but he had not played as significant a role in Democratic councils during the war as the Republicans claimed. That distinction disappeared in the guilt-by-association approach manifested here, familiar to all writers (and readers) of political party pamphlets over the years.

MR. TILDEN'S PAMPHLET

The letter, a *fac-simile* copy of which is annexed hereto [not included—*ed.*], was published on the eve of the Presidential Election of 1860, by Mr. Samuel J. Tilden, at this time candidate for the Presidency of the United States, and scattered broadcast by him, in the vain hope of defeating the election of Mr. Lincoln.

The Year 1860 the Great Crisis in Our History

The year 1860 was the great crisis in our history. With the election of Mr. Lincoln began the desperate military struggle for the maintenance of our national unity. It had for some time been evident that the North was about to pronounce against the creation of new Slave States. The exercise of such a right or power was met on the part of the South by threats of secession; the election of Mr. Lincoln, whose triumph foreshadowed that of the cause of freedom, to be the signal for their movement. It is unnecessary again to go over the ground so often gone over. The South seceded in a body. War followed with infinite waste of blood and treasure, and with all the pangs and heart-rendings that the death, in camp or in field, of half a million of men could cause.

The Authors of the War of the Rebellion

Who were the authors of this war, with all its waste of treasure and of life; which bereft almost every family in the land of some one of its members, and which turned the whole nation into a house of mourning? Those at the North who instructed the Southern States that *secession* was a right secured to them by the Constitution, and that they were the sole judges of the occasion, as well as the mode in which it was to be accomplished. Among the most conspicuous and criminal of them stands Mr. Tilden, who now asks the people to honor him with the highest office in their gift.

The Government of the United States—Is It a Confederation or a Nation?

The question always asked, from the adoption of the Constitution in 1788 to the present time, has been, "What is the nature of the government of the United States? Is it a confederation from which each State, as an integral party, may withdraw at pleasure; or is it a government of paramount powers from which no State can withdraw but by the consent of the whole?" Although the question had in itself nothing to do with geographical distinctions or boundaries, the South very soon came to give one answer, the North another, and each differing wholly and totally in kind. That of the South was formulated on the famous Virginia and Kentucky resolutions of 1798–99, directed against the Alien and Sedition laws, and of which Mr. Jefferson, though not a member of the Legislature of either State, was the author; and in the Report made by Mr. Madison upon the same to the Legislature of the former State. These Resolutions, among other things, declared:

The Resolutions of 1798–99

That the several States composing the United States of America are not united on the principle of unlimited submission to their general government, but that by a compact under the style and title of the Constitution for the United States, and of amendments thereto, they constituted a general government for special purposes; delegated to that government certain definite powers; reserving, each State to itself, the residuary measure of right to their own self-government; and that, whensoever the general government assumes undelegated powers, its acts are unauthoritative, void, and of no force; that to this compact each State acceded as a State, and is an integral party; that the government created by this compact was not made the exclusive or final judge of the extent of the powers delegated to itself, since that would have made its discretion, and not the Constitution, the measure of its powers; *but that, as in all other cases of compact among parties having no common judge, each party has an equal right to judge for itself; as well of infractions as of the mode and measure of redress,* . . . *"and that a nullification by those sovereignties of all unauthorized acts done under the color of that instrument is the rightful remedy."*

The Resolutions adopted by both States were similar in spirit, and, substantially, in form. Those submitted to, and finally passed by, the Legislature of Virginia were referred to a Committee, of which Mr. Madison was Chairman, who submitted an elaborate Report in their support, from which the following extract is given:—

Report of Mr. Madison on the Resolutions of 1798–99

It appears to your Committee to be a plain principle founded in common sense, illustrated by common practice, and essential to the nature of compacts, that where resort can be had to no tribunal superior to the authority of the parties, the parties themselves must be the rightful judges, in the last resort, whether the bargain made has been pursued or violated. The Constitution of the United States was formed by the sanction of the States given by each in its

SOVEREIGN capacity. The States, then, being parties to the constitutional compact, and in their sovereign capacity, it follows of necessity that there can be no tribunal above their authority to decide on the last resort whether the compact made by them be violated; and, consequently, that, as parties to it, they must themselves decide in the last resort such questions as may be of sufficient magnitude to require their interposition.

The preceding extracts sufficiently set forth the language and spirit of those Resolutions and that Report, which have exerted such a tremendous and baleful influence over the history and fortunes of the country. They include all that can be said in support of the interpretation of the Constitution by the Southern States, and by their adoption by the Democratic Party, as a fundamental article of its creed, prepared the way to their ultimate secession from the Union.

ACTS AGAINST WHICH THESE RESOLUTIONS WERE DIRECTED—ALIEN AND SEDITION LAWS

And what were the acts against which these Resolutions were directed, and which were regarded as sufficiently grave in their character to warrant the dissolution of the Union? There were four in all, the first three being termed the "Alien Acts," and the fourth, the "Sedition Act;" all passed in the summer of 1798. The first act provided for a residence in the country of fourteen years, as a condition of naturalization. The second, of which the continuance was limited to two years, gave the President authority to order out of the country all such aliens as he might judge dangerous to the peace and safety of the United States, or to be concerned in any treasonable or secret machinations. The third provided, that, in case of a declaration of war, or an invasion of the United States, all resident aliens, natives or citizens of the hostile nation, might, upon a proclamation to that effect, to be issued at the President's discretion, be apprehended, secured, or removed. The fourth, the Sedition Act, made it a high misdemeanor, punishable by a fine not exceeding $5,000, imprisonment from six months to five years, and binding to good behavior, at the discretion of the court, for any persons unlawfully to combine and conspire together, with intent to oppose any measures of the Government of the United States; or to intimidate or to prevent any person holding office under the Government of the United States, from executing his trust; or, with like intent, to commit, advise, or attempt to procure, any in surrection, riot, unlawful assembly or combination: and to punish by a fine not exceeding

$2,000, and imprisonment, not exceeding two years, the printing or publishing of any false, scandalous, and malicious writings against the government of the United States, or either House of Congress, or the President, with intent to defame them, or to bring them into contempt or disrepute, or to excite against them the hatred of the good people of the United States; or to stir up sedition, or with intent to excite any unlawful combination for opposing or resisting any law of United States, or any lawful act of the President; or to excite generally to oppose or resist any such law or act, or to aid, abet, or encourage any hostile design of any foreign nation against the United States. In all prosecutions, however, under the last act, the truth of the matter stated might be given in evidence as a good defence, the jury being made judges both of law and fact.

All these acts may have been very weak and foolish expedients, but they formed no better ground for the dissolution of the Union than the erection of a new collection district in any one of the Southern States. The utter absurdity of the pretexts put forth well illustrates the feebleness of the tie which, in the opinion of those who urged them, held the States together. The reason for the passage of the obnoxious measures was the great number of French and Irish emissaries then in the country, seeking to embroil it in a war with Great Britain. It would probably have been much better to have borne with their interference and impertinence, no matter how irritating or mischievous. They were, almost without exception, reckless adventurers, at war with all peace, order, and property in any community in which they might happen to be placed, and who would have soon become comparatively powerless, by the disgust created for them in the minds of all well-meaning citizens.

Washington's Opinion of the Character of These Resolutions—Letter to Patrick Henry

The publication of Mr. Jefferson's Resolutions, with the Report of Mr. Madison, created profound impression and alarm, and on the part of no one more than Washington. He regarded them as deliberate attempts to destroy the Union which he had labored so earnestly and untiringly to form and maintain, and whose preservation was always uppermost in his mind. Although he was in the last year of his life, and had sought to retire wholly from the turmoil of political life, he at once returned to it, and directed all his efforts to arouse the country to a sense of its dangers, and to urge men of character, experience and influence, to come forward to its rescue. Immediately upon their publication, he addressed a letter to the celebrated Patrick Henry, which, in earnestness of expression, zeal for the public welfare, appreciation of the dangers which threatened, and for the practical wisdom displayed, was never exceeded by any thing that came from his pen. As it is a document of the greatest value, not only as illustrating the history of the time, but of the whole career of "nullification," and should be in the hands, and uppermost in the minds, of every voter, it is here given in full.*

Mount Vernon, 15th of Jan'y, 1799.

My dear Sir,—At the threshold of this letter, I ought to make an apology for its contents; but if you will give me credit for my motives, I will contend for no more, however erroneous my sentiments may appear to you.

It would be a waste of time to attempt to bring to the view of a person of your observation and discernment the endeavors of a certain *party*[†] among us to disquiet the public mind with unfounded alarms; to arraign every act of the administration; to set the people at variance with their government, and to embarrass all its measures. Equally useless would it be to predict what must be the inevitable consequences of such a policy, if it cannot be arrested.

Unfortunately, and extremely do I regret it, the State of Virginia has taken the lead in this opposition. I have said the State, because the conduct of its Legislature in the eyes of the world will authorize the expression; and because it is an incontrovertible fact, that the principal leaders of the opposition dwell in it, and that, with the help of the chiefs in other States, all the plans are arranged and systematically pursued by their followers in other parts of the Union; though in no State except Kentucky, that I have heard of, has legislative countenance been obtained beyond Virginia.[‡]

It has been said that the great mass of the citizens of this State are well affected, notwithstanding, to the general government and to the Union; and I am willing to believe it, nay, do believe it; but how is this to be reconciled with their suffrages, at the election of Representatives, both to Congress and their State Legislatures, who are men opposed to the former, and by the tendency of

---

*See Sparks' Life and Writings of Washington, Vol. XI, p. 387.

[†]Mr. Jefferson.

[‡]The States of Delaware, Rhode Island, Massachusetts (then including Maine), New York, Connecticut, New Hampshire, and Vermont immediately and earnestly protested, in resolution addressed to Virginia, against the doctrines put forth by that State. The Resolution adopted by the State of Delaware may be given, as briefly expressing the sentiment of all:—

"*Resolved,* By the Senate and House of Representatives of the State of Delaware, in General Assembly met, that they seconsider the Resolutions from the State of Virginia as a very unjustifiable interference with the general government and constituted authorities of the United States, and of dangerous tendency, and therefore not a fit subject for the further consideration of this Assembly."

their measures would *destroy the latter?* Some among us have endeavored to account for this inconsistency, and though convinced themselves of its truth, they are unable to convince others who are unacquainted with the internal policy of the State.

One of the reasons assigned is, that the most respectable and best qualified among us will not come forward. Easy and happy in their circumstances at home, and believing themselves secure in their liberties and property, they will not forsake their occupations and engage in the turmoil of public business, or expose themselves to the calumnies of their opponents *whose weapons are detraction.*

But at such a crisis as this *when every thing dear and valuable to us is assailed,* when this party hangs upon the wheels of government as a dead weight, opposing every measure that is calculated for defence and self-preservation, abetting the nefarious views of another nation upon our rights; preferring, as long as they dare contend openly against the spirit and resentment of the people, the interests of France to the welfare of their own country, justifying the former at the expense of the latter; when every act of their own government is tortured by constructions they will not bear, into attempts to infringe and trample upon the Constitution with a view to introduce monarchy; when the most unceasing and the purest exertions which were making to maintain a neutrality proclaimed by the executive, approved unequivocally by Congress, by the State Legislatures, nay, by the people themselves in various meetings, and to preserve the country in peace, are charged with being measures calculated to favor Great Britain at the expense of France, and all those who had any agency in it are accused of being under the influence of the former, and her pensioners; *when measures are systematically and pertinaciously pursued which must eventually* DISSOLVE THE UNION OR PRODUCE COERCION; I say, when these things have become so obvious, ought characters who are best able to rescue the country from the pending evil to remain at home? Rather, ought they not to come forward, and by their talents and influence, stand in the breach which such conduct has made on the peace and happiness of this country, and oppose the widening of it?

Vain will it be to look for peace and happiness, or for the security of liberty or property, if civil discord should ensue. And *what else can result from the policy of those among us who, by all the measures in their power, are driving matters to extremity, if they cannot be counteracted effectually?* The views of men can only be known, or guessed at, by their words or actions. Can those of the leaders of this opposition be mistaken, then, if judged by this rule? That they are followed by numbers who are unacquainted with their designs, and suspect as little the tendency of their principles, I am fully persuaded. *But if their conduct is viewed with indifference; if there are activity and misrepresentation on one side, and supineness on the other, their numbers accumulated by intriguing and discontented foreigners under proscription, who are at war with their own governments, and the greater part of them with all governments, they will increase, and nothing short of Omniscience can foretell the consequences.*

I come, now, my good sir, to the object of my letter, which is to express a hope and an earnest wish that you should come forward at the ensuing elections, (if not for Congress, which you may think would take you too long from home), as a candidate for Representative in the General Assembly of this Commonwealth.

There are, I have no doubt, very many sensible men who oppose themselves to the torrent that carries away others who had rather swim with than stem it without an able pilot to conduct them; but these are neither old in legislation nor well known in the community. Your weight of character and influence in the House of Representatives would be a bulwark against such dangerous sentiments as are delivered there at present. It would be a rallying-point for the timid, and an attraction to the wavering. In a word, I conceive it to be of the utmost importance at this crisis that you should be there; and I would fain hope that all minor considerations will be made to yield to the measure.

If I have erroneously supposed that your sentiments on these subjects are in unison with mine; or if I have assumed a liberty which the occasion does not warrant, I must conclude as I began, with praying that my motives may be received as an apology. *My fear that the tranquility of the Union, and of this State in particular, is hastening to an awful crisis, has extorted them from me.*

(Signed)   GEO. WASHINGTON.

QUESTIONS RAISED BY THE FIRST SECESSION MOVEMENT

The Resolutions of 1798 and 1799, and the Report referred to, on one side, and the letter of General Washington, on the other, presented the first issue that was formally made after the adoption of the Constitution, as to the nature of the government of the United States; the former denying that it constituted a nation, and declaring that States might, at will, nullify any Act of Congress, and secede: the latter taking ground precisely the opposite,—that we were a nation, and that all refractory subjects, States as well as individuals, could be coerced into obedience to it. The issue joined was perfectly simple and intelligible, and went to the very root of the matter. It transcended all reasoning or argument. If we were not a nation, only a confederation, then no obedience to it could be enforced. If we were a nation, then disobedience to it became a crime which might be punished by taking the property or life of the offender.

The First Movement Allayed—Election of Mr. Jefferson to the Presidency

The movement in 1798–99 for a dissolution of the Union, which created such wide-spread alarm, ended with the expiration, or repeal, of the obnoxious acts, and by the election of Mr. Jefferson to the Presidency in 1800, which, to use his own words, "was as real a revolution in the principles of our Government as that of 1776 was in its form."

Revival of the Secession Movement by South Carolina, under Pretext of the Tariff Laws

Secession slumbered till 1832, when South Carolina made her first famous attempt to dissolve the Union, the alleged cause being the *Tariff.* In November of that year, she issued an Ordinance which, after reciting the grievances that led to its adoption, declared, among other things,—

Ordinance of Nullification and Secession by That State

That the several Acts of Congress of the United States, purporting to be laws for the imposing of duties and imposts on the importation of foreign commodities, and now having actual operation and effect within the United States; and more especially 'an Act in alteration of the several Acts imposing duties on imports approved 19th May, 1828;' also, an Act to amend the several acts imposing duties on imposts, passed 14th July, 1832,—are UNAUTHORIZED by the Constitution of the United States, and violate the true intent and meaning thereof; *and are null, void,* and no law binding upon this State, its officers or citizens; and all promises, contracts, and obligations made or entered into, or to be made or entered into, with the purpose to secure the duties imposed by said Acts; and all judicial proceedings which shall hereafter be had in affirmance thereof,—are and shall be held utterly null and void.

And we, the people of South Carolina, to the end that it may be fully understood by the Government of the United States, and the people of the co-States, that we are determined to maintain this our ordinance and declaration, at every hazard, do further declare that we will not submit to the application of *force* on the part of the Federal Government to reduce this State to obedience; but will consider the passage by Congress of any Act authorizing the employment of a military or naval force against the State of South Carolina, her constitutional authorities or citizens; or any Act abolishing or closing the ports of the States, or any of them, or otherwise obstructing the free ingress or egress of vessels to and from the said ports; or any other Act on the part of the Federal Government to COERCE the State, shut up her ports, destroy or harass her commerce, or to enforce the Acts hereby declared, to be null and void, otherwise than through the civil tribunals of the country, as inconsistent with the longer continuance of South Carolina in the Union; and that the people of this State will thenceforth hold themselves absolved from all further obligation to maintain or preserve their political connection with the people of the other States, and will forthwith proceed to organize a separate government, and do all other acts and things which sovereign and independent States may of right do.

Such was a part of the famous Ordinance of Nullification of South Carolina in 1832. It was instantly met by a proclamation against it by General Jackson, as President of United States, in which, among other things, he said:—

Counter Proclamation by General Jackson

This right to secede is deduced from the nature of the Constitution, which, they say, is a compact between *sovereign* States, who have preserved their whole *sovereignty,* and, therefore, are subject to no superior; that, because they made the compact, they can break it when, in their opinion, it has been departed from by the other States. Fallacious as this course of reasoning is, it enlists State pride, and finds advocates in the honest prejudices of those who have not studied the nature of our Government sufficiently to see the radical error on which it rests.

The people of the United States formed the Constitution, acting through the State Legislatures in making the compact, to meet and discuss its provisions, and acting in separate Conventions when they ratified those provisions; but the terms used in its construction show it to be a government in which the people of all the States *collectively* are represented. We are one people in the choice of the President and Vice-President. Here the States have no other agency than to direct the mode in which the votes shall be given. Candidates having the majority of all the votes are chosen. The electors of a majority of States may have given their votes for one candidate, and yet another may be chosen. The *people,* then, and not the States, are represented in the executive branch. . . .

The Constitution of the United States, then, forms a government, *not a league;* and whether it be formed by compact between the States, or in any other manner, its character is the same. It is a government in which all the people are represented, which operates directly on the people individually, not upon the States,—they retained all the power they did not grant. But that each State, having expressly parted with so many powers as to constitute, jointly with the other States, a single nation cannot, from that period, possess any right to secede, because such secession does not break a league, but destroys the unity of a nation; and any injury to that unity is not only a breach which would result from the contravention of a compact, but it is an offence against the *whole Union*. To say that any State may at pleasure secede from the Union, is to say that the United States are not a nation, because it would be a solecism to contend that any part of a nation might dissolve its connection with the other parts, to their injury or ruin, without committing any offence. Secession, like any other revolutionary act, may be morally justified by the extremity of oppression; but to call it a constitutional right is confounding the meaning of terms; and can be only done through gross error, or to deceive those who are willing to assert a right, but would pause before they made a revolution, or incur the penalties consequent on a failure.

The dictates of a high duty oblige me solemnly to announce that you cannot succeed. *The laws of the United States must be executed. I have no discretionary powers upon the subject; my duty is emphatically pronounced in the Constitution.* Those who told you that you might peaceably prevent their execution deceived you; they could not have deceived themselves. THEIR OBJECT IS DISUNION. Be not deceived by names. *Disunion by armed force is* TREASON! Are you ready to incur its guilt? If you are, on the heads of the instigators of the act be the dreadful consequences—on their heads be the dishonor, but on yours may fall the punishment. The chief magistrate of the nation cannot, if he would, avoid the performance of his duty.

Look back to what was first told you as an inducement to enter into this dangerous course. The great political truth was repeated to you, that you had the revolutionary right of resisting all laws that were palpably unconstitutional and intolerably oppressive; it was added that the right to nullify a law rested on the same principle, but that it was a peaceable remedy! This character which was given to it made you receive with too much confidence the assertions that were made of the unconstitutionality of the law and its oppressive effects. Mark, my fellow-citizens, that, by the admission of your leaders, the unconstitutionality must be palpable, or it will not justify either resistance or nullification! What is the meaning of the word "palpable," in the sense in which it is here used? That which is apparent to every one; that which no man of ordinary intellect will fail to perceive. Is the unconstitutionality of these laws of that description? Let those among your leaders who once approved and advocated the principle of protective duties, answer the question; and let them choose whether they will be considered as incapable, then, of perceiving that which must have been apparent to every man of common understanding, or as imposing upon your confidence, and endeavoring to mislead you now. In either case, they are unsafe guides in the perilous path they urge you to tread. Ponder well on this circumstance, and you will know how to appreciate the exaggerated language they address to you. They are not champions of liberty, emulating the fame of our revolutionary fathers; nor are you an oppressed people, contending, as they repeat to you, against worst than colonial vassalage. . . .

I adjure you, as you honor their memory; as you love the cause of freedom, to which they dedicated their lives; as you prize the peace of your country, the lives of its best citizens, and your own fair fame,—to retrace your steps. Snatch from the archives of your State the disorganizing edict of its Convention; bid its members to reassemble, and promulgate the decided expressions of your will to remain in the path which alone can conduct you to safety, prosperity, and honor. Tell them, that, compared to disunion, all other evils are light, because that brings with it an *accumulation of all. Declare that you will never take the field unless the star-spangled banner of your country shall float over you;* that you will not be stigmatized when dead, *and dishonored and scorned while you live,* as the authors of the first attack on the Constitution of your country. *Its destroyers you cannot be.* You may disturb its peace; you may interrupt the course of its prosperity; you may cloud its reputation for stability; but its tranquility will be restored, its prosperity will return and the stain upon its national character will be transferred, *and remain an eternal blot on the memory of those who caused the disorder.*

Fellow-citizens of the United States, the threat of unhallowed disunion, the names of those, once respected, by whom it is uttered, the array of military force to support it, denote the approach of a crisis in our affairs, on which the continuance of our unexampled prosperity, our political existence, and, perhaps, that of all free governments, may depend. The conjunctures demanded a full, free, and explicit enunciation, not only of my intentions, but of my principles of action; and, as the claim was asserted of a right by a State to annul the laws of the Union, and even to secede from it at pleasure, a frank exposition of my opinions in relation to the origin and form of our government, and the construction I give to the instrument by which it was created, seem to be proper. Having the fullest confidence in the justness of the legal and constitutional opinion of my duties which has been expressed, I rely, with equal confidence,on your undivided support in my determination to execute the laws; to preserve the Union by all constitutional means; to assert, if possible, by moderate but firm measures, the necessity of a recourse to *force;* and if it be the will of Heaven that the recurrence of its primeval curse on man for the shedding of a brother's blood should fall upon our land, that it be not called down by any offensive act on the part of the United States.

THESE ATTEMPTS AT SECESSION, IDENTICAL IN SPIRIT AND DOCTRINES

It will be seen that this *second* attempt at secession took precisely the same ground, and repeated, on both sides, the language of the first. On one side it was claimed that the States did not constitute a nation; were independent sovereignties, and could not be coerced; on the other, that the people of the

States did constitute a nation; that so far the sovereignty of the States was lost or merged in it, and that it could not be attacked or dissolved by any party or parties to it; and that such an attack was treason, and carried with it all the penalties attached to that great crime.

South Carolina Persists—The Force Bill Passed, and Secession Abandoned

The State reiterating its intention to dissolve the Union, in the event of the enforcement of the obnoxious laws, Congress speedily passed what was termed the Force Bill, and General Jackson, with that promptitude which characterized all his actions, particularly in military affairs, filled the forts and military posts of the State with troops and munitions, anchored a naval force off Charleston, and stood ready on the first act of resistance to the laws to "cry havoc, and let slip the dogs of war." It was well known that he made no secret of his intention to arrest Mr. Calhoun and all others implicated on the charge of HIGH TREASON the moment any overt act was committed. He swore, as was his wont, "by the Eternal," that he would hang the first man who raised his impious hand against the Union; "would shoot the first man who pulled down the American flag." He made no secret in after years of declaring that he ought to have hung Mr. Calhoun.* He was right. The seasonable example made of one man might have saved half a million of lives. The immunity accorded to Calhoun discharged every one who chose, from all sense of duty to his country and to his fellows, from all respect for law, and is the cause of no small part of the evils under which the nation is now laboring, and the demoralization witnessed on every side.

While no man was more loyal, no man ever penetrated the designs of the secessionists more clearly and thoroughly than General Jackson. Although he put down the rebellion with a high hand, he plainly saw that he had only "scotched" the snake of secession, not killed it. He knew that the Tariff was a mere pretext, and that slavery would be the next one as soon as the way could

---

*"The old Jackson men of the inner set still speak of Mr. Calhoun in terms that show that they consider him at once the most wicked and the most despicable of American statesmen. He was a coward, conspirator, hypocrite, traitor, and fool, say they. He strove, schemed, dreamed, and lived only for the Presidency; and when he despaired of reaching that office by honorable means, he sought to rise upon the ruins of his country,—thinking it better to reign in South Carolina than to serve in the United States. General Jackson lived and died in this opinion. In his last sickness he declared that, on reflecting upon his administration, he chiefly regretted that he had not had John C. Calhoun executed for treason. 'My country,' said the General, 'would have sustained me in the act, and his fate would have been a warning to traitors for all time to come.'"—Parton's Life of Jackson, vol. iii, p. 447.

be prepared.* He even lived to witness the beginning, under the administration of Mr. Polk, of the movement which was to end in an attempt to break up the Union by force, and to find himself deserted and deceived by the very man in whom he had so confided, and who, upon his election to the presidency, turned his back upon his old patron, and allied himself to that section of the party whose disunion scheme Jackson had so earnestly and persistently combatted. Under Pierce the triumph of the secessionists became complete, and their exactions, particularly in reference to the extension of slavery, so intolerable, that all the Northern Democracy that had any idea of justice, manliness, or shame left in them, broke from the party, and joining the best part of the old National Whigs, formed a new party, the Republican, which hurled the traitors from power, and saved the Nation.

CAUSE AND PROGRESS OF THE THIRD MOVEMENT TOWARDS SECESSION

The occasions which led to the threatened secession of 1798–99 and to that of 1832 were accidental in their character. The laws complained of might be injurious or beneficial, depending upon the ideas or fancy of those affected by them. Their expiration or repeal might remove all cause of complaint. Not so with the question of slavery, which was the cause that first carried the doctrine of secession to its overt act. This was really the imminent one from the very foundation of the Government. It was the greatest obstacle to the formation of the Constitution. At that time, through its influence, two nations were upon our soil, separated by a sharp and well-defined line. The two were

"MY DEAR SIR,—. . . I have had a laborious task here; but nullification is dead, and its actors and courtiers will only be remembered by the people to be *execrated* for their wicked designs to rise and destroy the only good government on the globe, and that prosperity and happiness which we enjoy over every other portion of the world. Haman's gallows ought to be the fate of all such ambitious men who would involve their country in civil war and all the evils in its train, that they might reign and ride in the whirlwind, and direct the storm. The free people of these United States have spoken, and consigned these wicked demagogues to their proper doom. Take care of your nullifiers: you have them among you. Let them meet the indignant frowns of every man who loves his country. The Tariff, it is *now* known, was a mere pretext: its burden was on your coarse woollens. By the law of July, 1832, coarse woollen was reduced to five per cent for the benefit of the South. Mr. Clay's bill takes it up and classes it with woollens at fifty per cent, reduces it gradually down to twenty-five per cent, and there it remains; and Mr. Calhoun and all the nullifiers agree to the principle. The cash duties and home valuation will be equal to fifteen per cent more; and, after the year 1842, you pay on coarse woollens thirty-five per cent. If this is not protection, I cannot understand; and, therefore, the Tariff was only the pretext, and disunion and a Southern Confederacy the real object. *The next pretext will be the negro or slavery question.*

(Signed)   ANDREW JACKSON.

[See letter to A. J. Howard, dated May 1, 1833, McPherson's Hist. Rebellion, p. 389.]

very nearly equal in numbers, and not very unequal in territory and natural resources. Totally dissimilar in ideas and institutions, they naturally viewed each other with jealousy; or rather the South the North, as the latter had nothing to fear from the former, while the former had a great deal to fear from the latter. Institutions and society at the South rested on force,—not on right. Should these become dislocated from any cause, no matter how accidental, they might never be restored. Those of the North, resting on natural laws, could never be imperilled by mere outward pressure. The North therefore freely committed itself to the influence and guidance of ideas, no matter the direction in which they might lead, confident they could only lead to good; and eagerly welcomed, and made the most of every suggestion, improvement, and invention, which promised to increase its wealth, its comforts, and its power. It allied itself with natural laws,—with steam and electricity,—and by such alliance acquired more than human strength. The South blindfolded labor, cut itself off from the spirit of progress, and deprived itself of the use of all those contrivances and inventions which, within the memory of man, have changed the whole face of society; and as a necessary consequence it soon fell far behind the North, so far as numbers were concerned, in the race for supremacy. It viewed with constantly increasing dread that mighty power which loomed up so majestically in the distance, and which might, some day, be directed against that institution upon which rested all its material interests. Conscious of its impotence to compete in numbers and wealth, its whole energy and skill were directed to compensate for their want by political finesse, and by the control of the government, so as to use it as the instrument for its own protection. It allied itself with the great Democratic party, which was dominant in most of the Northern States, and which, almost certain of remaining in power through the aid of its Southern allies, was content, for the privilege of the spoils, to concede any interpretation which the South might put upon the Constitution, and the direction and control of the party machinery.

The Two-Thirds Vote

With such concessions, the Southern people proceeded slowly but surely in their plans of committing the Democratic party, and through it the country, to the Resolutions of 1798–99. In the Convention of 1835, which nominated Mr. Van Buren for the Presidency, it secured an immense advantage by the adoption of a rule which required a two-thirds vote for the nomination of a candidate for the Presidency. By this rule, the whole form and spirit of our political institutions were changed. An oligarchy was substituted for the rule of the majority. This rule which has since prevailed in every national Democratic Convention, which has become a cardinal principle with the party, and which always enables a few adroit and unscrupulous managers to control the Conventions, gave to the Southern States the power to prevent the nomination of any person who was not fully committed to their interests, and in whom they could not implicitly confide.

The Secession Resolution of 1840

In the Convention which renominated Mr. Van Buren in 1840 another important step was gained by the adoption of a resolution which declared:—

That the Federal Government is one of *limited* powers, derived solely from the Constitution, and the grants of power shown therein ought to be strictly construed by all the departments and agents of the Government; and that it is inexpedient and dangerous to exercise doubtful constitutional powers.

Complete Triumph of the South in 1852

This resolution was repeated at the Conventions of 1844 and 1848. At the Convention of 1852, the South accomplished its grand purpose by committing the whole Democratic Party to the doctrines, in all their length and breadth, of the right of secession by the adoption of a resolution which declared,—

That the Democratic Party will faithfully abide by and uphold the principles laid down in the Kentucky and Virginia Resolutions of 1798 and 1799, and in the Report of Mr. Madison to the Virginia Legislature in 1799; that it adopts those principles as constituting one of the main foundations of its political creed; and is resolved to carry them out in their obvious meaning and import.

By the adoption of the two-thirds rule, and the resolution last recited, the South secured to itself a position in which it could with safety remain in the Union, so long as the Democratic Party could elect a President, always to be designated by itself; or could leave it so soon as it could no longer control its policy and action.

The election of Mr. Pierce by an almost unanimous vote in the Electoral

College, only four States voting against him, and by an overwhelming majority of the popular vote, was of itself received as full evidence of the entire acceptance by the North of the doctrine of the right of peaceable secession. It was reiterated and indorsed in all the States and in all the local ratifying Conventions; in all those held for the nomination of State officers and Members of Congress; so that there was hardly a Democrat in the whole United States who did not, in the course of the canvass, give repeated and emphatic "AYES" to the secession doctrine. Well might Mr. Calhoun, had he lived till then, have exclaimed, "Now let thy servant depart in peace!" for the defeat of the National Whig Party, in 1852, was a virtual annihilation of all effective opposition to the complete ascendancy of the Democratic Party, which ruled supreme till the organization of a new party,—the Republican,—upon the basis of Freedom, and its final triumph by the election of Mr. Lincoln, in 1860.

Mr. Tilden Comes to the Front, and Proclaims the Right of Secession—His Letter to Hon. William Kent

As the secession resolution of 1852 was repeated in 1856, and by both wings of the Democratic Party in 1860,—that which nominated Mr. Douglas at Baltimore, and that which nominated Mr. Breckinridge at Richmond,—the South, as far as the Democratic Party was concerned, was left, upon the election of Mr. Lincoln, free to choose whether it would remain in the Union, or peaceably secede from it. It was at this crisis that Mr. Tilden first became conspicuous in political affairs. His zeal and activity knew no bounds. His eloquence flamed, in the canvass, from every rostrum and stump. He asserted that the South had as much at stake in slavery as the North had in freedom; that it had as much right to pollute the Territories with its institutions as the North had to adorn it with its own; and that, unless the South was gratified in all its demands, it might and ought to retire from the Union; that there was no tie to hold it, no power to coerce it. His views were fully and carefully elaborated in the letter to the Hon. William Kent, already referred to. In that letter he says:—

> Each section is organized into States with complete governments, *holding the power and wielding the sword.* They are held together *only* by a compact of confederation. . . . The single, slender, conventional tie which holds the States in confederation has no strength compared with the compacted intertwining fibres which bind the atoms of human society into one formation of natural

growth. . . . The masters in political science who constructed our system preserved the State Governments as bulwarks of the freedom of individuals and localities against oppression from centralized power. They recognized no right of constitutional secession; BUT THEY LEFT REVOLUTION ORGANIZED WHENEVER IT SHOULD BE DEMANDED BY THE PUBLIC OPINION OF A STATE,—LEFT IT, WITH THE POWER TO SNAP THE TIE OF CONFEDERATION AS A NATION MIGHT BREAK A TREATY, AND TO REPEL COERCION AS A NATION MIGHT REPEL INVASION. They caused us to depend in great measure upon the public opinion of the States, in order to maintain a confederated union.

Again (page 7):—

As a rule of right and duty, for the construction and execution of the Constitution, the theory maintained by Mr. Seward, and too exclusively accepted (that the Government could exclude slavery from the Territories), is entirely fallacious. No contract governing complicated transactions or relations between men, and applying permanently through the changes inevitable in human affairs, can be effectual if either party intended to be bound by it is at liberty to construe or execute its provisions in a spirit of hostility to the substantial objects of those provisions,—*especially is this true of a compact of confederation between the States, where there can be no common arbiter invested with authorities and powers equally capable with those which courts possess between individuals for determining and enforcing a just construction and execution of the instrument.*

It will be observed that the latter part of the quotation reiterates almost in terms the language used by Mr. Madison in his report as to the want of a common arbiter between the States; and that each State, consequently, must be the sole judge of the emergency in which it may be called upon to act. The first part is even more emphatic than the secession Resolutions themselves in declaring, that, upon its mere motion, "A STATE MAY SNAP THE TIE OF CONFEDERATION AS A NATION MIGHT BREAK A TREATY, AND REPEL COERCION AS A NATION MIGHT REPEL INVASION."

THE SOUTH SECEDES, SOUTH CAROLINA
LEADING AS IN 1832

These words of encouragement and instruction for the Southern States had hardly fallen from Mr. Tilden's lips, than they proceeded to put them in practice. At that time Jackson no longer stood with flaming sword to bar the way. On the sixth day of November, 1860, before the election of Mr. Lincoln, the Legislature of the State of South Carolina assembled, and received a message from the Governor, in which he expressed his opinion that the only alternative left to it was secession from the Federal Union. On the 7th of November, the Postmaster, Collector, and other Federal officers in Charleston resigned their respective positions. On the 10th of November, the Senators from that State, in Congress, resigned. On the 13th of November, the collection of debts due to citizens of non-slaveholding States was prohibited. On the same day, Francis W. Pickens was elected Governor, and appointed, as a Cabinet, A. G. McGrath, Secretary of State; David F. Jamison, Secretary of War; C. G. Memminger, Secretary of the Treasury; William W. Harllee, Postmaster-General; and Albert C. Garlington, Secretary of the Interior. On the 17th of the same month, the ordinance of secession was unanimously adopted by a convention of delegates called for that purpose. On the 21st of November, commissioners were appointed to proceed to Washington to treat for the delivery to the State of the property of the United States within its limits. On the 24th of November, the Representatives of the State in Congress resigned their seats. And, on the 20th of December, 1860, the Governor of the State announced the repeal, by the people of South Carolina, of the ordinance (of the adoption of the Constitution) of May 23, 1788, and the dissolution of the Union between the State of South Carolina and other States, under the name of the United States of America; and proclaimed to the world that "the State of South Carolina is, as she has a right to be, a separate, sovereign, free, and independent State; and, as such, has the right to levy war, to conclude peace, to negotiate treaties, leagues, or covenants, and to do all acts whatsoever rightfully appertaining to a free and independent State."

The history of one seceding State will do for all. All the Southern States, as speedily as possible, followed the example of South Carolina, adopting her language and acts as precedents for theirs; so that, before Mr. Lincoln came to the Presidential Chair, nearly all of the Southern States had asserted, and apparently effected, the right of secession which Mr. Tilden proclaimed for them on every stump, and which he did all that lay in his power to forward.

THE SOUTH RIGHT IN SECEDING, ACCORDING TO MR. TILDEN AND THE NORTHERN DEMOCRACY

In looking back to this time, was not the conduct of the Southern States, from all the lights they could gather, perfectly justifiable and proper? A great party, existing from the foundation of the Government and embracing a large majority of the population of the Free States, had in almost every possible form declared their rights to be what by the act of secession they assumed them to be. It was not to be expected that they should recognize any duty of allegiance to the Republican Party, in case the latter came into power. It would be, in their view, the devotion to destruction of their dearest interests. The Republican Party proclaimed the incompatibility of Slavery with a free government; that the nation must, in time, become "all free or all slave." The South appreciated this great truth as well as the North. Such assumption rested not upon opinion, but upon natural law. They were content to remain in the Union so long as it could be made to protect slavery, and not a moment longer. They could judge of the sentiment of the North—of the Democratic party—only through its leaders,—through its exponents, among whom Mr. Tilden took a foremost rank. These leaders were unanimous as to the right of the Southern States to secede; and the multitude spoke only through them.

Franklin Pierce Asserts the Right of the South to Secede

Mr. Pierce, President of the United States from 1852 to 1856, wrote to his old friend, Jefferson Davis, his former Secretary of War, and the future President of the slave republic, under the date of Jan. 6, 1860, nearly a year before the election of Mr. Lincoln, in the following strain:*—

> I have just had a pleasant interview with Mr. ———, whose courage and fidelity are equal to his learning and talents. He says he would rather fight the battle under you as a standard-bearer in 1860, than under the auspices of any other leader. The feeling and judgment of Mr. ——— is, I am confident, rapidly gaining ground. Our people are looking for the "Coming Man," one who is raised by all the elements of his character above the atmosphere ordinarily breathed by politicians; a man really formed for this exigency, by his ability, courage, broad statesmanship, and patriotism. Colonel Thomas H. Seymour arrived here this morning, and expressed his views in this relation in almost the identical language used by Mr. ———. . . . I do not believe that our friends at the South have any just idea of the state of feeling, hurrying at this moment to the pitch of intense exasperation, between those who respect their political obligations and those who have apparently no impelling power but that which the

*See McPherson's History of the Rebellion, page 391.

fanatical passion on the subject of slavery imparts. Without discussing the question of right, of abstract power to secede, I have never believed that actual disruption of the Union can occur without blood; AND IF THROUGH THE MADNESS OF NORTHERN ABOLITIONISM, THAT DIRE CALAMITY MUST COME, THE fighting WILL NOT BE ALONG MASON AND DIXON'S LINE MERELY. IT WILL BE WITHIN OUR OWN BORDERS, IN OUR OWN STREETS, BETWEEN THE TWO CLASSES OF CITIZENS TO WHOM I HAVE REFERRED. THOSE WHO DEFY LAW, AND SCOUT CONSTITUTIONAL OBLIGATIONS, WILL, IF WE EVER REACH THE ARBITRAMENT OF ARMS, find OCCUPATION ENOUGH AT HOME. . . .

(Signed)   FRANKLIN PIERCE

To Hon JEFFERSON DAVIS, Washington, D.C.

BUCHANAN ON THE RIGHT OF THE SOUTH TO SECEDE

Mr. Buchanan, in his last message to the Congress of the United States, delivered on the 4th of December, 1860, and after the secession of South Carolina, took precisely the ground of Mr. Tilden, that the Federal Government could not coerce a seceding State.—

"The question fairly stated," said Mr. Buchanan, in the message referred to, "is: Has the Constitution delegated to Congress the power to *coerce* a State into submission which is attempting to withdraw, or has actually withdrawn, from the Confederacy? If answered in the affirmative, it must be on the principle that the power has been conferred on Congress to declare and to make war against a State. After much serious reflection, I HAVE ARRIVED AT THE CONCLUSION THAT NO SUCH POWER HAS BEEN DELEGATED TO CONGRESS NOR TO ANY OTHER DEPARTMENT OF THE FEDERAL GOVERNMENT. It is manifest, upon an inspection of the Constitution, that this power is not among the specific and enumerated powers granted to Congress; and it is equally apparent that its exercise is not necessary and proper for carrying into execution any one of its powers. . . .

"But, if we possessed this power, would it be wise to exercise it under existing circumstances? The object, doubtless, would be to preserve the Union. *War would not only present the most effectual means of destroying it, but would finish all hopes of its peaceful reconstruction.*

"The fact is, that our Union rests upon PUBLIC OPINION,* and can never be cemented by the blood of its citizens, shed in civil war. *If it cannot live in the affections of the people, it must one day perish.* Congress possesses many means of

---

*With Mr. Tilden, Mr. Buchanan, and the like, *influence* is government. Let us see what Washington said about influence being Government.

"The picture which you have exhibited, and the accounts which are published of the commotions and

preserving it by conciliation; but the sword was not placed in their hands to preserve it by force.

"In this conclusion, I shall merely call attention to the few sentences in *Mr. Madison's justly celebrated Report in 1799, to the Legislature of Virginia. In this he ably and conclusively defended the Resolutions of the preceding Legislature (of 1798) against the strictures of several other State Legislatures. These were mainly founded upon the protest of the Virginia Legislature against the Alien and Sedition Laws, as palpable and alarming infractions of the Constitution.* In pointing out the peaceful and constitutional remedies, and he referred to none other, to which the States were authorized to resort on such occasions, he concludes by saying that the Legislatures of the States might have made direct representation to Congress with a view to obtain a rescinding of the two offending acts; or they might have represented to their respective Senators in Congress their wish that two-thirds thereof would propose an explanatory amendment of the Constitution; or two-thirds of themselves, if such had been their option, might, by an application to Congress, have obtained a Convention for the same object."

It will be observed that Mr. Buchanan had "fully adopted the Resolutions of 1798 and 1799, and the Report of Mr. Madison* to the Virginia Legislature in 1799; and that he adopted the principle contained therein as constituting

---

temper of numerous parties in the Eastern States, present a state of things equally to be lamented and deprecated. They exhibit a melancholy proof of what our transatlantic foe has predicted; and of another thing, perhaps, which is still more to be regretted, and is yet more unaccountable, that mankind, when left to themselves, are unfit for their own government. I am mortified beyond expression when I view the clouds that have spread over the brightest morn that ever dawned upon any country. In a word, I am lost in amazement when I behold what intrigue, the interested views of desperate characters, ignorance, and jealousy of the minor part, are capable of effecting, as a scourge on the major part of our fellow-citizens of the Union; for it is hardly to be supposed, that the great body of the people, though they will not act, can be so short-sighted, or enveloped in darkness, as not to see rays of a distant sun through all this mist of intoxication and folly.

"You talk, my good sir, of employing influence to appease the present turmoils in Massachusetts. I now not where that influence is to be found; or, if attainable, that it would be a proper remedy for the disorders. Influence is not Government. Let us have a government by which our lives, liberties, and properties will be secured, or let us know the worst at once. Under these impressions, my humble opinion is, that there is a call for decision. Know precisely what the insurgents aim at. If they have *real* grievances, redress them if possible; or acknowledge the justice of them, and your inability to do it at the moment. If they have not, *employ the force of government against them at once.* If this is inadequate, *all* will be convinced that the superstructure is bad, or wants support. To be more exposed in the eyes of the world, and more contemptible than we already are, is hardly possible. To delay one or the other of these expedients, is to exasperate on the one hand, or to give confidence on the other, and will add to their numbers; for, like snowballs, such bodies increase by every movement, unless there is something in the way to obstruct and crumble them before their weight is too great and irresistible." (See Letter to Henry Lee, Wash. Works, (Sparks' ed.) vol. ix., p. 293.)

*It is proper to state, that, later in life, Mr. Madison fully recanted the doctrines of his Report, and the Resolutions of 1798–99. Mr. Jefferson adhered to them to the last, and even repeated them in 1824 with more emphasis than ever. Mr. Madison's recantation brought down upon him the most violent attacks and abuse from the nullification party.

one of the main foundations of the political creed of the Democratic Party, and had resolved to carry them out in their obvious meaning and import." And well did he carry them out. He folded his hands in impotent despair, and allowed the rebels to seize nearly every stronghold in the South, which were only regained by a cost of almost infinite blood and treasure.

J. S. Black, Buchanan's Attorney-General, on the Right of the South to Secede

Mr. J. S. Black, Attorney-General of the United States under Buchanan, in reply to an inquiry as to the right of the government to coerce the seceding States, replied in a similar strain:

> "If it be true," he said, "that war cannot be declared [as he had attempted to show in his letter that it could not], nor a system of general hostilities be carried on by the central government against a State, then it seems to follow that an attempt to do so would be *ipso facto* an expulsion of such State from the Union. Being treated as an alien and an enemy, she would be compelled to act accordingly. If Congress should break up the present Union, by unconstitutionally putting strife, and enmity, and armed hostility, between the different sections of the country, instead of '*domestic tranquility*,' which the Constitution was meant to insure, will not all the States be absolved from their Federal obligations? Is any portion of the people bound to contribute their money or their blood to carry on a contest like this?
>
> "If this view of the subject be as correct as I think it is, then the Union must perish. utterly perish, at the moment when Congress shall arm one portion of the people against another, for any purpose beyond that of merely protecting the General Government in the essence of its proper constitutional functions."

Fernando Wood on the Right of the South to Secede

In 1861, at the outbreak of the rebellion, Mr. Fernando Wood was mayor of the City of New York. At such a crisis, no position in the United States could be more important to the cause of nationality and freedom. He not only took the ground that the Union was rightfully and irreparable dissolved, but he was already forecasting the section or party with which the City of New York should cast its fortunes. That city was not only dissolved from allegiance to the Nation, but the State. On the 6th of May, 1861, he sent a message to its common council, in which he used the following language:—

It would seem the dissolution of the Federal Union is inevitable. Having been formed originally on the basis of general mutual protection, *but separate local independence,*—each State reserving the entire and absolute control of its own domestic affairs,—*it is evidently impossible to keep them together longer than they deem themselves fairly treated by each other, or longer than the interests, honor, and fraternity, of the people of the several States are satisfied. Being a government created by* OPINION, *its continuance is dependent upon the continuance of the sentiments which formed it. It cannot be preserved by coercion, or held together by force. A resort to this last dreaded alternative would, of itself, destroy not only the government, but the lives and property of the people.*

If these forebodings should be realized, and a separation of the States shall occur, momentous considerations will be presented to the corporate authorities of this city. We must provide for new relations, which will necessarily grow out of the new condition of public affairs.

It will be not only necessary for us to settle the relations which we shall hold to the other cities and States, but to establish new ones, if we can, with a POR-TION of our own State. . . .

California, and her sisters of the Pacific, will no doubt set up an independent Republic, and husband their own rich mineral resources. The Western States, equally rich in cereals and other agricultural products, will probably do the same. *Then it may be said, why should not New York City, instead of supporting by her contributions in revenue* TWO-THIRDS *the expenses of the United States, become also equally independent?* As a free city, with but nominal duty on her imports, her local government could be supported without taxation upon her people. Thus we could live free from taxes, and have cheap goods, nearly duty free. In this she would have the whole and united support of the SOUTHERN STATES, as well as all the other States to whose interest and rights under the Constitution she has always been true.

RODMAN M. PRICE ON THE RIGHT OF THE SOUTH TO SECEDE

In the spring of 1861, Mr. Rodman M. Price, who had recently been Governor of the State of New Jersey, in a letter addressed to Mr. L. W. Burnett, of Newark, in answer to the question, "What ought New Jersey to do?" replied:

I believe the Southern Confederation permanent. The proceeding has taken place with forethought and deliberation; it is no hurried impulse, but an irrevocable act, based upon the sacred, as was supposed, equality of the States; and, in my opinion, every Slave State will, in a short period of time, be united in one Confederacy. Before that event happens, we cannot act, however much we may suffer in our material interests. It is in that contingency, then, that I answer the second part of your question, What position for New Jersey will best accord with her interests, honor, and the patriotic instincts of her people? I say, emphatically, she would go with the South, from every wise, prudential, and patriotic reason.*

Leaders of the Northern Democracy Responsible for Secession

The preceding examples of the position of the leaders of the Northern Democracy at that time upon the subject of secession might be repeated without limit. The Southern people were told to go—were literally driven—out of the Union by their friends. They never would have raised the standard of the rebellion had they possessed the least idea of the real sentiment of the North. How could they get at that sentiment? Not through the Republican Party, which represented only a small majority of the North, and which, if war arose, was to be confronted by the Democrats in arms on their own soil. If fifty persons of the class we have quoted from had told the Southern people that they had no right to secede, that the attempt would be met by armed force, that the days and spirit of General Jackson were still remembered and revered, and that his denunciation of secession would become the watchwords of freedom, the South would never have taken the first step in rebellion.

What an infinite number of murders, of deaths in battle and camp, are to be laid to the charge of such men as Tilden, Buchanan, Wood, and the old leaders of Democracy, but for whom secession would have been but a dream! And one of these very men whose garments are most deeply dyed in the blood of his fellows is now to be made President of the United States,—to administer a government which he has spent a lifetime in attempting to undermine and overthrow!

Buchanan, Tilden, and Others Contrasted with Washington and Jackson

When we contrast the conduct of Mr. Buchanan and his government, in the third attempt at secession, with that of Washington and Jackson in the two preceding attempts, we can get some idea of the depth of the abyss of degra-

*See McPherson's Hist. of the Rebellion, p. 390.

dation into which the leaders of the Northern democracy had fallen. From the proclamation of General Jackson, in 1832, to the last message of Buchanan, in 1860, was a period of only twenty-eight years. Yet the conduct of the actors at these two periods was as unlike as if there had been centuries between them. One cannot imagine such a man as Jackson to belong to the same race with such as Buchanan, Tilden, Wood, and Franklin Pierce; one so patriotic, with such consciousness of the magnitude and importance of the issue before him, not only for his own people, but for mankind; knowing no duty for the moment but the preservation of the Union; the others so traitorous, so utterly lost to all sense of patriotism and humanity, that they would break up the government unless it could be made the instrument of polluting our virgin soil with slavery, and be made to minister to the ambitious and passions of those whose characters were the product of this accursed system. "Our Federal Union, it must be *preserved*," was Jackson's famous toast which, at the time, sent such a thrill through the hearts of his countrymen. Had secession become an overt act, he would have put into the field the last man, would have fired the last shot, and freely given up, if need be, his own life. What did Washington say in the letter to Henry Lee, already quoted? "If they (the malcontents in Massachusetts) have real grievances, *redress* them. If they have not, *employ the force of government against them at once!*" Contrast Washington and Jackson with such a wretched, sneaking, imbecile creature as Buchanan, who, when his trial came, sat motionless with terror, pleading as the excuse for his cowardice and inaction the Resolutions of 1798! Certainly, the great Revolution, which would have consigned such creatures to eternal obscurity, but for the infamy attached to them, came not a moment too soon. To what was that fall, which has no parallel in history, due? To slavery. The great reaction under the Stuarts, which seemed for a time to debauch all England, cannot for a moment compare with the utter demoralization of our public men in the time of Buchanan. The English soon became ashamed of their excesses, which were an accidental phase, partly due to the previous pressure and restraint. One reaction simply followed another. But slavery knew no change, and tolerated no compunctions or remorse. It exacted the daily sacrifice upon its altar of the little humanity or patriotism which the leaders of the Northern Democracy might still be supposed to feel. Without moral or political sense on the part of our rulers, the machinery of government refused to move longer. The very existence of society was threatened; and, but for the rise of the Republican Party to rescue the Government from the hands of traitors and imbeciles, we should already be repeating the examples of Mexico and those South American Republics where anarchy and rapine are not the exception, but the rule.

Mr. Tilden's Infamous Resolution at the Chicago Convention of 1864

The war into which the Nation was plunged by Mr. Tilden and his associates went on. In the dark days that followed, he gave to the cause of freedom and the Union no aid, no sympathy, no cheer. It was an unholy cause, an unrighteous war. Instead of going to the front, to encourage and sustain our soldiers, everywhere imperilling their lives, and falling in the cause of freedom, of humanity, and of the Union, he remained at home, far from danger, craven and terror-stricken, and hoarse with the cry of Peace! Peace! He would give up all for which so much life and treasure had been sacrificed, and for which so much had been suffered, and place the country still more under the feet of those who had poured contempt upon the Union, and upon the Northern Democracy, and upon none more than on those who, like Mr. Tilden, were traitors, not only to the supreme government, but to their own soil. The Convention at Chicago, in 1864, which nominated Mr. McClellan for the Presidency, again, as in 1860, became his opportunity. As a member of the Convention, he moved for the appointment of a committee on Resolutions, and was made one of its members. This Committee reported, among others, the *infamous* Resolution, reiterating, in terms, the doctrines of his letter, of which the following is a copy:—

> *Resolved, That this Convention does explicitly declare, as the sense of the American people, that, after four years of failure to restore the Union by the experiment of war,—during which, under the pretence of military necessity, or war power, higher than the Constitution, the Constitution itself has been disregarded in every part, and public liberty and private life alike trodden down, and the material prosperity of the country essentially impaired,—justice, humanity, liberty, and the public welfare, demand that immediate efforts be made for a cessation of hostilities, with a view to an ultimate convention of the States, or other peaceable means, to the end, that, at the earliest practical moment, peace may be restored on the basis of the Federal States.*

Proceedings of the Convention of 1864 in Reference to This Resolution

The Democratic National Convention of 1864, for the nomination of a candidate for the Presidency, met at Chicago, August 29. The following accounts of the proceedings, as far as relates to the matter of Resolutions or Platform, are copied *verbatim* from the Report of the same, transmitted to and published in the "New York World" of August 30 and August 31:—

Mr. Tilden, of New York, moved (Aug. 29) that one delegate be appointed by each delegation, to report Resolutions for the consideration of the Convention, and that all Resolutions be referred to said Committee without debate. Carried.

Mr. Guthrie, Chairman of the Committee on Resolutions, stated (Aug. 30) that several Resolutions offered to said Committee, yesterday, have been referred to a sub-Committee, and there was reason to believe that they would be ready to report this afternoon; and, furthermore, that there was a fair prospect of arriving at a harmonious conclusion.

Mr. Tilden, of New York, said that the Chairman of the sub-Committee, General John B. Weller, would probably be ready to report at four o'clock, P.M.; that Mr. Vallandigham was of opinion that they would not be ready at that hour, and that Mr. Guthrie hoped to be ready.

A motion was made to take a recess till four o'clock.

Mr. Cass moved to adjourn until to-morrow morning.

Mr. Brown, of Delaware (a member of the Committee), said THERE WAS NO DIFFERENCE OF OPINION AMONG THE MEMBERS OF THE COMMITTEE; nothing but a disposition, perhaps, on the part of a few to procrastinate; and there was no good reason why they should not be ready to report this afternoon.

Mr. McKeon said he would be in favor of instructing the Committee to report this afternoon. There was no need of further delay. *The sentiments of the members were alike; and, if there was any question at all, it was one of phraseology rather than of principles.*

Mr. Vallandigham thought it best to give the Committee further time, being satisfied that by to-morrow morning they will be able to bring in a Report upon which all Democrats and Conservatives in the country can cordially unite.

Several other members of the Convention said, that, whatever difference of opinion may exist among its members, they are as to the phraseology of the Resolutions rather than to the sentiment; and, if the Convention would immediately take a recess, the Committee would be able to conclude their labors by four o'clock P.M.

A motion for recess was put and carried.

Upon the reassembling of the Convention, at four o'clock, Mr. Guthrie stated that the Committee on Resolutions had agreed, and were now ready to report.

Mr. Cox moved the previous question.

Some discussion followed, but

Mr. Cox insisted upon his motion, and, the previous question being ordered, the Resolutions were adopted, with but *four* dissenting votes.

Mr. Tilden, as mover of the Committee on Resolutions, was, by courtesy, entitled to the chairmanship. The following despatch to the "New York World" explains the reasons why Mr. Guthrie was made Chairman:—

Mr. Samuel J. Tilden, of New York City, was the platform Committee-man selected by the New York Delegation, and, being the mover in the Convention of the Resolution for the appointment of the Committee on the platform (each State naming its man), became, by presumption of parliamentary strength, the Chairman of the Committee itself. The friends of Mr. Vallandigham pressed him for Chairman. Mr. Tilden, however, disclaiming any privilege for himself, Honorable James Guthrie, of Kentucky, was immediately elected by a large majority.

It will be remembered that Vallandigham, the associate of Mr. Tilden on this Committee, and his co-worker in the Chicago Convention, was drummed out of the Union lines, and sent into the camp of his friends, the rebels, for his notorious disloyalty, and the aid and comfort he gave the enemy.

Endorsement of the Resolution by the New York World

The great theme with the "New York World," upon the adjournment of the Convention, was its Resolutions or Platform; and, on the 1st of September, 1864, the following appeared in its columns as its leading editorial.

The Democratic Platform

The vigorous, patriotic, and conciliatory declaration of principles adopted at Chicago will be generally acceptable to the party. Not only all Democrats, but all Union-loving Conservatives, no matter of what political antecedents, can stand upon it with *honest approbation.* The Black Republicans carp at it,—as well they may. It was not made to please *them;* it is not calculated to promote the success of their party. They complain that it contains no invectives against the South; but it was by invectives against the South that the Union was destroyed. Democrats do not perceive that infuriated rant against the South has any tendency to bring its people to reason. The paramount aim of the Democratic Party is to restore the Union; the announcement of principles is intended to be such that when the South is tired of war, a repentant Union Party will have some tenable ground to stand upon. If they will accept of the Union, we offer them peace. If a controlling majority refuse, we still enable a minority to advocate the old Union without being hooted down; and, under the continued pressure of the war, a Union minority in the South may soon grow to a majority.

Besides objecting to the platform that it does not denounce those whom we wish to win back to the Union, its Republican critics say it is, in other respects, too negative. It is positive enough for the Union; and positive enough in its condemnation of the obstacles interposed by this recreant administration to the restoration of the Union. The things it insists on lie at the very roots of our Federative Republican system. The things it denounces are the chief dangers which, at the present time, assail that system. Southern arms would be powerless if they were not backed by Southern hatred. While stemming the stream, we aim to close up the fountain. While resisting Southern arms, we would remove all *just* causes of Southern dissatisfaction. We cannot ask the South, we will not ask *anybody,* to live contentedly under a government which does not permit free elections, *which violates State rights,* which throws men into prisons without informing them of their offence or allowing them a trial; which burdens white men with oppressive debt and grinding taxation to try an unconstitutional experiment of giving freedom to negroes. It is the government which our fathers made and administered, as the Democratic Party through the greater part of seventy years administered it, to which we invite the South to renew their allegiance; and we conceive it that they will prefer this to the prolongation of a civil, fratricidal war. If all do not, a part will; and no national man has any hope of restoring the Union without the co-operation of a Southern Union Party, which may in time grow to be a majority. The Democratic platform is calculated to remove the main obstacles to the formation of a Southern Union Party. When denunciation of the Confederate Government comes from *that* quarter, it will be of some value; and there is nothing for which the Southern people are so likely to denounce it, as for a refusal to make a reasonable peace, and relieve them from their cruel sufferings. But a proposal for an *abolition* peace can never gain a hearing in the South. If the Abolition Party continue in power, the separation is final, alike in feeling and in fact.

One might well suppose that Mr. Tilden wrote the editorial in the "World," as well as the Resolutions adopted by the Convention; for a more insidious, sneaking, hypocritical apology for the South and attack upon the Union cause than that contained in it, was never penned. It was wholly in keeping with the conduct of that class of nullifiers and disunionists of which Mr. Tilden was the appropriate exponent. How impotent all his plottings and machinations! and how true, applied to him, the burning words of General Jackson to all traitors to their country: "*Its destroyers you cannot be. You may disturb its peace; you may interrupt the course of its prosperity; you may* cloud its reputation for stability; but its tranquility will be restored, its prosperity will return, and the stain upon its national character will be transferred, *and remain an eternal blot on the memory of those who caused the disorder."*

The South Coerced into the Union

The cause of the Union and of freedom at last triumphed. The South was subdued, *coerced* back into the Union, nationality was restored by the sword, and the great obstacle to a true union, slavery, destroyed, in spite of all the efforts, the predictions, and the hopes of the Tildens, the Woods, the Buchanans, and the whole of that disloyal crew in which they stood conspicuous. Had Jackson lived and been at the head of affairs, not a few of them would have graced the gallows, or have been compelled to fly for escape to foreign lands. Calhoun was a model of patriotism and honor compared with them. He made a law which might have been, and perhaps was, justly obnoxious, the ground of secession. Tilden made the maintenance of the most accursed system that the world has ever seen—"the sum of all villanies"—his cause for secession, adding to his traitorous instincts an utter want of sympathy with oppressed humanity.

Mr. Tilden's Arraignment of the Republican Party on the Slavery Question

While Mr. Tilden proclaimed, on all occasions, the abstract right of the South to secede, the ground on which he justified the movement in which he was engaged was the conduct of the Republican party on the subject of slavery. He makes up his indictment by quotations from the speeches made by Mr. Seward and Mr. Lincoln in the canvass then pending. "The *rôle,*" he said, "of moral right and duty which may be fairly said to be adopted by the Republican party is stated by Mr. Seward at Lansing."

"I will favor," said Mr. Seward, "as long as I can within the limits of constitutional action, the decrease and limitation of African slavery."

"This sentiment," says Mr. Tilden, "runs through all Mr. Seward's speeches, and is, I think, the master-key to the whole argument by which the Republican leaders address the popular mind." He then proceeds to fortify his original charge, by giving the following quotations from different speeches made by Mr. Seward:—

"We do not *vote*," says Mr. Seward, "against slavery in Virginia. We do not authorize Abraham Lincoln or the Congress of the United States to *pass any laws* about slavery in Virginia.

"It is by a simple rule that I have studied the Constitution, which rule is, that no human being, no race, should be kept down in their efforts to rise to a higher state of liberty and happiness.

"It is true that they (the fathers) necessarily and wisely modified this policy of freedom, by leaving it to the several States, affected as they were by different circumstances, to abolish slavery in their own way and by their own pleasure, instead of confiding that duty to Congress.

*   *   *   *   *   *

"But the very nature of these modifications fortifies my position, that the fathers knew that *the two systems could not endure within the Union,* and expected that within a short period slavery would disappear for ever. Moreover, in order that these modifications might not altogether defeat their grand design of a republic maintaining *universal equality, they provided that two-thirds of the States might amend the Constitution.*

"It remains to say on this point only one word, to guard against misapprehension. If these States are to again become universally slaveholding, I do not pretend to say with what violations of the Constitution that end shall be accomplished. On the other hand, while I do confidently believe and hope that my country will yet become a land of universal freedom, I do not expect that it will be made so otherwise than through *the action of the several States co-operating with the Federal Government,* and all acting in strict conformity with their respective constitutions. I will favor, as long as I can, within the limits of constitutional action, the decrease and diminution of African slavery in all the States."

He quotes to the same effect from speeches of Mr. Lincoln, whose speeches, he says, are full of denunciations of "the further spread of slavery," the restriction of which will, he predicts, "place it where the public mind will rest in the belief that it is in the course of ultimate extinction." "We know," says he, "the opening of new countries tend to the perpetuation of the institution, and so does keep men in slavery who would otherwise be free." "Nothing," he again says, "will make you successful, but setting up a policy which shall treat the thing as wrong." . . . "This government is expressly charged with the duty of providing for the general welfare. We believe that the spreading out and perpetuity of the institution of slavery impairs the general welfare." . . . "To repress this thing, we think, is providing for the general welfare."

The italics, in the preceding quotations from Mr. Seward's speeches, are Mr. Tilden's. In commenting upon them, he replies:—

The mode provided by the Constitution for its own amendment, is not accurately stated by Mr. Seward in the above extract, but the plan of applying it so as to abolish slavery within the States is sufficiently disclosed. In a recent speech, he proposes to absolutely exclude from admission into the Union all new States having slaves, and to apply our northern system to all new States; evidently looking to the multiplication of the free States until their number shall enable them to alter the Constitution, and "the grand design of a republic maintaining universal equality" shall be consummated, without the consent and in defiance of the will of the Southern States.

Wisdom and Necessity of the Republican Organization

Could any sentiments be more just, humane, or wise than those upon which Mr. Seward and Mr. Lincoln proclaimed the Republican party to be founded? Was it not desirable that African slavery should come to an end? Was it not proper that the Constitution should be invoked for such an object? Our fathers provided for the amendment of that instrument to meet any great inconvenience or grievance, not sufficiently provided against. If, in such matter, two-thirds of the States propose, and three-fourths ratify, must not the minority of one-fourth, yield? Is not this a government of majorities? Does not a minority of one always have to yield, on all occasions, to a majority of one? If there could be no progress, no change, the nation would surely die: An inexorable code is always death. All codes and all constitutions must change with the change of the national life. The code of the ten tables, the foundation of, and at one time the only source of, Roman law, almost wholly disappeared in the subsequent codes of the Empire. The English Constitution always yields to supreme necessity. Our Constitution can only yield to such necessity by its formal amendment. This was the only way, the only mode, at the time, by which the question of slavery could be met. It was in harmony with the instrument itself, with the habits and thoughts of our people, and with that necessity of progress, consequently of change, inherent in our race. There was no suggestion of unfair dealing of covert design. Every thing was open and manly. Whether the object sought to be gained was wise, humane, and useful, I will not at this late day attempt to show. The demonstration transcends words.

But Mr. Tilden joins issue, not only on the constitutionality, but the *policy,* of such an amendment. He would keep the negro perpetually in chains, as a matter of principle, for the benefit of the white race, and as the best condition of the black. "They (the Republicans) ask," he says, "Have we not a right to elect a President in a constitutional manner by our own votes?" "You have," he replies, "in obedience to the fundamental ideas of our *Confederation,* no more moral right to do so on the basis of your present party organization than you have to do a thousand other things which the laws and Constitution allow, but which reason, justice, public policy, and fraternal sympathy, forbid."

> "The Northern States," he continues, "have a direct and important interest in keeping the natural course of their emigration into the territories substantially undisturbed, with freedom to such of their people as overflow into the territories to establish in their new seats such systems of industry and society as they have been accustomed to at home.
> "The Southern States have exactly the same interest. *Both have an indirect interest in the formation of new States, as it affects the balance of power between the two classes in the Confederation.*"

Balance of power between the two classes of the Confederation! What two classes? Slave and free. Then we are a nation of *classes,* not of individuals. Has it come to this, that we must nurture and maintain on our own soil the antagonisms and rivalries of the Old World, for which millions of men are kept constantly under arms, and which stand as the great blot upon, and the great obstacle to, the progress of humanity? What kind of a Government, and what kind of a nation, is this, in which the different members are to checkmate, overreach, and, if they cannot succeed in this way, to attack and destroy each other? Is this Mr. Tilden's statesmanship, of which he makes such boast,—this the kind of Nation whose affairs he is to be called upon to administer? God, in his infinite mercy, forbid!

MR. TILDEN DECLARES THAT THE REPUBLICAN
MOVEMENT MUST END IN UTTER
FAILURE AND DISGRACE

But suppose the Republican party elects Mr. Lincoln, what then? "I will tell you," says Mr. Tilden.

"The Southern States," to quote from his letter, "will not, by any possibility, accept the avowed creed of the Republican Party as the permanent policy of the federative government as to slavery, either in the States or Territories. . . ."

Nothing short of the recession of the Republican party to the point of total and absolute non-action on the subject of slavery in the States and Territories could enable it to reconcile to itself the people of the South. Even then it would have great and fixed antipathies to overcome; and men and parties act chiefly from habit. . . .

Will the Republican Party submit itself to this inevitable necessity to revolutionize its whole character? To attempt this change, and not to perish as a dominant party, is barely possible. Not to attempt and accomplish it, and yet to live as an ascendant power in our Union, is totally impossible. . . .

It must travel through the entire cycle of retrogression, and demonstrate that its existence in its present form was a mistake. . . .

What will Mr. Lincoln do? Can he be expected, as President, to understand the state of things in any other sense than that of his own partisan policy? Can he avoid the attempt to maintain the power of his party by the same means which will have acquired it? Can he emancipate himself from the dominion of the ideas, associations, and influences which will have accompanied him in his rise to power? Can he be expected to act in any new direction with sufficient breadth of view and firmness of purpose?

If he shall fail adequately to respond to these great exigencies, the inevitable result, as it presents itself to my judgment, has been already sufficiently indicated. . . .

Elect Lincoln, and we invite those perils which we cannot measure; we attempt in vain to conquer the submission of the South to an impracticable and intolerable policy; our only hope must be, that, as President, he will abandon the creed, the principles, and pledges on which he will have been elected. . . .

Defeat Lincoln, and all our great interests and hopes are, unquestionably, safe.

If thus, or in any mode, we escape the perils of which his election will be the signal, our noble ship of state will issue forth from the breakers now foaming around and ahead, and spring forward into the open sea in all the majesty of her strength and beauty.

But if the Providence which has hitherto guided and guarded our country shall at last abandon us to our foolish and wicked strifes, I behold a far different scene.

The Success Achieved

Unintimidated by this fearful picture of ruin and woe, the Republicans did elect Mr. Lincoln President of the United States. The Southern States seceded. War followed. The rebellion was utterly subdued. The Union was not only preserved, but, by the removal of the cause of the rebellion, was made stronger than ever. The seceding States were only too glad to re-enter it, exclaiming like the prodigal son: "I have sinned against Heaven and in thy sight, and am no more worthy to be called thy son." The worst place in the Union was infinitely better than the best place outside of it.

Utter Failure of All Mr. Tilden's Predictions

Not a prediction of this great philosopher and statesman was realized. He estimated the character of the North by that of the degraded populace of New York; of the poltroons that hung round the purlieus of Tammany Hall. In his view of the ordering of human affairs, God had no place or hand. Tammany Hall was his deity,—his all in all. The result was to be what Tammany Hall would have achieved. He wholly counted out of the struggle the sense of duty in the human soul. He knew the impotence of Tammany Hall for such a contest, and knew nothing better. Is this statesmanship? What is statesmanship but the recognition of a Divine rule to which all human conduct must conform; and an attempt to direct all life, public and private, according to that rule? Was it statesmanship to plunge the States into a fratricidal war,—a war which wasted the fields of the South, decimated its people, received and inflicted a waste and loss which a generation cannot restore? If this is statesmanship, it is an inspiration borrowed from Satan himself.

Mr. Lincoln's Statesmanship

Compare this statesmanship with that displayed by Mr. Lincoln in his second inaugural message.

On the occasion corresponding to this four years ago, all thoughts were anxiously directed to an impending civil war. All dreaded it; all sought to avert it. While the inaugural address was being delivered from this place, devoted altogether to *saving* the Union without war, insurgent agents were in the city seeking to *destroy* it without war,—seeking to dissolve the Union, and divide effects by negotiation. Both parties deprecated war; but one of them would *make* war rather than let the nation survive; and the other would *accept* war rather than let it perish. And the war came.

One-eighth of the whole population were colored slaves, not distributed generally over the Union, but localized in the southern part of it. These slaves constituted a peculiar and powerful interest. All knew that this interest was, somehow, the cause of the war. To strengthen, perpetuate, and extend this interest, was the object for which the insurgents would rend the Union, even by war, while the Government claimed no right to do more than to restrict the territorial enlargement of it. Neither party expected for the war the magnitude or the duration which it has already attained. Neither anticipated that the cause of the conflict might cease with, or even before, the conflict itself should cease. Each looked for an easier triumph, and a result less fundamental and astounding. Both read the same Bible, and pray to the same God; and each invokes His aid against the other. It may seem strange that any men should dare to ask a just God's assistance in wringing their bread from the sweat of other men's faces; but let us judge not, that we be not judged. The prayers of both could not be answered; that of neither has been answered fully. The Almighty has his own purposes, "Woe unto the world because of offences! for it must needs be that offences come: but woe unto that man by whom the offence cometh!" If we shall suppose American slavery is one of those offences which, in the providence of God, must needs come, but which, having continued through His appointed time He now wills to remove, and that He gives to both North and South this terrible war, as the woe due to those by whom the offence came, shall we discern therein any departure from those Divine attributes which the believers in a living God always ascribe to Him? Fondly do we hope, fervently do we pray, that this mighty scourge of war may speedily pass away. Yet, if God wills that it continue until all the wealth piled by the bondsman's two hundred and fifty years of unrequited toil shall be sunk, and until every drop of blood drawn with the lash shall be paid by another drawn with the sword, as was said three thousand years ago, so still it must be said, "The judgments of the Lord are true and righteous altogether."

With malice toward none, with charity for all, with firmness in the right as God gives us to see the right, let us strive on to finish the work we are in; to bind up the nation's wounds; to care for him who shall have borne the battle; and for his widow and his orphan; to do all which may achieve and cherish a just and lasting peace among ourselves and with all nations.

What was Mr. Lincoln's statesmanship? The recognition of a Providence in human affairs,—of a Law, far higher than that of man's choice, and an obligation, or duty, to obey his Law, no matter at what cost. And was there not a Providence that sustained our country, and, through terrible trial and suffering, guided it at last to glorious victory,—not by immolating myriads of our fellow-beings upon the altar of an insatiable avarice and lust, but by raising and elevating them, so that, in time, they may hail, in the spirit in which it was proclaimed, the words of the Great Charter of human freedom which so thrilled the world a hundred years ago, that "all men have an equal right to life, liberty, and the pursuit of happiness." Was there ever a higher statesmanship than Mr. Lincoln's, and did ever one reap so rich a reward? This was a statesmanship to which Mr. Tilden was wholly blind. All Europe, echoing him, predicted the ignominious failure of our government in its contest against such apparently overwhelming odds,—an united South excited to the highest pitch of rage, allied to the traitors and malcontents so numerous at the North, all seeking to "*rend*" the Union that slavery might spread itself over our fair domain. How were all these predictions falsified, the schemes of the conspirators brought to naught, their armies broken in pieces, and the Union restored upon the basis of equal rights to all, by Him who at last heard the cry of his people that for one hundred and fifty years had groaned beneath the oppressor's lash! If in the future we would do any thing worthy a great nation,—of the hopes of humanity,—is Mr. Lincoln's statesmanship, or that of Mr. Tilden, born of Tammany Hall and of the lowest and most selfish instincts of our nature, to become our inspiration and guide?

Mr. Tilden, in his letter of acceptance, will undoubtedly be loud in denouncing the financial policy of the Republicans, and in vaunting his own, carefully avoiding the record of his political life. But for him and the like of him we should have had no war, and no financial policy to denounce. Would not his statesmanship have been far better employed in preventing the evils under which the nation is now laboring, than in proposing his nostrums for their cure? Can there be statesmanship without a nation?

MR. TILDEN THE MOST OBNOXIOUS PERSON IN THE NATION TO ALL PRINCIPLES OF ORDER AND GOOD GOVERNMENT

Certainly no man in the country is so obnoxious to all the principles and ideas which should, and do, characterize the better portion of our people, and especially to the Republican Party, as Mr. Tilden. His nomination revived all the issues which involved such a waste of life and treasure, and such unspeakable suffering. The effect of his election would be to undo all that had, in principle, been accomplished by the war. It would be far worse than was the election of Polk, in whose administration the secession element finally got full control of the Government; for the presidency of Tyler was an accident, and, though himself a secessionist, he had no following. The election of General Taylor was also an accident, growing out of a quarrel in the Democracy for the spoils. Even Mr. Tilden, in his letter, says, that no principle, only spoils, was involved in the movement which nominated Van Buren for the third time, and in which he took a conspicuous part. With Pierce, told dynasty was restored to power by a majority which had no parallel in our history. So rapid had been the process of demoralization that all sections and wings of the party, North and South, united upon a man who, when elected, incarnated the slaveholders' highest idea. But the slaveholders soon tired of him, and, with that inconstancy which always characterizes such a class, remorsely "whistled him down the wind," when his four years had expired. Buchanan, whom they took in his place, was still worse. The rebels at the expiration of his term, regarded his paltering imbecility with still greater contempt than the Republicans. Polk, Pierce, and Buchanan, all illustrate the common fate of men who, in affairs, ignore the sentiments of humanity and of justice. As a penalty, men are always bereft of all wisdom to act, when they have lost all sense of duty and obligation to a higher power. In Tilden is concentrated all that was wrong-headed, perverse, unpatriotic, and inhumane in all three of his precedessors. His election would fully restore that corrupt and effete dynasty which, in the triumph of Lincoln, was with such scorn and indignation hurled from power.

Is the country sufficiently recovered from the effects of the war that it can afford to put the high priest of secession at the head of the Government? Suppose the Southern people should some day take it into their heads not to pay their quota of the interest or principle of the debt which was created to subdue them. What could Mr. Tilden do to coerce them into payment? Coercion with him would be the "violation of the Constitution in every part." If a crisis came, would he not become as imbecile and emasculated as Buchanan, or Pierce, or Polk? Such a crisis may speedily happen. The State of Alabama, soon after the war, went into the Northern markets, and borrowed $20,000,000 on her bonds, and with the money constructed 1,000 miles of railroad, in order to "develop her resources." These bonds are largely held by Northern savings-banks. They have all been repudiated for no other reason than it does not suit her dignity or convenience to pay them! A sponge has been put over the whole. In this case the people of the State received full consideration,—a dollar in hand for every dollar promised to be repaid; and in fact received five-fold consideration in a magnificent system of public works which this money served to construct. How long will such a people stand the debt of the United States after they get into power? Not an hour. They could, following Mr. Tilden's law, plead the very Constitution in full bar to any claim to be made upon them. "Coercion was without warrant in law: the contract to pay was made under duress. The State was unconstitutionally driven and held out of the Union when the debt was contracted."
No action would hold morally or legally with such a defense. Mr. Tilden as

judge would have to admit the defence, and give judgment accordingly. If the South are to be let off, why not the North? Admit Mr. Tilden's construction, and the Constitution is feebler than any rope of sand.

Mr. Tilden the Political Reformer

Do reformers circulate such documents as the following?

Rooms of the Democratic State Committee,
Oct. 27, 1868.

My dear sir,—Please at once to communicate with some reliable person in three or four principal towns, and in each city of your county; and request him (*expenses duly arranged for this end*) to telegraph to William M. Tweed, Tammany Hall, at the minute of closing the polls, *not waiting for the count*, such person's estimate of the vote. Let the telegraph be as follows: "This town will show Democratic gain (or loss) over last year of—(number)." Or this one, if sufficiently certain: "This town will give a Republican (or Democratic) majority of—." There is, of course, an important object to be attained by *a simultaneous transmission at the hour of closing the polls, but not longer waiting. Opportunity can be taken of the usual half-hour lull in telegraphic communication over lines before actual results begin to be declared, and before the Associated Press absorb the telegraph with returns, and interfere with individual messages,* and give orders to watch carefully the count.

Very truly yours,
Samuel J. Tilden,
Chairman.

What was the object in ascertaining how the towns outside the city of New York had gone the moment the polls in them were closed? To create fraudulent votes in the City of New York, in number sufficient to overbalance any majority that the country might throw. In the country, one need not wait till the votes are counted to know the result. There every man's preference is known, and freely expressed. The yearly canvass taken in New Hampshire, completed a week before election, has never failed to show the final result, within one thousand votes, in a poll of seventy-five thousand. So in the agricultural counties of the State of New York. It is as substantially known what the result will be days before the election as when it is actually declared. Far different are the lower wards of the City of New York, where no one knows who the voters are, nor how many. Two things, however, are always known:

they will cast just as many votes as Tammany Hall dictates, and for just the person that Tammany Hall names; it can have twenty thousand votes with the same ease that it can have five thousand or ten thousand. Mr. Greeley, when in the Constitutional Convention with Mr. Tilden, endeavored to do something to stop the gigantic evil of fraudulent voting in the City of New York. Failing in this, he made a personal appeal to Mr. Tilden, in an open letter, which appeared in the columns of the "Tribune," under date of Oct. 20, 1869, to put a stop to it.

Letter of Mr. Greeley to Mr. Tilden

Letter to a Politician.

To Samuel J. Tilden,
Chairman Democratic State Committee.

Sir,—You hold a most responsible and influential position in the councils of a great party. You could make that party content itself with the polling of legal votes, if you only would. In our late Constitutional Convention, I tried to erect some fresh barriers against election frauds,—did you? The very little that I was enabled to effect in this direction I shall try to have ratified by the people at our ensuing election,—will you? Mr. Tilden, you cannot escape responsibility by saying, with the guilty Macbeth,

> Thou canst not say I did it: never shake
> Those gory locks at *me!*

for you were, at least, a passive accomplice in the giant frauds of last November. Your name was used, without public protest on your part, in circulars sowed broadcast over the State, whereof the manifest intent was to *make assurance doubly sure that the friends here perpetrated should not be overborne by the honest vote of the rural districts.* And you, not merely by silence, but by positive assumption, have covered those frauds with the mantle of your respectability. On the principle that *"the receiver is as bad as the thief,"* you are as deeply implicated in them to-day as though your name were Tweed, O'Brien, or Oakey Hall.

And, though our city has since largely increased its population, the *lower wards* were quite as populous then (1840) as they are to-day,—several of them more so. . . .

Now look at the vote of four of these Wards in 1840 and 1868 respectively:—

	President, 1840.		Governor, 1868.	
Four Wards.	4,793	5,521	2,840	20,283

Van Buren's majority, 726; Hoffman's majority, 17,443.

Mr. Tilden, you know what this contrast attests. Right well do you comprehend the means whereby the vote of 1868 was thus swelled out of all proportions. There are not 12,000 legal voters living in those wards to-day, though they gave Hoffman 17,443 majority. Had the day been of average length, it would doubtless have been swelled to at least 20,000. There was nothing but time needed to make it 100,000,—*if so many had been wanted and paid for.* Now, Mr. Tilden, I call on you to put a stop to this business. You have but to walk into the sheriff's, the Mayor's, and the Supervisor's offices, in the City Hall Park, and say that there must be no more of it; SAY IT SO THAT THERE SHALL BE NO DOUBT THAT YOU MEAN IT, and we shall have a tolerably fair election once more.

Will you do it? If we Republicans are swindled again, as we were swindled last Fall, you and such as you will be responsible to God and man for the outrage.

Yours,
HORACE GREELEY.

NEW YORK, Oct. 20, 1869.

Although the circulars to which Mr. Tilden's name was attached, had been previously published by the Tribune, and fully implicated him in the frauds charged, yet he was as silent under the accusations as a stone. Had he been innocent of the charge, and had he been desirous of purging the ballot-boxes, he would instantly have come to the front, demanded an investigation, and volunteered to go all lengths in their correction. But had he done so, he never would have been Governor of the State of New York, nor would he have had the least show for the Presidency. He, of all men, was the most interested in perpetuating them, as a means of climbing to political power.

MR. TILDEN THE REFORMER OF MUNICIPAL CORRUPTION

Mr. Tilden the municipal reformer! When was that discovery made? The first ever heard of him in that relation was after the exposure of his old friend and confidant, Tweed; Tweed had acquired an enormous fortune by his robberies. Every man in New York was interested in making him disgorge,—the keepers of gambling-houses, according to their means, equally with merchant princes, for the purpose of lightening their taxes. After the frauds of Tweed and his associates had been discovered, it became the fashion to pursue such sort of game. Tilden joined the crowd, and in the hue-and-cry. He, from his connection with the railroads, was almost as suddenly gorged with wealth as

Tweed; as a very rich man, it was for his interest to catch the thief who had broken into his enclosure. His spirit of reform was precisely that of a Turkish Bashaw, who occasionally takes off the heads of a few of his followers and officials, for no other reason than that they have taken to themselves more than their full share of the plunder. The difference between him who loses his head and him that keeps it is luck,—the accidental possession of power. Tilden's love of reform never went an inch beyond this. If he were such a reformer, there was no need to wait sixty years for an opportunity. There were plenty in the city of New York. There was Tammany Hall, of which he has so long been a member, which has done more to corrupt the politics and debauch the morals of the country than any ten other causes put together, slavery excepted. Tammany Hall a reformer! It has been seethed in corruption for a half century past. What are reforms? Temperance: a mitigation of social abuses by which the laboring man may be better fed, sheltered, and clothed; which shall prevent his dwelling from being the hotbed of disease; which shall give to the children of the poorer classes an occasional breath of fresh air and a sight of green fields; which shall make provision for those who, from any cause, are no longer able to care for themselves; which shall train those for whom reforms are inaugurated, to take them up and carry them forward; and, more than all, which shall attack in every manner possible that evil of evils,—that curse of all curses,—slavery. If that be dead and gone, are there not still crying evils and abuses to fight against, as firmly intrenched, and perilous to attack, as was slavery? If a man saw in that monstrous wrong nothing to condemn; if, on the contrary, it was to be encouraged to spread itself over the whole land; if, for its support, the Government was to be broken up, and the fairest hope of humanity destroyed,—is he likely to have much of the spirit of a reformer in his blood? When such a man moves, it is always from interest or policy; never from sympathy with any good cause. The true reformer is always, in the outset, in a minority,—often wholly alone in battling against some gigantic abuse, hoary and reverend with age. When he has brought the world over to his side, he ceases, in that particular, to be the reformer. Show us an instance in which Tilden has taken the reformer's first part? If a member of Tammany Hall steal any of its property, are the other members made reformers by seeking to recover it, or by punishing the thief? If persons employed in a gambling-house should steal and carry off the implements of their trade, would its owners be *reformers* for seeking to reclaim them? Yet such are the precise grounds upon which Tilden bases all his right to be called one. It is as impossible that he, with his surroundings, should have been a reformer as that the Sultan should. Is it a reformer's instinct to crib with such fellows as Tweed, Field, Connolly, and Genet, and a host of that ilk? How did all these men get their power and plunder? By playing like Mr. Tilden, upon the prejudices and passions of the ignorant and degraded populace of the city of New York. In that city, the *rôle* of a great leader is very simple and easy,—to glory over the beauties of Democracy, and to stuff it with bad whiskey. Such a populace are the tools of Mr. Tilden's trade,—the counters by which he hopes to reach the highest office in the gift of the people. All he wants is votes; and he is twice as sure of them so long as those who cast them remain ignorant and degraded, as he would be if they became intelligent and acted upon their own convictions. The moment they gain such a position, his occupation is gone, and his political aspirations vanish in empty air.

Is Tilden the Fit Man for President of the United States.

Is this the man to fill the seat once occupied by Washington and Jackson? Imagine him in the Presidential Chair, with these august figures on either side of him. The scorn of Washington might be shown by his majestic silence; but how would the eyes of Jackson glare with fury on the man who had been guilty, in a tenfold degree, if possible, of the crime for which he always regretted he had not hung Calhoun, and who, by helping to make secession a fact, had thrilled the chord nearest the old hero's heart. Will the nation honor such a man with the highest office in its gift? Will those whose lives were long spent amid persecution and obloquy, in the battle against slavery, help to raise to the Presidency him who was, of all others, the great advocate and support of that accursed system which it cost so many sacrifices, and so much blood and treasure, to overthrow? Are those fathers who sent their sons to die on the battle-field, or to return home, if they escaped, only to drag out a miserable existence from the effect of wounds, or diseases caught in camp, to do homage to one of the chief instruments of their bereavements, and of the living deaths which they still see on every side? Will the soldiers themselves, take as their standard-bearer the man who did more than any other to precipitate the rebellion; who gave it all his countenance and moral support; who, when they were confronting the enemy in the field, was threatening their rear with a still more dangerous enemy,—encouragement of secession at the *North;* and who proclaimed far and wide that all their sacrifices and heroism had resulted and could result only in defeat and shame? Will the young men coming forward to take upon themselves the duties and responsibilities of life and of public affairs, full of life and generous hope, take for their guide and example the man who has always been allied with that element of American life from which our political and social corruptions have almost wholly sprung, and who has never displayed the least interest or sympathy in those questions which more deeply concerned their own welfare and that of society? Is such to be the ideal,—"the coming man"? If so, God save the country, for which there is no human help. Is there not something better for their inspiration and imitation than slavery, the Resolutions of 1798, the right of secession, or the drunken orgies of Tammany Hall? Do not they want a government which shall throw its broad ægis over them, in whatever part of our wide domain they may happen to be placed? If not, we cannot too soon cast in our lot with Mexico, and with those South American States, where anarchy is the rule, and where life is hardly worth the possession. Would not the election of Mr. Tilden, in view of the past as well as the future, sound a lower depth in our political history than has yet been touched? Would it not show that we had no government worth preserving; no humanity; no political principles but the right of secession; no aspirations for a higher and purer system and life than that which allies us with slavery, with all its degradation and crimes? If nothing better be in store for us, we cannot too soon commit ourselves to the downward current, if only to escape the shame which our corruptions and demoralizations yet excite, but which is powerless for our rescue.

This present year is our National Centennial Birthday! Had Mr. Tilden been able, the eighty-fourth year of our national life would have been its last. Shall we desecrate this birthday, which every one is celebrating with such earnestness and joy, by electing as our Chief Magistrate a man who proclaims that our national existence may at any moment be brought to an end, by the fancied interests, the caprice, or the whim of any one of its members? that the nation of to-day may cease to be the nation of to-morrow? that its life hangs upon a single thread, which any State, ill-affected for the moment, may sever? Are we, by one act, to undo all that is glorious in our history, all that is valuable in our acquisitions and achievements, and show ourselves to the world a people without principle, without conviction, without aspiration, driven hither and thither by every lawless impulse, as if to verify the predictions of the enemies of freedom that Republics are but the nurseries of license and insubordination, and have only to run their course to destroy the fairest hopes of humanity? Shall we not rather crown the year with an utterance which shall go round the world to cheer the heart of every lover of freedom, that "THE NATION, NOT THE STATES, IS SUPREME."